REPUBLICAN POPULIST

REPUBLICAN POPULIST

Spiro Agnew and the Origins
of Donald Trump's America

Charles J. Holden, Zach Messitte,

and Jerald Podair

University of Virginia Press

CHARLOTTESVILLE AND LONDON

University of Virginia Press
© 2019 by the Rector and Visitors of the University of Virginia
All rights reserved
Printed in the United States of America on acid-free paper

First published 2019

9 8 7 6 5 4 3 2 1

Library of Congress Cataloging-in-Publication Data

Names: Holden, Charles J., author. | Messitte, Zach P., author. | Podair, Jerald, author.
Title: Republican populist : Spiro Agnew and the origins of Donald Trump's America /
  Charles J. Holden, Zach Messitte, and Jerald Podair.
Description: Charlottesville : University of Virginia Press, 2019. | Includes bibliographical
  references and index. |
Identifiers: LCCN 2019006956 (print) | LCCN 2019010741 (ebook) | ISBN 9780813943275
  (ebook) | ISBN 9780813943268 (cloth : alk. paper)
Subjects: LCSH: Agnew, Spiro T., 1918–1996. | Vice-Presidents—United States—
  Biography. | Populism—United States—History—20th century. | Conservatism—
  United States—History—20th century. | Political culture—United States—History—
  20th century. | Right and left (Political science)—United States—History—20th
  century. | Republican Party (U.S. : 1854–)—History—20th century. | United States—
  Politics and government—1969–1974.
Classification: LCC E840.8.A34 (ebook) | LCC E840.8.A34 H65 2019 (print) | DDC
  973.924092 [B]—dc23
LC record available at https://lccn.loc.gov/2019006956

Cover art: "Agnew," drawing by Edmund S. Valtman, 1970. (Courtesy of the Library of
Congress, Prints and Photographs Division)

CONTENTS

ACKNOWLEDGMENTS

The germination of this book began on November 11, 2005. That evening two of us, Chuck Holden and Zach Messitte, spent a couple of hours with the late *Washington Post* editor Ben Bradlee and syndicated columnist Richard Cohen at Bradlee's home, Porto Bello, on the banks of the St. Mary's River in southern Maryland. Cohen, who had been the Annapolis correspondent for the *Post* at the time of Agnew's downfall in 1973, described "a golden age of corruption in Maryland politics" to us; later that same night he delivered the fourth Ben Bradlee Lecture in Journalism at St. Mary's College of Maryland. We realized immediately that there was a larger story that had not yet been told. There was more to Spiro Agnew than just his alliterative speeches and his resignation. Then in 2014 we had the great fortune of befriending Jerry Podair, and our writing team was in place.

Over the course of the past few years, as the Republican Party continued to shift toward its so-called silent majority supporters, and as the Donald Trump campaign emerged, Agnew's political trajectory took on even greater significance. We continued our discussions—during baseball games at Miller Park in Milwaukee, on summer days by Green Lake in Wisconsin, and over lunches and dinners at Lawrence University and Ripon College—until the three of us had mapped out the book you have in your hands now.

As with any research project of this size and scope, many people and institutions deserve our thanks and appreciation.

The staff at the University of Maryland's Hornbake Library, which houses Agnew's papers, was unfailingly helpful and well organized. Special thanks go to Eric Stoykovich and Elizabeth Novara for helping us navigate the huge Agnew collection.

The University of Virginia Press, and in particular Dick Holway, the senior executive editor for history and the social sciences, saw the relevance early on of Agnew's political story and his relationship to the modern Republican Party.

We also owe a special debt of gratitude to our former and current colleagues and friends at St. Mary's College of Maryland, Lawrence University, the University of Oklahoma, and Ripon College who have encouraged our work and served as sounding boards as we progressed with the project. Our wonderful and smart student researchers over many years helped us track down details large and small. Our thanks goes to Alexa Beck, Tori Braun, Holly Chase, Reshma McHale, Ceren Oney, Natalie Reese, Joseph Rieu, Emma Saiz, and Megan Root.

The hard work and care of several administrative assistants allowed us to focus on the book even as we continued with our teaching, service, and other research roles: Erin Berry, Valerie Carlow, Donna Cline, Danielle Ficek, Claudia Leistikow, Lori Rose, and Abby Meatyard Thompson.

We would also like to add a few individual acknowledgments:

Zach Messitte: I am thankful as always for the love, support, and wisdom of my family: Julia Messitte, Peter and Susan Messitte, and Sam and Jules Messitte.

Jerry Podair: I would like to thank Lawrence University provost David Burrows for his friendship and support over the years, and my research assistant Emma Saiz for her indispensable help in bringing this book to fruition. I remain grateful to James McPherson and the late Alan Brinkley for the examples they have set for me and for all historians. As always, this book is for Caren and Julie.

Chuck Holden: Thanks to the coffee group and the history department at St. Mary's College of Maryland for being wonderful scholars, teachers, and friends. Other friends have been encouraging throughout, especially Chris and Tracy Adams, Glen Hoyt, Rick and Kathy Morain, and Gene Blanshan. Finally, thanks always to my family: Rosemary and David Hoyt, Mike and Sue Holden, Mary Jo and Roger Kluesner, Ann and Gary Kendell, Bill Brunner, and all my nieces and nephews.

REPUBLICAN POPULIST

INTRODUCTION

In the spring of 2016 the American Political Science Association polled forty scholars to name the worst vice president of the last century. Their consensus choice was an easy one: Spiro Agnew.[1] We disagree. Richard Nixon's selection of Spiro Agnew to be his running mate in August 1968 proved to be one of the most underrated, consequential decisions in modern American politics, and it still reverberates a half century later. Although Agnew's policy contributions during his five years in office were limited, he took on the important role of reshaping the trajectory of the Republican Party. His suburban, middle-class image, blended with his sharp-edged, anti-elite political style, launched his meteoric rise from an obscure county executive in a small border state to the man who was a heartbeat away from the presidency.

While there is no shortage of books about Richard Nixon, Bobby Kennedy, and the importance of the year 1968, scholarly work about Spiro Agnew is almost nonexistent. We hope that this book will help give Agnew's historical significance—for better or worse—its rightful place. We situate Agnew squarely, and prominently, in the lineage birthed by Barry Goldwater that is now ascendant in the GOP. It is a lineage that runs through Pat Buchanan's presidential primary bids in 1992 and 1996, Sarah Palin's brief star turn, the Tea Party, and most recently, Trumpism.

Since the 1960s the Republican Party has been based around a loose philosophy that has espoused support for smaller government, lower taxes, and a perceived toughness in foreign policy, particularly regarding the Soviet Union during the Cold War. The party found success at the national level in the past fifty years that had eluded it in the previous half century. And it has succeeded in achieving some of its primary policy purpose: the rollback of the New Deal/Great Society policy dominance that the Franklin Roosevelt/LBJ Democrats enjoyed from the 1930s through the 1960s.

Vice presidential scholars Christopher Devine and Kyle Kopko argue that the selection of the vice president often is justified on political, geographic, or policy grounds, but the electoral impact has been far from clear.[2] The GOP establishment during these years nodded toward its populist wing by selective use of ticket balancing, best personified by vice presidential nominees like Bob Dole (1976), Dick Cheney (2000 and 2004), and Palin (2008). But in 2016 Trump was the firebrand at the top of the ticket. The more establishment figure (in this case Mike Pence) received the No. 2 spot to soothe the party's old guard. In 1968 it was precisely this act of ticket balancing that helped launch Agnew's career.

Agnew's selection allowed Nixon to appear to be (at least in public) the establishment's candidate. The Nixon tapes reveal that privately the president was always, in his own mind at least, on the outside of the establishment looking in. But with Agnew on the ticket, the Republicans embraced an anti-elitism that they had been wary of in past elections. With his classically good looks, slicked-back hair, and dark suits, Agnew talked sports with the passion of the average fan, which he was; he claimed to bear the attacks on him by the "elite" on behalf of his fellow frustrated middle-class citizens throughout the land; he loyally did his time supporting the president on the chicken-dinner circuit from Iowa to Idaho; and he played a key role in turning the white South toward the Republican Party. It was Agnew who spoke most directly to the emerging Republican base because he, unlike Trump's faux blue-collar billionaire persona, was truly one of them. Agnew's core anti-elite message, while perhaps short on conservative ideology, was long on the politics of anti-establishment, white working- and middle-class resentment. It has since become an article of faith. Trump and Pence bottled the same magic in 2016, and it helped them capture the White House by turning Rust Belt swing states like Ohio, Michigan, Pennsylvania, and Wisconsin to the Republican column.

In 1968 and again in 1972 the Nixon-Agnew combination worked like a charm. While he was not an Ivy Leaguer, Nixon, having moved to Manhattan in 1963, was acceptable enough to the New England prep school wing of the Republican Party, which included legacies like the Bushes, the Lodges, and the Rockefellers. But Nixon could still connect with white, hardscrabble America in a way that spoke to his humble California upbringing. Agnew was something altogether different and new for the Republicans. Unlike the blue-blooded Henry Cabot Lodge, Nixon's running mate in the 1960 presidential election, Agnew came straight out of Towson, Maryland. *Time* magazine dubbed him "Suburbman," the type "whose life revolved around [his] four kids and [his] home, and who preferred family domestic life which, in years past, consisted largely of lawn sprinklers, pizza, ping pong in the basement rec room, Sunday afternoons watching the Baltimore Colts on color TV."[3]

Agnew's lasting influence was his ability to mix politics and emotion; indeed, his scrappy temperament was arguably his most effective political weapon. Here he also shares the stage with Trump. While Nixon's foreign and domestic policymaking legacy (obscured still by Watergate) included, among other achievements, the opening to China, the creation of significant environmental legislation, the signing of Title IX, and the negotiation of the Anti-Ballistic Missile Treaty, it was Agnew, by giving voice to those anxious white middle- and working-class voters, who played a primary role in forging a new Republican electoral majority. This same deal appears to be taking form in the first term of the Trump administration, where the policy details are being left to congressional Republicans while the president continues to cement an emotional bond with his voters, seemingly no matter what he does.

Just eight years removed from a seat on the Baltimore County zoning board and a single term as Baltimore County executive, Agnew had served fewer than two years as governor of Maryland when Nixon nominated him to be vice president in 1968. He was a national candidate with such a weak political resume that there is almost no historical parallel.[4] That such a political novice could by 1969 become the third-most respected man in the country behind Richard Nixon and Billy Graham speaks volumes to the chord he quickly struck with the American people.[5]

This book leaves the task of a full-on biography to others. Instead, we offer the following chapters as tight, selective snapshots from Agnew's career framed within a larger political narrative. Together they reveal Agnew's surprising ability to navigate the changing tides of post–World War II American politics. As his aide David Keene explained, "He was sort of a self-made guy who grew up on the block in Baltimore and went to night school, and people talked about how he'd studied his list of words in *Reader's Digest*."[6] The future vice president's father was a diner-owning Greek immigrant. Agnew became a decorated World War II soldier, then moved on to law school, the suburbs, and to lawyering and eventually into politics. Nixon and his closest aides realized early on that Agnew was out of his league on policy matters and had very little idea of how to operate in the White House environment. In April 1969, just three months into the Nixon-Agnew team's first term, H. R. Haldeman, Nixon's chief of staff, wrote in his diary: "VP called just before dinner and said he had to talk to Nixon. . . . Later [Nixon] called me into bedroom to report, furious, that all he wanted was some guy to be Director of the Space Council. May turn out to be straw that breaks the camel's back. [Agnew] just has no sensitivity, or judgment about his relationship with Nixon. After movie we were walking home and Nixon called me back, again to ponder the Agnew problem."[7]

Agnew never made it into Nixon's inner circle on foreign or domestic policy and later slammed his former boss for having "an inherent distrust of anyone who had an independent political identity."[8] Nixon's staff thought even less of Agnew, but that would later play out in the vice president's favor. He was so far out of Nixon's orbit that he had absolutely nothing to do with the Watergate scandal. Instead, he seemed destined to attend state funerals, take long goodwill trips abroad, and represent the White House on low-priority domestic issues.[9] Nixon couldn't stand Agnew personally, and he seriously contemplated replacing him in 1972 with Texas governor John Connolly, a conservative Democrat who would later become a Republican. He ultimately decided otherwise, conceding correctly that Agnew, in the meantime and much to everyone's surprise, had become an icon to the GOP base.

Instead of dwelling in vice presidential obscurity, Agnew in 1969–70 turned himself into a valuable ambassador to the white South and the great silent majority. He was a leading fund-raiser at Lincoln Day dinners and the like, speaking to adoring crowds in places including Des Moines, Birmingham, and Boise. At these events he injected into the national dialogue the idea that the media was biased against conservatives. He attacked the Democratic Party for taking white southerners for granted, and he lashed out at the culture of permissiveness and the antiwar protests on college campuses. Agnew's best-known speech on what he saw as the corrupting power of television network news identified a "small group of men, numbering perhaps no more than a dozen anchormen, commentators, and executive producers, [who] settle upon the 20 minutes or so of film and commentary that's to reach the public." The 1969 speech became an instant classic, and while it is now a shibboleth of the Republican Party, it was originally met with hue and cry from the very media "elite" Agnew attacked—proving to his followers his point.[10] But it also built a foundation, just as Pat Buchanan prophesized in 1970, for conservatives to "give consideration to ways and means if necessary to acquire either a government or other network through which we can tell our story," thus connecting Agnew's take on the media to the creation of Fox News and the alt-right.[11]

His attacks on the media catapulted Agnew to a new level of national political prominence. Forgotten now is that he was legitimately being touted, along with Ronald Reagan and Nelson Rockefeller, as an early leader for the 1976 Republican presidential nomination. But with George Wallace ready to make another run in 1972, it remained critically important for Nixon's reelection that the emerging southern leadership of the Republican Party, including politicians like South Carolina senator Strom Thurmond, was behind the national ticket. Thurmond was on record as saying, "South Carolina will favor Spiro Agnew for president in 1976."[12] And it helped that Senator Barry Goldwater, the 1964 GOP nominee and spiritual godfather of the emerging conservative movement, also supported retaining the sitting vice president, pointedly arguing, "Agnew's popularity equals that of the President."[13]

Of course, there would be no "Spiro of '76," as the early bumper stickers proclaimed. The presidential talk was aborted by Agnew's resignation in October 1973 and his replacement by Gerald Ford. As legendary *Washington Post* editor Ben Bradlee noted, "It is a measure of the darkness of the Watergate cloud that in only a few days, Agnew was history. The country welcomed the new Vice President, and returned to their seats to await the start of the final act."[14] Watergate consumed all the political oxygen in the aftermath of Agnew's departure. Nixon resigned just ten months later.

The sordid details of Agnew's sudden resignation—he was charged with tax evasion in October 1973—explain part of his quick fade into history and his lack of historical recognition. And while our work will touch upon his downfall, it is not the focus of our effort. The end of Agnew's public life is ground well-plowed by journalists Richard Cohen and Jules Witcover in *A Heartbeat Away*, which was written shortly after his resignation, and more recently by MSNBC's Rachel Maddow in her podcast "Bag Man." Agnew's own memoir, *Go Quietly . . . or Else*, focuses on his side of the resignation story. While there is some speculation as to why he capitulated to the prosecutors so suddenly, there is little ambiguity about Agnew's guilt. Nixon's solicitor general, Robert Bork, argued that Agnew "had to resign; otherwise, he was going to jail."[15] While the vice president would later maintain that he was innocent of the allegations that compelled him to resign, his primary line of defense in private during the summer and fall of 1973 was that everyone else in Maryland took kickbacks, too.[16] Agnew accepted what amounted to bribes for construction contracts that started while he was in Towson and continued in Annapolis and during his time as vice president. As Cohen, who covered the investigation for the *Washington Post*, later said, "This was a thoroughly corrupt man. He shook down everybody. . . . He was shameless."[17]

After pleading nolo contendere for failing to declare the bribes as income, Agnew disappeared suddenly from the political scene. He lived out an odd couple of decades, playing golf in Palm Springs with his pal Frank Sinatra and authoring a steamy spy novel that he tried to turn into a movie, as well as a memoir that focused on his version of the events that led to his resignation. His attempts to find work as a disbarred lawyer-turned-lobbyist for Middle Eastern princes and other international strongmen were embarrassing. Public appearances were rare. There was, as he wrote later, a "more subtle punishment" inflicted upon him: "I cannot walk through a hotel lobby or down a street and simply be one of the crowd. Although I have none of the benefits of public life—no pension, no former statesman status, no diplomatic passport to ease my comings and goings in my international business affairs—I have retained a major impediment of public life. I have no privacy because I am recognized all over the world. When people stop and stare at you, you know some are thinking: 'there goes Agnew, the guy who was kicked out of the vice-presidency.'"[18]

Even the U.S. Senate, where Agnew had presided from 1969 to 1973 as vice president, seemed to wish him away. The Senate withheld the traditional installation of his bust in its antechambers for more than two decades. When the statue was finally unveiled in 1995, the ceremony was pointedly not attended by either of Maryland's U.S. senators. Agnew acknowledged mournfully, "I'm not blind or deaf to the fact that some people feel that this is a ceremony that should not take place."[19] He died a year later near his beach home in Ocean City, Maryland.

The vice president's swift departure from the national spotlight, his sad plea bargain deal (which came on the heels of a public vow to fight until the bitter end), and his lack of any lasting policy legacy certainly are contributing reasons for his ghosting from American political history. The same handful of Agnew anecdotes and conversations are recycled in most biographies of Nixon. Agnew is occasionally worth a mention for pundits wishing to illustrate the perils of choosing an unknown running mate with little national experience.[20] We believe, however, that the current narrative is incomplete.

Looking back now, we can see that Agnew's nomination and ascendance as a national political figure helped fuse a broad-based coalition that connected Wall Street with the growing suburban middle class and a disgruntled white working class. It helped create a bond of political and cultural convenience between conservative country clubbers, a growing religious movement, and "betrayed" white southerners looking for a new home after Lyndon Johnson's decision to back civil rights in 1964. Agnew made the most of his time in office to blaze a political trail that his protégé and speechwriter, Pat Buchanan, would reprise in his own presidential campaigns in 1992 and 1996. But many Republicans originally met Agnew's selection as vice president with deep skepticism.

Indeed, Agnew was as surprised as anyone to be chosen. After being nominated by Nixon at the Republican National Convention in Miami in August 1968, he told reporters that the selection had come "like a bolt out of the blue." He also knew that "the name Spiro Agnew is not a household name. I certainly hope it will become one within the next couple of months."[21] In his acceptance speech he stated outright, "I stand here with a deep sense of the improbability of this moment."[22] Many mainstream Republicans agreed. Michigan governor George Romney got 186 delegates (14 percent of the total) from the floor during the nomination process despite Nixon's endorsement. Maryland congressman Rogers Morton, who knew Agnew well and would later be appointed chair of the Republican National Committee, privately told Nixon that while Agnew was potentially a very good candidate, he had a tendency to be "lazy."[23] But as Richard Scammon and Ben Wattenberg pointed out in their examination of the Nixon coalition, "Strom Thurmond may have liked John Tower on the ticket. Nelson Rockefeller might have liked Mark Hatfield on the ticket—but Thurmond couldn't go home with Hatfield and Rockefeller couldn't go home with Tower. Everyone could go home with Agnew— maybe grumpily . . . but it was a livable arrangement."[24]

Almost immediately after his nomination, and again after the victorious election, Agnew began to blaze a rhetorical path on race, culture, and the frustrations of Middle America. It got him on the cover of *Life* magazine in 1970, arms folded and peering out under the headline "Stern Voice of the Silent Majority: Spiro Agnew Knows Best."[25] He insulted and talked tough. Speaking to the GOP faithful and the newly converted at overflow crowds throughout the South and rural America, he went after the apostates in his own party and his perceived enemies with a vengeance. Agnew spoke directly to "the great majority of the voters in America [in 1968 who] are un-young, un-poor, and un-black; they are middle-aged, middle-class, middle-minded."[26] By 1969 Agnew was calling the news media biased and criticizing intellectuals and war protesters as "an impudent corps of effete snobs." He stood for law and order and against anyone who opposed the Vietnam War. During the 1970 midterm elections Nixon deployed him as an attack dog not only against Democrats but against liberal Republicans who dared to challenge his administration. Politically and strategically, Agnew discovered how to make himself essential both to Nixon and to the creation of the modern Republican Party.

A half century later Donald Trump followed Agnew's playbook, likely without knowing it, in order to consolidate political support and national media attention. Denigrate minorities? Take on the news media and the biases of academics and intellectuals? Knock "political correctness" and elites? Publicly admonish members of your own party? Trump and Agnew could answer affirmatively to all these questions, separated by nearly fifty years.

Trump's campaign made explicit use of the Nixon-era buzzwords "silent majority" and "law and order." Trump routinely used Agnew-like attacks on the perceived bias of the liberal media.[27] Both men excelled at the political counterpunch and tilted against sacred norms and traditions of American political life. They each employed a slash-and-burn campaign style, carried their lack of elected political experience around as badges of honor, and are (or will be) remembered as overwhelmingly prideful men who lacked the humility to admit their mistakes.[28] Put the similarities together and it is hard to deny that Spiro Agnew was a harbinger of things to come in American politics.

Agnew and Trump come together perhaps most closely as cultural critics for the white working class. As champions of the white everyman against Democratic Party liberal elites—the professional classes, the media, the entertainment community, the intellectuals, and the bienpensants of the coasts—Agnew and Trump were viewed as heroes not just for their own personas but for the enemies they made. As Trump pointed out during the primaries, his followers were so loyal, he "could stand in the middle of 5th Avenue and shoot somebody and [not] lose voters."[29] And even after having resigned and pled nolo contendere to tax evasion, Agnew received thousands of letters from supporters pledging their undying allegiance. Both Agnew and Trump made it possible for a working stiff or a middle-level office worker to vote Republican, because they countered the charge that the GOP was the party of the rich by pointing out the snobbery and elitism of liberal Democrats and their politically correct supporters.

Like Agnew, Trump had been a registered Democrat before switching parties. He had also been critical of Ronald Reagan.[30] But Trump's entrance and elevation into Republican Party politics was colored by the politics of race, much like Agnew's sudden rise to national attention after the riots in Baltimore following the assassination of Martin Luther King Jr. in 1968. As early as 2011 Trump challenged the legitimacy of Barack Obama's citizenship.[31] And the centerpiece of his speech announcing his candidacy focused on building a wall and making a broad-brush dog-whistle generalization about Mexican immigrants in the United States.

Trump's political use of racialized offensive language is well documented. The list includes, but is not exclusive to, impugning a U.S. District Court judge of Mexican descent, responding only tepidly to the white nationalist rally in Charlottesville, Virginia, where a counter-protester was killed, calling Haiti and African nations "shitholes," mocking the way Asians speak English, and giving shout-outs to "my African Americans."[32] He even went out of his way to insult the intelligence of African American politicians and sports heroes, including basketball star LeBron James. In this way Trump's playbook mimics Agnew's in style and substance. And he is speaking to a similar constituency; the one-third to 40 percent of American voters who are Trump supporters resemble Agnew's old silent majority population.[33] Trump's speeches have been given almost exclusively in Agnew's old political stomping grounds—far from the East and West Coasts.

Agnew and Trump's relationship with the press and the intellectual elites is also a core part of their political identities. Trump's all-out assault on the veracity of the news media is in many ways the apotheosis of Agnew's assertions in 1969 about the power of network news to shape public opinion. Trump's pronouncements, like Agnew's, are peppered with the law and order tilt of ending "American carnage," calling out the media as "the enemy of the people," and branding those that don't agree with his immigration policies as politically correct. Like Agnew, Trump plays up his unfamiliarity with the ways of Washington, D.C., and rallies those left behind by the postwar/post-recession boom that exacerbated the divide between rich and poor, black and white, and urban and rural America.[34]

The Agnew and Trump messages were, and are, angrier, edgier, and more accusatory than the Eisenhower or the Bush Republicans were used to, but they resonated with white America because they reinforced a perception that the civil rights movement or the Black Lives Matter drive was too militant, that intellectuals were too liberal, and that the media was too self-righteous and opinionated. The modern Republican Party, which in 2016 attained a position of dominance not seen since before Franklin Roosevelt's presidency, owes Spiro Agnew a debt of gratitude. Whether this makes Agnew the worst vice president or not, it certainly makes him deeply and historically significant.

Our book is organized into seven chapters that focus on Agnew's legacy and importance to modern American political history. Chapter 1 introduces his personal story and examines his political career up to his nomination for the vice presidency. It traces the arc of his early life, including his mixed religious/ethnic identity (Greek immigrant father and Episcopalian mother with Revolutionary-era Virginia roots), his marginal academic record at the University of Baltimore and Johns Hopkins University, his dignified and decorated service in World War II, and his struggles as a lawyer. The chapter's focus, however, is on his postwar arrival in the suburbs, where he made the shift from immigrant's son to Kiwanis Club mainstay. Agnew represented the post–World War II generation of white men who emerged from the war to build lives as members of a broad, respectable, and upwardly mobile middle class. While this "gray flannel suit" America was often lampooned by critics as bland, shallow, and conformist, it developed a distinct cultural approach based on "traditional" values—work, family, and community—that formed the basis of what would be known as the silent majority. Moreover, by the early 1960s members of this silent majority were becoming increasingly anxious about the rapidly changing society around them. Agnew, an undistinguished, resolutely average "man from nowhere," became their sharp-tongued champion, not in spite of these qualities but because of them. There were millions of "Spiro Agnews" across America by the late 1960s, and they helped transform the Republican Party.

Agnew's rise in Maryland was also enmeshed in the state's political, economic, and cultural makeover, which started in earnest in the 1950s and '60s. After World War II Maryland evolved from a sleepy border state with strong southern roots to one of the wealthiest and most educated suburban centers in the nation in the space of a generation.[35] Statewide elections today are won and lost in the affluent counties of metropolitan Washington, D.C., and suburban Baltimore, but that was not the case in the middle of the twentieth century, when the city of Baltimore and the rural counties dominated. The demographic changes and rapid economic growth of the suburban areas that began in earnest in the 1960s accelerated their newfound influence. Agnew was well positioned to take full political advantage of these changes.

In chapter 2 we pay attention to the shifts that occurred in the national political environment that would, by the time of Agnew's ascension to the Republican ticket in 1968, reverse the public's perception of the two major parties. The political wisdom of the time was that America was living through an era of Democratic Party dominance that began with the election of Franklin Roosevelt in 1932 and continued through LBJ's 1964 landslide, punctuated only by the "personal victories" of popular war hero Dwight Eisenhower in 1952 and 1956.[36] Beneath the surface, however, liberals and intellectuals within the Democratic Party were traumatized by the excesses of McCarthyism and the John Birch Society and fearful of their popular resonance. They began to back away from New Deal–era professions of faith in "the people" and become more skeptical of the wisdom and judgment of the "average American." This vacuum created an opening for what Kevin Phillips called the emerging Republican majority and included a "popular upheaval which would overthrow the obsolescent 'liberal ideology and interests of today's Establishment.'"[37] Agnew emerged as a champion of this backlash during his five years as vice president.

The second chapter will also examine how the Democratic Party of the 1950s and '60s began to move toward positions of cultural elitism, as Republicans pushed the GOP in the opposite direction. The cultural stresses of the 1960s certainly accelerated this process, making it possible for Agnew to become the Republican governor of a deeply Democratic state, and again reinforced the mantle of the people's party for the GOP in the tumultuous political year of 1968. As the social scientists Richard

Scammon and Ben Wattenberg explained, more than any other national political figure, Agnew represented "social stolidity" and "conformity with the attitudes of 'plain folks' who are the great majority of voters.... [T]he Silent Majority."[38] The second chapter ends with the 1964 presidential election.

The third chapter covers Agnew's ascent from local to state to national leader, culminating with his vice presidential nomination and the 1968 campaign. While no one had more firsthand experience with the pros and cons of the vice presidential selection process than Richard Nixon, Agnew was a complete unknown to the public, and his selection shocked political insiders. A poll found that a surprising number of people thought "Spiro Agnew" was some kind of shellfish.[39] House Republican leader Gerald Ford was gobsmacked by the choice. "I couldn't believe it," he later wrote. "Here was a man who had risen from total obscurity a few years earlier to become governor of a border state.... He seemed like a nice enough person, but he lacked national experience or recognition. And now, after just two years as governor, he was going to run for Vice President? I shook my head in disbelief. This was the reaction of many of my House colleagues."[40] But others, such as Lyndon Johnson, saw a certain shrewdness in Nixon's move and believed that Agnew was responsible for delivering the border states of Tennessee and Kentucky to Nixon, as well as securing the Carolinas and Virginia.[41]

In the fourth chapter we unpack Agnew's early travails in office and his search for political relevance in the Nixon administration. Agnew's initial months in Washington were difficult. In their first meeting in Key Biscayne, Florida, after the election, Nixon asked Agnew to establish his office in the West Wing (unprecedented for a vice president) and to play an active role in federal/state issues and relations with Congress, a seemingly promising portfolio. The reality of his early public appearances and speeches tells a different story. Agnew quickly fell down the ladder of importance with Nixon and his closest aides. The vice president's speeches during his first few weeks in office focused on issues like maritime affairs, urban renewal, and Native Americans. He often was sent in to repeat what Nixon had said the week before or to attend ribbon cuttings that allowed him to recite accomplishments for the party faithful.

Beginning in the spring of 1969, growing bored and increasingly uneasy about his irrelevance, Agnew went rogue with some help from Nixon's speechwriters. By the 1970 midterm election he had become an attack dog, hammering home the message that the GOP was the true party of the people and the Democratic Party the bastion of the cultural elite. Speechwriters including Pat Buchanan and William Safire deliberately took aim at the media, academics, and the anti–Vietnam War movement. The speeches made Agnew a household name and earned him magazine covers. He became a favorite on the luncheon circuit, particularly in more conservative midwestern and southern venues.

During his five years as vice president, Agnew developed a niche as a vocal defender of the emerging silent majority. Race was crucial to this project, and Nixon learned fast that in Agnew he had a winner when it came to recruiting the white South. Chapter 5 explores Agnew's overlooked legacy in this regard. As he became the administration's most prominent articulator of aggrieved white sensibilities, he connected with a growing number of Dixiecrats such as Strom Thurmond who had already switched parties or who began supporting conservative causes in the 1960s. He also struck a chord with those middle-class white voters of the "new," more suburban South. Known most for their opposition to civil rights, these white southerners openly supported the American escalation in Vietnam and were outraged by the growing cultural permissiveness in the country. In this way Agnew was again a forerunner of an important wing of the modern Republican Party. He was a veteran himself, and his son served in Vietnam during his term. Agnew combined his patriotism and pro-military record with a populist appeal that connected to patriotic rural and suburban southern voters alike. He and Nixon managed to overcome their mutual suspicions to steer the Old Confederacy into becoming the GOP's stalwart base.

Agnew's political end was swift, and in chapter 6 we look at his final year in office, his resignation, and his post-1973 career. His future—and that of the Republican Party—certainly looked bright in November 1972 as the Nixon-Agnew ticket was overwhelmingly reelected and the Republicans picked up seats in Congress. As the Watergate scandal began to unspool, Agnew's national standing actually strengthened. Marginalized from the beginning and an outcast in Nixon's inner circle, Agnew had nothing to do with the break-in and the ensuing cover-up. For a moment it even seemed possible that Agnew might replace Nixon as president before 1976.

Agnew's downfall and the major players in the drama that unfolded in the late summer and early fall of 1973 shine a light on a Republican Party riven by factionalism. Those players—Nixon; Attorney General Elliot Richardson; George Beall, the U.S. attorney for Maryland; Senator Barry Goldwater; and even the presiding judge in the case, Walter Hoffman—are part of an illustrative story of the emerging debate within the party that would play out in the coming decades. All were seen as establishment Republicans. Their contribution to Agnew's sudden fall stunned and angered his faithful followers.

Agnew's post–vice presidential career was undistinguished and obscure. He remained largely out of the public eye until his death in 1996. But despite his ignominious end, he exited the national stage having bolstered the Republican Party for the future. He had helped establish a national cultural paradigm of Republican populism (and conversely, Democratic elitism) that would make the GOP a potent electoral force for the next half century. He showed how a national political figure could become a conduit for the frustrations of those who believed the Democratic Party had left them behind.

We conclude in chapter 7 by taking stock of Agnew's impact on the current Republican Party. Agnew helped alter the national political landscape to construct a governing coalition that was as powerful, consequential, and long-lived as the New Deal coalition it supplanted. He also embodied the tensions and contradictions of his party's rival wings. Neither Agnew nor any other Republican leader—even Ronald Reagan—completely reconciled them, and their simmering disagreements continue into the twenty-first century, where they burst to the surface again during the bitter internecine Republican presidential primaries in 2016.

Like Joseph McCarthy, to whom he is often compared, Spiro Agnew was much less significant as a man than as a phenomenon. In the 2016 presidential election cycle, as pundits and pollsters predicted Hillary Clinton's victory, many were tempted to say that demographic shifts, the gender gap, and a coalition of urban elites and minority voters portended long-term Democratic success. The results of the election proved otherwise. Donald Trump's victory in the electoral college exposed the political math that a new Democratic "coalition of the ascendant" is not yet able to rebrand the GOP as the party of economic elites and "the 1 percent." Now more than ever, Spiro Agnew's Republican Party governs America. The new political roads Americans will travel in the twenty-first century will be across terrain shaped at least in part by this most unlikely of forgotten politicians who had no comeback or second act. His unprepossessing life has produced an oddly enduring legacy.

1

REFUSING TO KNUCKLE UNDER

A Political Temperament Forged Early

A 1962 picture of Spiro and Judy Agnew's family in the *Baltimore Sun* is a study in post–World War II suburban stability and conformity. The three older children — Pamela, Sue, and Randy — stand in back, while the youngest, Kimberly, kneels in front between her parents, who are seated. The men are in dark suits, and the women wear tasteful dresses. All are smiling more or less comfortably.[1] The recently elected executive of Baltimore County, readers learned, was also a World War II veteran, a past president of the local junior high PTA, and a member of the Kiwanis "with a seven-year perfect attendance record." There is not the slightest hint in this nice family portrait that the father would soon embark on one of the most dramatic rise-and-fall careers in American political history.

There is also nothing in Agnew's story up to this point to suggest anything other than a lifetime of sturdy, respectable anonymity. Agnew was born in Baltimore city in 1918, the son of a Greek immigrant, Theophrastos Spiro Anagnostopoulos, and Margaret Pollard, whose parents were Virginians. Theirs was, by the standards of a century ago, a mixed marriage in that Theophrastos was Greek Orthodox and Margaret was Episcopalian. She had one son from a previous marriage. Her first husband, William Pollard, died in 1917, and she married the elder Agnew the next year.

The Agnews tried their hands at a number of business ventures, running at various times a restaurant, a grocery store, and a confectionary.[2] Among his peers, young Spiro was embarrassed by his father's accent and his habit of speaking Greek to his old friends. The son was at best an indifferent student at Baltimore's Forest Park High School, where he "took part in no activities, won no honors, played no sports, made no endur-ing friendships."[3] He attended Johns Hopkins University, where again he made little impression and by his own admission was "more interested in having a good time than studying."[4] After deciding college was not for him at that time, Agnew dropped out and worked for an insurance com-pany, Maryland Casualty, before he was drafted into the army in August 1941. The time at Maryland Casualty was well spent in at least one regard: Agnew met Elinor "Judy" Judefind there, and they married in 1942.[5] His military service led him to the European Theater of Operations in 1944, where he endured the siege of Bastogne with the 54th Armored Infantry Battalion. He later recalled that he "slept on ice for a week" at one point.[6] Decorated with the Bronze Star, he was discharged in November 1945 and returned home to Baltimore city.

After the war Agnew considered whether politics could be the "vehicle to lift him out of mediocrity and obscurity."[7] His big break came when an older lawyer and mentor, Lester Barrett, a staunch Republican, was appointed chief judge of Baltimore County Circuit Court and moved to Towson, the county seat.[8] Agnew followed Barrett to the suburbs and opened a law office across from the courthouse. But as important as leav-ing Baltimore city was for Agnew's future as a "creature of suburbia," he also left behind the Democratic Party of his immigrant, urban father. According to Richard Cohen and Jules Witcover, it was Barrett, "rather than any great ideological pull," who brought Agnew into the Republican Party. Agnew asked his mentor "how a young man got started in county politics. Become a Republican, Barrett had told him: the field of competi-tion is smaller, and although the odds of winning public office are longer, there are other benefits, not the least of which is the law business Repub-lican contacts can bring."[9] And with that, Spiro Agnew became a big fish in the small pond of the Baltimore County Republican Party.

This chapter picks up Agnew's story in 1962, just after his election to head the government of the fast-growing suburban county surrounding Maryland's largest city. Baltimore County's population more than tripled after World War II, from 155,825 in 1940 to 492,428 in 1960.[10] One profile of Agnew noted that the county now had "steel mills [and] farm fields" as well as "split-level homes [and] manor estates." It had a "burgeoning population and a forest of industrial smokestacks growing along Chesapeake Bay." In a matter of a few years, Baltimore County "seemed less rural than urban," and it now "had all the problems of the big city—traffic, schools, taxes, crime."[11]

Since Democrats in Baltimore County outnumbered Republicans nearly four to one, Agnew's election as county executive came as a surprise to many. In other ways, however, he seemed the perfect fit for his time and place: a pragmatic, white-collar, middle-class man elected to lead a booming suburban county in need of order and direction. The Agnew Bi-Partisan Committee of supporters hailed the candidate as "The Man with the Plan."[12] The *Sun* described him as a "tall, unassuming, young Republican." His election, it continued, "surprising as it seems, couldn't have happened in a more likely setting than in Baltimore county, which, in shaking off its rural characteristics, is 'busting out all over,' and moving toward a position of leadership in the metropolitan area."[13]

Agnew biographers portray him during these years as a results-oriented moderate, or even liberal, Republican.[14] Indeed, Agnew described himself in 1962 as an Eisenhower Republican, saying, "It is possible to be liberal on one issue and conservative on another."[15] As county executive, he pushed for an open accommodations law against racist housing practices. He favored gun control. He supported antipollution measures. He was the only Republican county executive in the state—and in the state's largest county, at that—and his election instantly launched him into the upper ranks of the party in Maryland.[16] He immediately started receiving attention from national GOP leaders, especially those from the Eastern Establishment wing of the party. Nelson Rockefeller invited Agnew and other Maryland Republican leaders to New York City for lunch in 1963.[17] In the 1964 presidential election Agnew first supported California senator Ted Kuchel and then Pennsylvania governor William Scranton, both moderates, but remained unenthusiastic about the successful hard-right campaign of Barry Goldwater, saying he "would much prefer a candidate of more moderate viewpoint."[18]

But whether Agnew was a moderate or a conservative Republican overlooks what is his lasting legacy: his fighting political temperament, one particularly suited to his time and place. Cohen and Witcover, looking back in 1974 over Agnew's rise and fall, observed that in the early days "contentiousness and righteousness" were "the man's trademarks, trademarks that stayed with him throughout his political career."[19]

Over time as he took on the press, academics, the antiwar movement, and liberals generally, this bare-fisted, everyman political style earned Agnew a loyal following, first among his fellow suburbanites and later among the white working-class "hard hats" as well. Behind the image of the Baltimore Colts–loving, Ping-Pong–playing suburban dad was a "tough, cold, and aggressive" political counterpuncher.[20] His followers wrote to him of their adoration of "men like you who are not afraid to speak up, that will tell it like it is."[21] These characteristics surfaced early in his career, especially when Agnew spoke out against black activism. An examination of his pre–vice president years, therefore, sheds light on how Agnew became both a model and a magnet for those seeking a more confrontational political style, a blunt suburban populism from someone "like them."[22]

Agnew possessed a keen sense of his image as a "normal" guy for his time and place. Sometime in late 1964 or early 1965 he received a draft of an article that chronicled his recent emergence in the state Republican Party. The piece, which was set to run in *Kiwanis Magazine*, portrayed a man who was impressive but not extraordinary; he was the "man of modest means" Richard Nixon had invoked in his famous Checkers speech. Agnew personified the civic-minded yet accomplished men of the Kiwanis. It was "more than a little tempting to Horatio-Algerize the arrival of the eminence of Spiro T. Agnew, son of a Greek immigrant," the article said. Instead, the writer stuck to the era's dominant middle-class themes of competency and pragmatism. Agnew personified "the new 'commuter citizen'—men of moderate wealth, who have doubled the County's population in the last decade by moving from the city and who . . . are interested in schools, highways, taxes and civic issues." Agnew "was the right man for the job."[23]

The article was happy to report that "Ted Agnew has not disappointed his supporters." The accomplishments listed bolstered his image as a level-headed administrator in touch with the growing suburban county's needs and problems. For example, Agnew "did not make job appointments on a strict party basis. Instead, he initiated a bi-partisan regime emphasizing ability rather than party label." As a result, the county had launched efforts rejuvenating "blighted sections," dealing with water pollution, starting "no less than 32 separate neighborhood sewer projects," and getting "excess" tax revenues collected by the state returned to the county.[24]

Not surprisingly for an article highlighting the sterling qualities of a Kiwanian, Agnew's personal characteristics figured into the piece even more than his political accomplishments. He was a "confident, well-dressed, soft-spoken man" with hair "greying at the temples." He appeared "a foot taller" than he really was, and his most distinctive feature was "his eyes, sharp and penetrating under heavy brows." The article also noted how "through the corridors of antiquity" the men in Agnew's family had been named some variation of Spiro Theodore or Theodore Spiro. But befitting the post–World War II middle-class desire to fit in, the "latest Spiro Theodore, after having had to fight his way through grammar school in this country, decided to be the last. He named his one son among three daughters Randy."[25]

The profile next covered Agnew's military service and early professional career, a story that certainly would have struck a chord with millions of men of his generation. Drafted into the army in 1941, Agnew fought at the Battle of the Bulge, but "today [he] doesn't dwell on his war experiences." He used the G.I. Bill to enter the University of Baltimore's law school, where he completed his degree by taking night classes. (The University of Baltimore was not accredited by the American Bar Association until 1972.[26] If Richard Nixon felt snubbed by the Ivy League–trained elite because of his Duke University law degree, one can imagine the size of the chip on Agnew's shoulder when he became a household name in the late 1960s.) Elected office was nowhere in his future, he was sure: "If people at that time had told me I would be in politics, I would have said they were crazy." With the number of practicing attorneys rising steadily, Agnew took on a series of undistinguished yet respectable middle-management jobs in other fields. He worked as a claims adjustor for an insurance company and as a personnel director for a grocery store chain. After being called back into the army during the Korean War and relocating to Baltimore County, he finally returned to law in the early

1950s. By the end of the decade Agnew was the chair of the county's first board of appeals, where he handled disputed zoning cases, an important and often contentious issue in fast-developing suburban areas.[27]

A close look at Agnew's edits to the *Kiwanis* profile reveals a political savvy and self-awareness that challenges the later historical narrative of Agnew as a witless tool of Richard Nixon. For example, where the article noted Agnew's creation of a "bi-partisan regime emphasizing ability rather than party label," he edited out the next line: "'One of these days I must appoint some Republicans,' he said only half-jokingly."[28] More revealing, however, are the changes he made to the biographical facts; his attention to detail is impressive and his edits are canny, shaping the positive yet relatable image he wanted to portray. The original draft explained that "he is called Ted by almost everybody except his wife Judy and friends of his father from the old neighborhood, who are often disappointed to discover he can't even speak Greek." Agnew cut "from the old neighborhood," likely sensing that he had done enough to embrace his background in a place where many upwardly mobile families had said a happy good-bye to the old neighborhood.[29]

In an environment where military service—and the experience of actual combat—was not uncommon, Agnew also knew better than to make too much of his time in the army. The original draft read: "Overseas in 1944 he fought in the Battle of the Bulge, but today doesn't dwell on his war experiences. 'I won four battle stars, but I can't remember now for which battles. I was never wounded to the extent of reporting it.' He earned the combat infantry badge and was discharged in 1946." Agnew deleted his humble brag about winning four battle stars in now-forgotten military campaigns. But he kept the sentence about earning the combat infantry badge; it meant that he had come under fire in an active combat situation, as every veteran of his generation would have known.[30]

Finally, and wisely, Agnew reined in an overly enthusiastic description of his physical appearance. The draft read, "Ted Agnew is a serious, confident, well-dressed, heavy-necked, handsome, soft-spoken man with straight black hair greying at the temples, who, because of his erect carriage and quiet, yet not mirthless, manner, gives the impression of being something of a cross between John Wayne and [comic strip hero] Steven

Canyon." "Oh God!" Agnew penciled in the margin. Out went "heavy-necked, handsome," his black hair became "brown," and he cut the remainder of the sentence.[31] The reader is left with a deftly created image of Spiro Agnew that fit the World War II generation in the postwar era: successful but not a show-off, a veteran but not a hero, a family man, and a capable administrator more interested in doing a good job for his fellow citizens than in personal accolades.

Despite his later reputation for not being an especially deep thinker, Agnew was notably attuned to the quickening pace of life Americans faced as the 1960s began. In addition to the existential anxieties caused by the Cold War threat of nuclear annihilation, the postwar explosion of new technology, the dizzying power and reach of consumerism, and the rise of the suburbs left many middle-class citizens with an uneasy feeling of rootlessness amid their many material comforts. As sociologist William Whyte, author of *The Organization Man*, observed in the mid-1950s, suburban life encouraged in those new to the middle class a "strong impulse to upgrade themselves" materially, culturally, and socially. The result made for a strange new kind of anxiety. Somewhere "lies the good life," Whyte wrote, "but . . . it vanishes as quickly as one finds it."[32]

Well before his turn on the national stage, Agnew had developed an effective way of describing the middle-class experience that felt so precarious to so many. For them, the early 1960s seemed to reveal disturbing evidence that the "good life" that Whyte described was in danger of slipping from their grasp. Worries over the fragility of their newly achieved prosperity would later meld seamlessly with their alarm over the rise of the antiwar movement, the student movement, and the black power movement. It all spoke to a fear of disorder and loss of control. Recognizing these anxieties, Agnew had already formulated a critique of modern society and a rhetoric of toughness that fed perfectly into his law and order speeches less than a decade later as Richard Nixon's vice president.

In 1964, at the Masons' thirty-sixth annual Cornhusking-Harvest Home Day, Agnew delivered a detailed—and inexplicably long, given the setting—address on the challenges of the modern world. The event was held in Cockeysville, outside of Baltimore County, indicating Agnew's rise in statewide recognition and, perhaps, his interest in running for governor. Throughout the history of the United States, he began, the country had "moved in the direction of grandeur and power, marked by an increased technology, a larger population and greater complexity in every aspect of life." Undeniable success created new and often baffling circumstances: "Methods of mass communication, rapid transportation, and nuclear warfare, undreamed of by our forefathers, have actually succeeded in shrinking the world while at the same time multiplying its problems and the difficulties of legislation." Meanwhile the rise of a consumer economy encouraged a narrow preoccupation with lives Agnew described as "full of our own small busy-nesses." "As our country has progressed and encompassed newer, better, and bigger things," he said, "we have had to adapt ourselves to a fast-paced 20th century world which demands greater intelligence, more creative thinking and forward-looking ideas than before." Speaking in terms that would soon resonate with the silent majority, he added, "While living in today's world may well be a unique and marvelous experience in many ways, it is certainly not easy to be forced to reevaluate traditional standards and update long-standing concepts. The 20th century is not only moving swiftly in every direction—it is sweeping us in a considerable state of bewilderment, along with it."[33]

Despite the modern American ideal of the middle-class home as a safe, calming space, Agnew saw how "in our home, too, we are bombarded with demands, as conflicting groups and interests constantly vie for our attention—watch this show, read that book, listen to this program, attend that meeting, go to this lecture, take that course, join this club, play with the children, mow the lawn, fix that screen! The list seems endless." It was "no wonder we feel harassed and frustrated. We barely have time to think and we resent any intrusion—no matter how worthwhile—which forces its way into our hard-earned moments of privacy."[34] Here Agnew sounds remarkably like a character in Sloan Wilson's famous 1955 novel about the anxieties of middle-class striving. In the opening scene of *The Man in the Gray Flannel Suit*, Betsy Rath, surveying all that she and her husband have—a nice home, steady job, healthy kids—laments, "I don't know what's the matter with us. . . . We shouldn't be so discontented all the time."[35]

Agnew's solution to these challenges can be found in a commencement address he delivered in 1963 at Essex Community College (known today as the Community College of Baltimore County). He began with the usual thanks and congratulations before offering a blunt analysis of the rising generation: "We cannot spoon-feed, we cannot mass-produce, we cannot guarantee that you will be a productive citizen." Agnew was echoing the growing criticism of the baby boomer generation as over-indulged and entitled. He confronted the happy graduates by adding: "I am sometimes fearful, looking about me, that we are producing generations of timid organization people, born to be commanded. I fear we are losing our appreciation for hard work and independent thought." There-fore, "I suggest that it is an attitude of mental toughness that each of you *must* acquire if you are not to fall *victim* to an easy world in which easy opportunities, and security, are so readily available."[36]

The themes that dominate these speeches — that life in the post–World War II era was "moving swiftly in every direction," making the next gen-eration soft but leaving Americans like him in a "state of bewilderment" and "frequently suspicious" — served as a constant backdrop to Agnew's outlook on life. As a product of the suburbs with all their new trappings, he certainly could not reject this modern world; but he also acknowl-edged that his generation was having to reevaluate traditional concepts. And he conceded that making these adjustments was not easy. Respond-ing to this often unspoken middle-class unease, he offered himself as the tough truth-teller, wielding bluntness and certainty to cut through the era's complexities.

Out of this context was Agnew's political style born. Throughout his career, when challenged on almost any subject, he responded with biting verbal attacks he defended as necessary candor. In doing so he routinely defined his critics as unreasonable, overly sensitive, and out of touch with "normal" Americans like himself. Plus, he discovered early, it was good politics. Picturing him early in his political career as a moderate, results-oriented Republican thus overlooks the abundant evidence of the hard-hitting, suburban populist style that later made Agnew an icon to the silent majority. His first foray into elective politics made it clear to him that he started from outside the establishment.

When Agnew ran for Baltimore County Circuit Court judge in 1960, he found himself opposed by the local Democratic Party's sitting judge principle, meaning support for the incumbent (and Democratic) judges. The *Sun*, too, backed the sitting judges, prompting Agnew to accuse the newspaper of pressuring politicians to agree in order to assure good treatment in the press. To him, the sitting judge principle was simply a means to keep Republicans off the circuit court. In a published letter to the *Sun*, Agnew unleashed his style of attack, combining sarcasm and victimhood. The "sitting judge bandwagon" was, he charged, "in danger of collapsing from the weight of all the politicians who have jumped aboard hoping . . . to enjoy the obvious benefits of 'togetherness' with your editorial position." There had been, Agnew continued mockingly, "a veritable frenzy of indorsement [*sic*] as the vote seekers grab for hand-holds on the chosen vehicle, which they hope will transport them to the Valhalla where dwell all public office holders." The idea that the sitting judge principle led to a "nonpartisan judiciary" was "a beautiful mirage," he wrote. Partisanship was precisely the issue. Sitting Republican judges in past elections, Agnew noted, had been defeated. Why? Because "each suffered from a disease of the registration glands, feared by the organization to be communicable, known as 'Republicanitis.'"[37] Agnew lost that race and all three incumbents were reelected.[38]

Local Democrats flexed their muscle again the next year when Agnew was not reappointed to the county Board of Appeals. The Baltimore County Council, all Democrats, made the appointments to the board, and Agnew blamed his removal on their desire for total control. He had considerable support, including endorsements from "numerous civic organizations and 71 prominent lawyers."[39] Already sounding like the Agnew of later years, he again portrayed himself as an aggrieved warrior for justice pitted against darker forces. He charged that an "undercover campaign" had been waged to remove him from the board. He had become a target to his "foes" because they were "afraid they can't control me." He "represented a lack of control, as far as they are concerned." But, Agnew assured his supporters, "I am not going to lie down and take it."[40]

Agnew's slashing rhetoric revealed early an ability to stir passions. At the session where the county council announced that he was being replaced, the *Sun* reported, the "meeting room [was] jammed with Agnew partisans" who "sent up cries" of protest. Sharp words flew for and against Agnew. The article quoted council members on why they had made their decision. Robert Gill, a Democrat, explained that he had changed his vote when "Mr. Agnew chastized [*sic*] us all in the press and burned his bridges."[41]

Agnew may have burned his bridges with the local establishment, but he remained a popular figure among the voters who elected him county executive in 1962, a victory that he found deeply satisfying given his past dust-up with the council. The win also elevated his profile in the state overnight. As the head of a growing, modernizing county, he was in greater demand as a speaker, and he used his new platform to weigh in on issues of the day. Despite Agnew's burgeoning reputation as a moderate Republican, his combative style and his articulation of middle-class worries remained on clear display.

Agnew's early political style in addressing civil rights and race relations is especially important to examine because it would later have national repercussions. As the 1960s began Maryland was slowly dismantling its Jim Crow laws. Officials in John F. Kennedy's administration were inquiring into the discrimination African diplomats experienced while driving through Baltimore County on their way from Washington, D.C., to the United Nations in New York City.[42] In 1961 three writers from the *Baltimore Afro American* reported on progress of a sort. The journalists "dressed as diplomats from the mythical country of Goban, visited restaurants along U.S. Route 40 last week, and were mistaken for African diplomats and served." This ended up being a hollow victory, however, because for members of the local African American community, the article continued, "You just don't get served period."[43]

Even though the county's African American population was small, Agnew knew that its proximity to the nation's capital meant he was going to have to contend with local incidents of racial discrimination. Agnew considered himself liberal-minded on the issue of segregation; that is, he thought it was wrong and had to end. But it is equally clear that dealing with the issue caused him great discomfort. He claimed to support the movement toward desegregation in the early 1960s, but that support was cautious and contingent. Agnew represented the commonly held view that racial inequality was best addressed in procedural terms: for example, by establishing legal protections in public activities and accommodations. But like so many others, he drew the line at redistributing resources to address past injustices. Nonetheless, from this position Agnew could claim that he had always supported civil rights even as the ground shifted between 1963 and 1968. Additionally, and not surprisingly, from the beginning of his political career as county executive Agnew's commitment to civil rights warred with his counterpunching style of attacking those who questioned his actions. As early as 1963, even as he was instrumental in an important settlement in favor of the local civil rights community, he lashed out with dismissive and often insulting language when challenged over the pace of change and the tactics used by activists.

The still-segregated Gwynn Oak Amusement Park opened its 1963 season as a target of activists. Gwynn Oak's owners, brothers Arthur, David, and James Price, had made it clear they had no intention of integrating. Protests led by the local chapter of the Congress of Racial Equality (CORE) on July 7 ended in more than a hundred arrests.[44] The *Sun* also reported on racists threatening violence. During a "tension-packed two hours" Baltimore County chief of police Robert Lally wrestled to control the situation, "his voice nearly drowned in a cacophony of 'kill all them Niggers' and 'get Nigger lovers.'"[45]

Afro American editor James Williams was among those arrested. He recounted how "a group of young toughs with their duckbill hats and pinched faces, stepped out on the sidewalk to block our way. I saw one of them take a heavy leather belt in his hands and snap it, again and again." Later, as the protesters were arrested and held in the Pikesville Armory for processing, he saw the injuries inflicted on some of the marchers, including a woman who was "struck in the head with a piece of paving block thrown by a female spectator in a red dress. Having once thrown the rock, the girl with the red dress showed her courage by running."[46]

Agnew, in office only since January, contributed to the eventual integration of the amusement park. He and the county council called for the formation of a group to help resolve such potentially explosive situations. Despite tension between CORE, Agnew, the Price brothers, and the new Human Relations Council, Gwynn Oak Amusement Park finally integrated on August 28, 1963, the same day as the now legendary March on Washington.[47] The *Sun* reported that it came off without incident. One story focused on the Langley family: Charles, Marian, and daughter Sharon. The Langleys lived in Baltimore and personified the African American middle class; Charles worked for the Social Security Administration in Washington, D.C., and Marian was a nurse. Charles, who "wore a clasped-hand Freedom March badge on his jacket," explained that although he did not belong to any civil rights organizations, the family had planned to go to the March on Washington until they decided to go to Gwynn Oak instead. The article indicated that a "few sotto voce comments from white patrons were heard," but "in general the Negro patrons, once the photographers left, attracted little more attention than anyone else." The Langleys pronounced Gwynn Oak "a very nice park" and said they hoped they would become regular visitors.[48]

The successful integration of the Gwynn Oak Amusement Park undergirds the narrative about Agnew as a pragmatic leader who sought fairness and results over scoring political points. However, when looking at Agnew's public statements at this time, one can plainly see a certain brittleness with those who questioned his lead. While the Gwynn Oak negotiations were underway, local activists announced their intention to picket the park again despite Agnew's request that they not do so. He responded by attacking their credibility, reasonableness, and what he perceived as over-emotionalism. "Although I am in sympathy with the goal of the demonstrators," Agnew stated in a press release, "I seriously question the wisdom of their actions." The protesters had "thrown, through [their] hasty and immature decision, an undeserved burden upon the Baltimore County Police Force" and "wasted the money of the taxpayers of Baltimore County." "Regrettably, fairness and restraint" had "lost out to ill-advised haste and emotional self-hypnosis."[49]

Notes from a statement Agnew made on the civil rights movement in December 1963 again reveal a narrow range of acceptable activism from his perspective. Employing false equivalencies, he said that the issue of civil rights made "fertile soil for the malcontent opportunists." Now, he complained, he had to contend with the "hatreds of segregationist dogma" and also the "unreasonable ultimatums of some power crazed integrationist leaders." After this brief balancing act Agnew reserved his criticism for the nonviolent civil rights community rather than those who threatened to murder black people over access to an amusement park. He accused the leaders of creating "popularity cheaply purchased by boldly assuming over-simplified positions on highly complex, volatile issues." Agnew was presumably referring to himself when he cited the "obliga-tion . . . to protect our Negro community against exploitation by selfishly motivated opportunists," in particular those who "come from afar to lash emotions to a frenzy with unlawful demonstrations, who substitute slo-gans for logic, who create crises where none exist."[50]

Agnew already relished being provocative, especially when talking about civil rights and race relations. At a local testimonial dinner in his honor on May 5, 1964, he acknowledged that "you might logically ex-pect that, having basked a while in this pleasant and non-controversial atmosphere, I would avoid anything as volatile as the icy needle-shower of public reaction to any statement on civil rights. Illogical or not, I cannot resist the temptation to use this occasion . . . to amplify a few simple state-ments that need saying and need listening to by all citizens." Agnew trot-ted out his "someone has to say it" theme as he instructed and warned the civil rights community: "Negroes must educate their followers that gov-ernment cannot . . . legislate social acceptance."[51] On another note card of the same date, he wrote that "emphasis should be placed on Negroes with intelligence, stature, & acceptance not wildmen." The final text, released to the press, claimed to know the mind of the black community, if not all the names of its leaders, and took a shot at the media along the way: "Many of the more sensational self-styled Negro leaders do not command the respect of Negroes. The news media would perform a great service by concentrating on the intelligent and accepted Negro leaders, such as King, Wilkinson [sic: NAACP leader Roy Wilkins], and [CORE leader James] Farmer—and ignoring the wild men."[52] He concluded that there was a "great need for calm & moderate leadership." In the only underlined sentence on the note card, Agnew emphasized a point he would return to later in the decade: "Civil disobedience is just a fancy way of saying law-breaking."[53] Here was Agnew the civil rights proceduralist: equal rights for all within the law, and if the law needed to be changed to achieve equal rights, so be it. But in his view, behavior that violated the law, even on behalf of the cause of racial justice, could not logically claim to be done on behalf of "civil rights."

Certainly part of the touchiness Agnew showed in the Gwynn Oak incident and its aftermath was due to the fact that there was already speculation about a future run for governor. The *Kiwanis* profile reported that he "had been . . . non-committal on his future political ambitions," although among friends he shared his thoughts more freely. As a Baltimore city native and a Baltimore County leader, Agnew pointed out that around "82 percent of the voters are from Baltimore and environs." He felt confident about getting good press, the article said, "if he could get the support of the *Sunpapers*, the *Washington Post*, and one or two others—maybe." In an observation that would look ironic in just a few years, the *Kiwanis* writer noted that "Ted always has had good public relations with the press, not because he is patronizing but because he is friendly—and because he suspects he learns as much from reporters as they from him." But the open speculation in front of friends—and that particular reporter— on a race for governor then ended abruptly: "'It depends on timing,' he said. 'You have to be in the right place and at the right time.' Then he lapsed into silence."[54] Given that Baltimore County Democrats had unified behind a single strong candidate, Dale Anderson, and that reelection as county executive therefore looked unlikely, Agnew determined that 1966 was indeed the right time to make a statewide run.

The Maryland governor's race of 1966 offers a useful snapshot of the swirling national currents at mid-decade, especially in light of the passage of the Civil Rights Act of 1964 and the Voting Rights Act of 1965. The summers were marked by headline-grabbing urban riots in places like Newark in 1964 and, more famously, the Watts neighborhood in Los Angeles in 1965—unrest often explained as African American frustration boiling over. A growing number of white moderates now questioned the direction of the civil rights movement as Martin Luther King Jr. and other leaders took on urban poverty and black nationalist organizations like the Black Panthers began to appear. Tom Wicker of the *New York Times* wrote in 1966 that "while most people may talk more about Vietnam and inflation, they worry more about Negroes moving into the block, taking over their jobs, and making their streets a battleground. Thus backlash, as so long predicted, may become a major element in American politics this year."[55] Gene Roberts of the *Times* observed similarly: "Public support for the Negro and his problems is waning, white opposition is growing, and the civil rights movement is falling into increasing disarray. Many white liberals are confused; others have become preoccupied with Vietnam. And white moderates, disturbed by Negro riots and mounting pressure for housing desegregation, are becoming apathetic, or hostile." Roberts also cited others "who identified with the Negro when he was under physical attack in the South" but who had "switched their identification when riots erupted in Northern cities."[56]

What the political fallout from the urban rioting would be was still anyone's guess, as both parties seemed to be in flux ideologically (as will be discussed more thoroughly in subsequent chapters). Despite legislative progress on civil rights, the failed attempt to rid the party of segregationist delegates at the 1964 Democratic National Convention caused some black activists to question their faith in the political system. At the same time, conservatives such as John Tower and Strom Thurmond became Republicans because the Democratic Party had become *too* liberal. One thing was clear as the 1966 midterm elections neared. As Wicker noted, "backlash" was the word of the day.

These trends were evident in Maryland, too. In 1964, for instance, Jane Zantzinger held a Democrats for Goldwater fund-raiser in conservative southern Maryland. Her husband, William Zantzinger, had killed Hattie Carroll, an African American woman, the year before at a Baltimore charity ball. When Carroll, who was working at the event, did not prepare a drink fast enough for the already-drunk tobacco farmer, he beat her with a cane. She died shortly thereafter of a brain hemorrhage. Zantzinger was found guilty only of assault and served six months in a county jail. The light sentence outraged civil rights activists, and the episode became more widely known thanks to Bob Dylan's song "The Lonesome Death of Hattie Carroll." When the *Baltimore Afro American* contacted Jane Zantzinger about the Goldwater fund-raiser and whether her husband would be attending, she shot back, "He has nothing to do with it. . . . Are you trying to make a stink out of this?" before adding, "I don't trust newspapers."[57] Other white conservative Maryland Democrats had a candidate of their own. George Wallace, the segregationist governor of Alabama, posted a strong showing in the state's Democratic primary that year, finishing second but carrying sixteen of twenty-three counties.[58]

Two years later, in 1966, George Mahoney, an unabashed segregationist and a backlash-driven candidate, captured the Democratic nomination for governor, much to the horror of the pro–civil rights wing of the party in places like Montgomery County and the African American precincts of Baltimore city. Mahoney's nomination reverberated, and "Washington buzzed with discussion" of the upset win. Lyndon Johnson himself was reported to be "disturbed at the 'white backlash'" in Maryland.[59] But as the Zantzinger for Goldwater story shows, Maryland was still home to thousands of old southern Democrats on the Eastern Shore and in the rural southern counties of St. Mary's, Calvert, and Charles. Appealing to white urban and suburban voters also, Mahoney ran on a George Wallace–like message against a pending state law regarding fair housing. For some white Marylanders a law mandating fair housing practices was a bridge too far, and they responded positively to Mahoney's campaign slogan: "Your home is your castle; protect it." Mahoney's success offered a clear sign that the white backlash was not just southern and rural. A 1975 study concluded that he received 46 percent of the white working-class vote in Baltimore city, and that elsewhere in the state "the greater the black population in a white majority region, the greater the white attraction to Mahoney."[60] The *Sun* reported that the "similarities" between Mahoney's victorious vote totals in Agnew's home of Baltimore County and those of George Wallace in 1964 were "particularly striking."[61]

Meanwhile, Agnew crushed four other candidates in the Republican primary, winning more than 83 percent of the vote.[62] Agnew, the *Sun* reported, was now a "by-word in the Republican Party in Maryland." Voters found him a "pleasant, direct sort of man" but also "somewhat thinskinned—and quite pugnacious."[63] Mahoney's nomination suddenly made an Agnew victory possible, even likely, as he observed with his "cat-who-ate-the-canary smile of a man quietly waiting to rake in the chips."[64] Given this remarkable turn of events, Agnew's campaign strategy was to offer himself as a capable, experienced administrator and as a moderate on civil rights. His campaign literature, it was noted at the time, "pointedly avoids mention of party affiliation,"[65] and he welcomed the support of the Democrats for Agnew clubs organized to defeat Mahoney.[66]

Even as Agnew occupied the moral high ground on race relations over his opponent, he remained sensitive to the growing white moderate unease over civil rights; indeed, he shared it. Thus, while Agnew was campaigning not to lose, he still took care to send a consistently guarded message on civil rights even as he drew in African American and white liberal voters. In a July 27 speech, for instance, he observed that "there are many who would agree with me that the civil rights movement has lost much of its momentum because it has become a 'house divided.' Some of its leaders are turning in one direction, and some in other directions. Some are turning to violence, and others to moderation." But now he worried about the "pell-mell haste to take *yet another and another* giant step forward." Below that line on his note card, Agnew penciled in, "We must not drop the tool of moral persuasion. Black power in the finest sense will come from responsible black leadership and total community." He then capitalized for emphasis his view on appropriate civil rights activism. The Congress of Racial Equality, he concluded, "can be very helpful indeed in some of its QUIETER causes—for its efforts in Baltimore to help get Negroes started as owners of small businesses and as operators, through franchises, of gas stations, dry-cleaning shops, and other establishments."[67]

Against a backdrop of sharply increasing crime rates nationwide, Agnew also effectively combined his guarded message on civil rights with an increasingly popular law and order theme. In a news release he stated: "Crime is a frightened housewife, afraid to leave her home either by day or night—and it is this kind of citizen, living in terror for herself and her children, who we must protect." He referred to a letter he had received from a "family living in [a] lovely suburban Washington community" who had written: "We no longer feel safe residing with our children in Silver Spring, which is certainly a sad commentary on our times." Agnew's message, targeted here to the white middle class, was none too subtle: "There is no escape to the suburbs to avoid crime for it is becoming nearly as prevalent there as on the streets of our suffering cities."[68]

In the end Agnew won comfortably, 49.5 percent to 40.6 percent, with Mahoney having been "buried under an avalanche of Negro and suburban 'white collar' voters."[69] Revealingly, however, given the context of the "backlash" vote, Agnew's home base of Baltimore County voted for Mahoney by nearly 13,000 votes — 81,570 to 68,596.[70] Nonetheless, it marked the second time in his short political career that Agnew had pulled off the unlikely, scoring a Republican victory in a heavily Democratic state. The pragmatic, capable moderate was now also perceived as a winner.

Agnew's term as governor, less than two years, was in many ways similar to his experience as county executive. He could point to his work with the Democratic-controlled assembly and claim real accomplishments, such as ending the state ban on biracial marriage and, significantly, passing a fair housing law. As late as September 30, 1967, the *Afro American* applauded Agnew's "impressive civil rights accomplishment record" in his short time in office.[71] Despite this seemingly progressive track record, Agnew proposed slashing $30 million from the state welfare department's budget increase request for 1967, while approving a pay raise for the state police.[72] Given that Agnew had promised to support increasing public assistance, this switch angered many who had recently voted for him. The new governor did not do himself any favors with his liberal supporters when he refused at first to meet with those protesting the cut to the budget increase. Agnew was "apparently annoyed by the picketing and demonstrating" outside his office.[73]

Indeed, Agnew's by now well-established political style ripened during his brief governorship. His biographers point to incidents like the racial unrest in the Eastern Shore town of Cambridge in 1967, the African American student uprising at Bowie State University beginning in March 1968, and his notorious hectoring of Baltimore's civil rights leaders in the aftermath of Martin Luther King Jr.'s assassination as turning points in his evolution into a conservative. Justin Coffey argues that the Cambridge incident in particular was "a defining moment" when Agnew "began to move to the right and was increasingly critical of not just the civil rights movement but liberalism in general."[74] But Agnew's reaction to the activists of 1967 and 1968 was essentially, and at times literally, no different from his reaction to CORE's efforts to integrate Gwynn Oaks in 1963.

The stakes were certainly higher, and the size of the stage had changed from Towson to Annapolis, but the national Republican Party establishment had taken note of how he handled the race issue in Maryland.

Cambridge had a history of racial tensions prior to 1967, but that summer they flared again over a range of issues. The points of friction included access to a public swimming pool and multiple charges of "discrimination at all levels of the city's seasonally limited job market, discrimination in the local agency of the Office of Economic Opportunity, discrimination by employers on Federal contracts and discrimination at all levels of law enforcement in Dorchester county."[75] Agnew's early efforts to "head off racial strife" got off to what appeared to be an encouraging start as representatives from his office worked with local black leaders to effectively end segregation in the community pool. But more difficult issues lay ahead. Tensions escalated when H. Rap Brown, the new leader of the Student Nonviolent Coordinating Committee (SNCC), came to the Eastern Shore in late July. Using the harder-edged rhetoric of the black power movement, Brown proclaimed, "Don't be trying to love that honky to death. . . . Shoot him to death. Shoot him to death, brother, because that's what he is out to do to you. Do to him like he would do to you, but do it to him first." Brown talked about how slowly Cambridge was changing from its racist past and concluded, "If this town don't come around, this town should be burned down."[76] Later that night, Cambridge did indeed explode in fire and gunshots. Two blocks were burned to the ground, and the cause and effect of Brown's visit and the subsequent destruction were fixed in the public's, and Agnew's, eye.

Agnew toured the burned-out area and urged "citizens of both races to remain calm and reaffirm their commitment to uphold law and order." Agnew's own calm slipped, however, as he pinned the blame on Brown, "a professional agitator whose inflammatory statements deliberately provoked this outbreak of violence." As governor, he continued, "I cannot and will not tolerate riot induced felonies which verge on anarchy, nor will I allow the individuals who maliciously inspire such action to slip away unchallenged. I have directed the authorities to seek out H. Rap Brown and bring him to justice. Such a person cannot be permitted to enter a State with the intention to destroy and then sneak away leaving these poor people with the results of his evil scheme."[77] The next week Agnew announced a new policy that authorized law enforcement to arrest immediately "any person inciting to riot" and thus shutting down "his vicious speech."[78]

The governor continued to use Brown as his stalking horse throughout the fall. In September he took his message to an audience he knew would be receptive, the Southern Governors' Conference. In his law and order address, Agnew again dismissed the notion that Brown's language in Cambridge was simply a matter of free speech. There was a critical difference between "free speech and excuses or rationalization to permit criminal conduct," he said. While there is no question that by 1967 the civil rights struggle had taken a radical turn from the nonviolent ethics of the early 1960s, Agnew's response was the same; he remained "angry at civil disobedience when it is used as a claim to be able to break laws."[79]

Agnew's attempts to put down civil disorder shifted from Cambridge to campus in March 1968 when students at predominantly African American Bowie State University began to press for improvements to their underfunded institution. Their efforts included a multiday boycott of classes and occupation of the president's office. On April 2 Agnew responded with threats and by discrediting the students' activism. He warned that "'force would have been used' had the need arisen." He also replayed his 1963 complaint about CORE at Gwynn Oaks: "It is time public officials in this country stop yielding to pressures and threats by those who would take the law into their own hands. . . . I certainly don't intend to yield to such pressures."[80]

When the students went to Annapolis on April 4 and conducted a "study-in" in the state capitol, Agnew had more than two hundred of them arrested and announced he was closing Bowie State for the time being. In his statement he again denounced civil disobedience and called for more law and order. The issue was "whether or not to condone a deliberate flouting and defiance of law" by "young people who confused provocation with principle—who were deliberately inflamed by outside influences, influences which all too often thrive on chaos and disrespect of the law." Agnew was "certain" that "they—the public—do not want the Governor of this State, or any other elected official in whom they have reposed this confidence, to yield to unlawful and illegal tactics such as those that the State has seen in the past few days. I am fully aware that these students have been orderly in their disorder, but I do not find that an excuse for breaking the law."[81]

Agnew's Bowie State problem was swept aside by the shocking news of Martin Luther King Jr.'s assassination that same day. On April 6 Baltimore erupted in violence and civil unrest. The governor called out the Maryland National Guard and then received additional federal troops. By the time the unrest ended three days later, the damage included more than a thousand businesses destroyed, at least six persons killed, and more than seven hundred injured. Looking back on the tenth anniversary in 1978, former Baltimore mayor Thomas D'Alesandro III conceded, "I don't think that a large segment of the population knew how bad it was in those [black] neighborhoods, how deep the problems were. Jobs, housing, medical care, all the essentials for life were missing down there."[82] Out of this nerve-wracking context came Agnew's sit-down with the local black leadership of Baltimore, a meeting that would have, as it turned out, national political implications.

Some one hundred local African American leaders received invitations to meet with Agnew at the State Office Building in Baltimore on April 11. Television stations aired the meeting live, a clear indication of its importance. Agnew opened by assuring his listeners that "hard on the heels of tragedy come that assignment of blame and the excuses. I did not invite you here for either purpose. I did not ask you here to recount previous depravations, nor to hear me enumerate prior attempts to correct them." But then Agnew did just that. Acknowledging that "every one here is a leader," he contrasted those present to "the ready-mix, instantaneous type of leader" who was, by Agnew's own design, "not present." The governor once again showed his ability to turn a phrase, sneering, "The circuit-riding, Hanoi-visiting type of leader is missing from this assembly. The caterwauling, riot-inciting, burn-America-down type of leader is conspicuous by his absence. That is no accident, ladies and gentlemen, it is just good planning." Agnew then added awkwardly, "All in the vernacular of today—'that's what it's all about, baby.'"[83]

Things went downhill quickly, and members of the audience began to walk out in protest of what they were hearing.[84] Referring to local SNCC leader Robert Moore, Agnew said, "Some weeks ago, a reckless stranger to this city, carrying the credentials of a well known civil rights organization, characterized the Baltimore police as 'enemies of the black man.'"[85] To the credit of some of those present, Moore's comments had been condemned, he added. But when "white leaders openly complimented you for your objective, courageous action, you immediately encountered a storm of censure from parts of the Negro community. The criticism was born of a perverted concept of race loyalty and inflamed by the type of leader whom I earlier mentioned is not here today. And you ran."[86]

Not only did the leaders run, according to Agnew's information, but they met with "that demagogue and others like him," and all agreed not to "criticize any black spokesman, regardless of the content of his remarks." Agnew continued to pour on the blame: "You were beguiled by the rationalizations of unity; you were intimidated by veiled threats; you were stung by insinuations that you were Mr. Charlie's boy, by epithets like 'Uncle Tom.'" The leaders of the black community had given in to lawbreakers, the governor said. "But actually it was only the opinions of those who depend on chaos and tumult for leadership—those who deliberately were not invited today. It was the opinion of a few, distorted and magnified by the *silence* of most of you here today. Now, parts of many of our cities lie in ruins." Of the destruction in Baltimore, Agnew said, "you know who lit the fires. They were not lit in honor of your great fallen leader. Nor were they lit from an overwhelming sense of frustration and despair." It was lawlessness, plain and simple, "kindled at the suggestion and with the instruction of the advocates of violence."[87]

Again recycling almost verbatim his criticisms from 1963–64, Agnew lectured the leaders of the black community on the wrong turns their movement had made:

> Somewhere the objectives of the civil rights movement have been obscured in a surge of emotional oversimplification. Somewhere the goal of equal opportunity has been replaced by the goal of instantaneous economic equality. . . . I readily admit that this equal opportunity has not always been present for Negroes—that it is not still totally present for Negroes. But I

say that we have come a long way. And I say that the road we have trod-den is built with the sweat of the Roy Wilkenses [*sic*] and the Whitney Youngs—and the spiritual leadership of Dr. Martin Luther King—and not with violence.[88]

As he drew to a close, Agnew proclaimed, "I publicly repudiate, con-demn and reject all white racists." But he followed this with, "I call upon you to publicly repudiate, condemn and reject all black racists. This, so far, you have not been willing to do." And therefore, as a result of *their* failure, the future looked bleak. "I call upon you as Americans to speak out now against the treason and hate of Stokely Carmichael and Rap Brown. . . . I submit to you that these men and others like them represent a malig-nancy out of control; that they will lead us to a devastating racial civil war" in which "the heaviest losers will be the Negro citizens of America."[89]

The optics were dramatic. In addition to running the text of his re-marks, the *Sun* included a photograph of an agitated Agnew pointing his finger at the leaders of the black community, along with shots of men leaving the room and a powerful one of a group of black leaders gathered elsewhere to watch the address on television. This photo captures vividly the anger and disbelief of those watching and listening to Agnew's state-ment. It focuses on a number of middle-aged and older African American men, eyes riveted on the television screen, some standing and some seated, many with arms folded, but all with looks that burned with indignation.

The moment highlights the building tension between local, usually white, government officials and the civil rights community through the middle years of the decade. Agnew's timeline in relationship to this story, starting in 1963, parallels the shifting focus and tactics of the movement itself. During this fraught time, meanings of racial justice diverged and began to collide, often violently. While the earlier phase of the movement achieved truly significant victories over legal segregation and voter sup-pression, King himself by the end had moved on to address economic and structural racism, while new leaders such as Stokely Carmichael began to promote a more separatist black nationalism. The annual summer unrest in places including Newark and Detroit warned that a breaking point was fast approaching. Many were convinced that with King's murder at the hands of a white man, that point had already arrived. Black moderates like those Agnew harangued were in an enormously difficult bind. Showing up to hear Agnew out signaled that they were anxious to work with the government to address the unrest and destruction taking place in their community. But to stay and be lectured to—and blamed—was asking too much of these leaders at this time. Their walkout demonstrated their long-held exasperation and anger at the white power structure's knee-jerk habit of yet again blaming the black community for its own difficulties.

The blowback was instantaneous; so too was the support for Agnew. A statement on behalf of those in the audience read, "We are shocked at the gall of the Governor suggesting that only he can define the nature of the leadership of the black community."[90] The sense of betrayal, given the strong African American vote for Agnew in 1966, was palpable. In a letter to Agnew published in the *Afro American*, Helen Shaw wrote, "Each time I see your face on television or in the papers, I become sick, knowing that I am guilty of helping a person like you obtain public office." Agnew was both "cowardly and rude" and "not only a disgrace to the State of Maryland, but to the whole human race." Shaw now saw Agnew's "true colors" as a politician, she wrote, and in a bit of foreshadowing she suggested he "contact George Wallace of Alabama."[91]

But, as the *Sun* reported, the episode also produced a wave of praise for Agnew, whose "popularity was greatly enhanced, at least among the white middle class." His office received a deluge of telegrams, calls, and letters, overwhelmingly positive. The article included quotes from the respondents, such as "We're proud to be Republicans" and "[I'm] thankful to hear that the white people will have a strong voice in government." Those rallying to Agnew's side included fifty Baltimore law enforcement officers who wrote, "It has been a long time since we have heard a politician who had the guts to bring it out in the open and lay it on the line as you did yesterday."[92]

The *Sun* reported that Agnew tried immediately—although in hindsight it appears halfheartedly—to repair some of the damage, promising another meeting "in the very near future." It was, the paper noted, "apparent from the shocked reaction of those who came yesterday that much fence mending would be required before many of them would come to another such gathering." Meanwhile, Agnew employed other elements of his political style in his defense. Mindful that he had been elected "largely by the overwhelming support of the Negro community, [he] then added: 'Don't you think I know I'm committing political suicide when I sit here and do this? I know it.'" While he said he was surprised that so many walked out—the paper estimated seventy of the one hundred invited—he "felt no apology was needed" because it "clearly needed to be said."[93]

Agnew's claim of being taken aback by the walkout strains credulity. After all, he acknowledged in his text that "I am sure that these remarks come as somewhat of a surprise to you." And at this extraordinarily delicate moment in the city's race relations, he chose to deliver his speech flanked by three white leaders from law enforcement: the head of the Maryland National Guard, the head of the state police, and the Baltimore City police commissioner. Moreover, Mayor D'Alesandro had read a copy of the speech ahead of time and advised that it be "cooled down."[94] It therefore is hard to escape the conclusion that Agnew knew what he wanted to say and what the reaction was likely to be. The *Sun* at least suspected as much; it observed that "the tenor of the overwhelming support he got from the white community today only indicates that he might have precipitated exactly what he said he was trying to avoid."[95]

The incident did not represent a "new" and harder-edged Agnew. From the days of nonviolent protest in 1963 to the black power–driven unrest of 1967–68, he used the same words, phrases, and logic to push back against civil rights activism that confronted him in any way. What happened in front of the leaders of Baltimore's African American community, and in front of the thousands watching on television, echoed Agnew's well-practiced response to political challenges. And broadening the lens a bit further, this was the same Spiro Agnew who in 1961 had proclaimed he was "not going to lie down and take it" when challenged by the local establishment. The line connects directly to the same bare-fisted vice president who would take on the national media, intellectuals, and anti–Vietnam War protesters within the same decade.

Spiro Agnew would likely have remained a forgettable, small-state governor had Martin Luther King Jr. not been assassinated. Instead, in the aftermath of Agnew's bullying appearance before Baltimore's African American leaders, Pat Buchanan began to feed information about the pugnacious governor to his boss, Richard Nixon. But before we resume telling that story, it is necessary to step back and consider the changing political landscape that Agnew entered in 1960. Starting in the 1930s, both major parties were undergoing a significant reorientation. These tectonic shifts created uncertainties, but they also created opportunities for a new kind of GOP — one that Spiro Agnew helped shape.

2

ROLE REVERSAL

The Roots of the Republican Revival

The Republican Party of 1936 had an image problem. While its base among the plain-folks Protestants of the small-town and rural Midwest gave it the patina of the common touch, there was little question that the party's power center lay with the big, moneyed interests who were now being blamed for the Great Depression. During the 1936 presidential campaign, almost half of the contributions to the Republican National Committee came from the banking and brokerage sectors.[1] The party's presidential candidate that year, Kansas governor Alf Landon, ran on a platform of "individual responsibility, fiscal restraint, efficiency and government decentralism." He was crushed by Franklin Roosevelt and his Democratic New Deal coalition, which employed the interventionist state, government deficit spending, administrative bureaucracy, and pro-labor policies to win a close-to-unanimous electoral college victory.[2] FDR and his party won every state except Maine and Vermont.

Roosevelt's position, and that of Democrats generally, was that the Republican Party bore responsibility for the plight of the "forgotten man." Having yoked themselves during the 1920s to the image of the businessman as the exemplar of American progress and prosperity, the Republicans were trapped on the wrong side of an elemental economic shift after the stock market crash of October 1929 and the onset of the Great Depression. Calvin Coolidge's "the business of America is business" and the "American Individualism" of Herbert Hoover were empty bromides by March 1933, as FDR took the oath of office with the national unemployment rate hovering in the midtwenties. Democrats such as Huey Long pounced; in his stump speech, Long would refer to "Mr. Herbert Hoover of London, England."[3] By 1936 Roosevelt had succeeded in linking the ongoing depression inextricably to the GOP. Republican "economic royalists," as Roosevelt labeled them in his speech accepting renomination for the presidency that year, were out-of-touch elitists. With their insistence on a gold-based currency, a balanced budget, private property rights, and free markets, they were as far removed from the common man and the concerns of everyday life in America as one could be and still reside in the same country. "Roosevelt," one working-class supporter declared, "is the only man we ever had in the White House who would understand that my boss is a son-of-a-bitch."[4] His boss, it may be presumed, was a Republican.

The American Liberty League—an amalgamation of business leaders, financiers, and right-leaning politicians that purported to oppose the New Deal's economic interventionism on philosophical grounds, but whose membership evoked an almost cartoonish vision of plutocratic avarice—epitomized the popular image of Republicans and Republicanism during the first two terms of the Roosevelt administration.[5] On November 4, 1936, the day after suffering the most lopsided defeat in the history of American political parties, and after losing 19 congressional seats to the Democrats, the GOP faced representational deficits in the House and Senate—334 to 88 and 76 to 16, respectively—that appeared to consign it to irrelevancy or perhaps even extinction.[6]

On that November day it would have been risible to predict that some thirty years later the Republican Party would have recast its political image from economic royalism to cultural populism and taken on the role of champion of the common folk against the elite class. Yet by April 11, 1968, the day Spiro Agnew delivered the most important public statement of his career thus far—the angry tongue-lashing of Baltimore's moderate black leaders in the wake of the riots precipitated by the assassination of Martin Luther King Jr.—that transformation had indeed taken place. It made possible the meeting of man and moment, as a suburban everyman Republican governor of a traditionally Democratic state claimed the mantle of spokesperson for the average American. By 1968, thanks largely to a role reversal driven by an increasingly defensive middle-class cultural outlook and changing attitudes toward race relations, Republicans could savage Democrats as out-of-touch elitists blind to the concerns and needs of the everyday people who would soon be known as the silent majority. That reversal made Agnew's political career possible. It allowed him to embark on the same passage from urban Democrat during the depression and war years to suburban Republicanism afterward that hundreds of thousands of other gray-flannel homeowners with mortgages, rec rooms, and lodge memberships had undertaken. Agnew's surpassing averageness thus offers him a representative quality. His story belongs to many others as well.

The Republican Party's road from economic royalism to cultural populism began in an unlikely place. Early in 1937 the newly reinaugurated Roosevelt proposed legislation to radically reconfigure the Supreme Court, which had invalidated a number of core New Deal enactments.[7] While on the surface the president's plan to add a new Supreme Court justice for each one serving past the age of seventy appeared to promote the popular will against an unelected elite, it was also perceived to be itself a form of elitist overreach. Roosevelt's heavy-handed attempt to pass the "court-packing bill" during the spring and early summer of 1937 appeared to many—including many Democrats—to threaten traditional constitutional protections of the separation of powers. Even while the immediate issue of saving New Deal achievements resonated with the American public, Roosevelt's strategies and methods evoked anti-democratic images of overweening executive power. By the time the bill failed in the Senate in July, FDR's national popularity, which had peaked with the election of the previous year, had taken a hit. Roosevelt also put forth a series of executive branch reorganization proposals that would consolidate even more power in his hands.[8] In November 1938 Republicans gained seventy-one seats in the House and six in the Senate, forging an anti–New Deal electoral coalition with southern Democrats on an agenda of localism and anti-statism.

By 1939 and the advent of the new Congress, the tide of New Deal legislation had crested and war preparation was soon to begin. The conversion to a war economy would require a rapprochement with the business community whose hatred Roosevelt had claimed to welcome during the 1936 presidential campaign. During World War II Republicans and southern Democrats pushed back against the Roosevelt administration to limit expansions of state power. The war stimulated a vast expansion of national productive capacity, driven by government-sponsored military spending, but opportunities for broadening the scope of the New Deal welfare state to include universal human services—including guaranteed jobs, incomes, and health care—were lost in the face of Republican and southern opposition.

The Republicans finally won back control of Congress in 1946, and in the ensuing legislative session they reinforced their image as the party of big business. The Taft-Hartley Act, passed over Harry Truman's veto in 1947, authorized state right-to-work laws, classified shop floor foremen and supervisors as part of management, outlawed sympathy strikes, and forced the CIO (Congress of Industrial Organizations) to expel almost 20 percent of its members by mandating loyalty oaths as a condition of affiliation with the union.[9] The Republican-controlled Congress also enacted balanced budget legislation, a tax cut, and a presidential term limit, all aimed at satisfying its corporate constituency seeking to put the New Deal to rest.

Congress was a perfect target for Truman in his uphill, populist-themed reelection campaign of 1948. When he called the "do-nothing" Republican Congress back into summer session that year to consider his Fair Deal program containing expansions of New Deal social, labor, and housing initiatives—a gesture he knew would not result in any substantive legislation—he intended to drive home the message that Republicans were economic elitists. "The people know that the Democratic Party is the people's party, and the Republican Party is the party of special interest," the president told convention delegates as he accepted the nomination, "and it always has been and always will be."[10]

During the campaign, Truman excoriated Republicans as "gluttons of privilege" and "blood suckers with offices in Wall Street" to devastating effect.[11] The Republican presidential nominee, New York governor Thomas Dewey, was associated with the Eastern Establishment wing of his party, the least hostile strain of the GOP toward the policies of the New Deal. Nonetheless, Truman succeeded in linking Dewey to the economic royalist trope with which the GOP had been burdened since the beginning of the Great Depression. Truman's upset victory over Dewey in November 1948 seemed to confirm and reinforce the image of Republican corporate elitism. The president carried every state west of the Rockies except Oregon and most of the Midwest. He was able to win without four traditionally Democratic southern states whose electoral votes went to States' Rights Party candidate Strom Thurmond, governor of South Carolina and leader of a walkout at the Democratic National Convention to protest a platform plank supporting civil rights. The Democrats also regained control of both houses of Congress.

But even as the Democratic Party celebrated the continuation of its national electoral hegemony, the seeds of a Republican revival were being planted. They began in the South. The white southern element of the New Deal coalition was anomalous, a reflexive residue of an earlier time. FDR took care to ensure that his New Deal initiatives funneled money to the region without substantially disturbing the racial status quo. His political bargain kept the South loyal to the Democratic Party through the war years, during which defense spending in the region buoyed the economy.

By 1948, however, with black voting power growing in the North and increasing pressure from the left/liberal wing of the party on civil rights, it had become impossible for the national Democrats to elide the issue of race. Truman, a savvy vote-counter from his days as a Kansas City machine pol, knew that a commitment to racial equality by the national party would eventually trade white southern support for increased strength in northern urban areas. The Thurmond-led walkout at the 1948 Democratic Convention set that process in motion. When Minnesotan Hubert Humphrey, supporting a civil rights platform plank and speaking directly to the southern delegates, proclaimed that "the time has arrived in America for the Democratic Party to get out of the shadow of states' rights and walk forthrightly into the bright sunshine of human rights," he was announcing a fundamental shift in the party's position on race.[12]

The Deep South's response was the creation of a splinter "Dixiecrat" party that carried South Carolina, Mississippi, Alabama, and Louisiana. Four years later, those states were back in the Democratic column in the presidential race, but Republican candidate Dwight Eisenhower carried Virginia, Tennessee, Florida, and Texas. The white South was changing, and a window of opportunity was opening for the Republican Party.

The South was also changing economically, as the forces and effects of development in the long-dormant region drove white voters toward the GOP. The postwar South was the beneficiary of capital flight from the North and Midwest as companies lured by low taxes and weak unions relocated, introducing a new economy built on manufacturing, finance, defense, and construction. The region now possessed a viable and growing white-collar urban middle class, one that began to replicate northern patterns of outmigration and suburbanization. As their incomes rose, these southerners gravitated toward the GOP, pulled by class aspirations as much as they were pushed by racial concerns.[13]

Class, in fact, was the leading edge of the southern Republican revival. Eisenhower's regional successes in the 1952 and 1956 presidential elections came from the outer South states in districts characterized by business expansion and suburban growth. Higher-income Truman voters in the South in 1948 were much more likely to support Eisenhower than the Deep South working-class Thurmond voters, who remained loyal to the Democratic Party of the New Deal and backed its nominee, Adlai Stevenson.[14] But upscale southern whites were not merely seeking to match their lifestyles to their incomes by relocating to the suburbs in the 1950s. They were also attempting to escape the reach of the burgeoning civil rights movement. By the 1960s their class and racial interests had melded into an identification with a southern Republican Party that appeared to accommodate both.[15]

The white North was changing as well. Since the nineteenth century the Democratic Party had traditionally been the party of urban Catholics, and it had served as the electoral bedrock of the Democratic machines that offered a counterweight to a hostile and exclusionary Protestant order. Thanks to the New Deal and its support for unions and Keynesian stimulus spending, urban Catholics had secured a place in a rising postwar middle class that would ironically begin to unmoor them from the party of their fathers and grandfathers. By the time of the Democratic Convention of 1948, the shift of party liberals from a concern with class politics and economic equality to cultural politics and race was apparent. African Americans who had moved North during the depression and war years were now in uneasy proximity to ethnic Catholics. They competed for jobs, services, power, and often urban space itself. The racial initiatives of the Truman administration, which in addition to the convention's civil rights platform plank included the desegregation of the armed forces and the formation of the President's Committee on Civil Rights, put Catholics on notice that the party's priorities were shifting.

The GOP was also gaining ground in the rapidly developing southwestern portion of the Sun Belt—most notably the greater Los Angeles area, known as the Southland—where a populist conservatism was growing on a grassroots level. A steady stream of midwesterners and southerners had flowed west beginning in the 1920s and continuing throughout the Great Depression and war years. While the economic radicalism of John Steinbeck's Dust Bowl "Okies" is the stuff of legend, a less remarked-upon aspect of his novel *The Grapes of Wrath* is the cultural and social conservatism of most of its protagonists. By the postwar years the children of poor farm or factory workers who had assailed "the boss" were often white-collar employees of defense contractors and oil and real estate companies or small-scale entrepreneurs or professionals living in suburban tract homes. They possessed a fierce sense of independence and a desire to manage their own lives. In a region lacking a well-developed party structure, they turned to ground-level political organizing, frequently led by women.[16] For these "suburban warriors" of the Sun Belt, "union leaders, international bankers, and New Deal administrators replaced corporate oligarchs as the autocrats, while the middle class replaced farmers and the proletariat as 'the people.'"[17]

This view largely blunted the raw class resentments that traditionally underlay American labor relations and upon which the Democratic Party had built its appeal since the New Deal. It substituted an overweening central state for avaricious big business as the primary threat to the freedom and autonomous individualism the suburban Southlanders craved.[18] Indeed, there emerged "an expansive definition of the middle class to include anyone who valued individualism, upward mobility, organized religion, and the Protestant work ethic. An assembly-line worker, small-town dentist or CEO of a multinational corporation could be middle class as long as he lived by [this] simple code."[19] Control of life circumstances — families, schools, homes — was paramount, more so than any notion of equality, especially racial equality, put forth by liberal Democrats.

For these grassroots Republicans, Cold War anticommunism, while important, was less pressing as a cause than the issues that were of more personal and immediate concern: crime, progressive education, school prayer, parental authority, integration, and open housing. A nexus of businessmen, religious leaders, homeowners, and housewives coalesced around free enterprise principles, anti-statism, and cultural traditionalism.[20] Organizing into an array of overlapping ground-level advocacy groups to pursue these goals, they would prove instrumental to the rise of both Barry Goldwater and Ronald Reagan in the Republican Party.

Different from the eastern and midwestern ethnics who were beginning to shift toward the GOP, the Sun Belters were more middle-class, more Protestant, and more economically conservative. They shared a sense of localism, of moralism, and of antipathy toward far-removed elites who threatened their homes, children, and lives. While Sun Belt conservatism led to a different wing of the Republican Party than did the ethnic working-class populism of the East and Midwest, they both led to the GOP. They would eventually converge in the candidacy of Richard Nixon, separate routes to the same destination.

At the same time, as Kevin Phillips and others have noted, eastern-based Protestants — New England Yankees, "silk-stocking" New Yorkers, and professionals, academics, journalists, theologians, administrators, technocrats, even some representatives of the business and corporate classes — were peeling away from their Republican roots and moving toward Democratic affiliations.[21] They took their cultural attitudes with them as they did so. Anti-Catholic prejudices among Protestants had traditionally included a strong element of elitism. By the middle of the twentieth century, there was little support for the idea that Catholics were something less than "true" Americans, but what remained was the Protestant impulse of cultural superiority that had divided the two faiths for a century or more. Driven in part by the movement of their perceived rivals—Protestants as well as African Americans—toward the Democratic Party, Catholics were beginning their journey to the GOP.

They were also moving toward the Republican Party because it seemed to best accommodate the powerful anticommunist impulse that ran through the American Catholic community during the early Cold War years. Every one of the eastern European nations that fell within the orbit of the Soviet Union after World War II had either Catholic majorities or substantial Catholic populations. For American Catholics anticommunism served multiple purposes. It was a political statement. It was a profession of religious faith. It also expressed the class and status grievances of the newly arrived. It was a way to turn the tables on those who had questioned their worth as citizens and Americans. Through anticommunism Catholics could question the patriotism of their "betters" among eastern Protestant elites.

An accelerating northern white movement to the suburbs in the immediate postwar years also facilitated Republican gains. During the 1950s, 85 percent of the nation's new homes were constructed in the suburbs.[22] Traditionally enclaves of old-line wealth and status, the suburbs were now attracting a new white middle class, often fleeing the presence of minorities in the cities. Once arrived, suburban migrants like the Spiro Agnew family of Baltimore County, Maryland, began shedding their Democratic allegiances. It was not lost on newly arrived suburbanites seeking to distance themselves from people of color that the national Democratic Party was increasingly concerned with issues of race. Under the circumstances it was less important that the Republicans were the party of big business than that they were the party of smaller government that promised to leave them alone.

Kevin Phillips has aptly described a postwar suburbia of "subdivisions populated by salesmen, electricians, and supermarket managers" whose parents had been poor or working class and who were resolutely determined to put space between their new lives and their old ones.[23] The economic and labor policies of the Democratic New Deal that had made their new suburban lives possible were now outweighed by racial concerns and fears. As a result the Republican Party no longer seemed the alien force it had been when they lived in the cities. In their old neighbor-hoods it had been possible to walk down the street and never encounter a Republican voter. In the new air of the suburbs anything was possible.

The path of the Republican Party from economic royalism to cultural populism can be traced through two pairs of opposed political figures. Alger Hiss and Dean Acheson were well born, urbane, and Ivy League–educated. Richard Nixon and Joseph McCarthy were common folk, with-out pretensions and pedigrees. In another time, the first pair likely would have been Republicans and the second Democrats. Now their affiliations were reversed.

Alger Hiss was a Harvard Law School graduate who had clerked for a Supreme Court justice, worked in a Wall Street firm, served in various high-ranking government positions during the New Deal, and advised Roosevelt during the February 1945 Yalta Conference at which the struc-tures of the postwar world were negotiated. In 1948 he was accused of spy-ing for the Soviet Union by Whittaker Chambers, one of his former espi-onage contacts. Chambers's accusations elicited an outpouring of support for Hiss from the highest reaches of government, academia, and philan-thropy, including President Truman, Supreme Court justice Felix Frank-furter, who had taught and mentored Hiss at Harvard, Secretary of State Dean Acheson, and Illinois governor Adlai Stevenson. Hiss's dogged pur-suer on the House Un-American Activities Committee (HUAC), Con-gressman Richard Nixon, was the son of a failed grocer and a graduate of decidedly non–Ivy League Whittier College who had been rejected by every Wall Street law firm to which he had applied out of school.

The confrontation between Hiss and Nixon was that of a "made" man who was a Democrat and a "self-made" one who was a Republican. At one point during his HUAC examination by Nixon, Hiss imperiously cited his Harvard legal education and contrasted it with Nixon's degree from lowly Whittier College.[24] Even Hiss's initial accuser, the communist-turned-conservative Chambers, was decidedly plebian, a college dropout from a nondescript background whose self-proclaimed mission was to warn ordinary Americans away from Marxism.

After his conviction for perjury in 1950, Hiss's innocence of all espi-onage charges was an article of faith among the eastern educated class, the members of which in turn despised Nixon as the embodiment of the common and vulgar. Nixon was especially dangerous to them because he represented a form of Republicanism that was anticommunist but not overtly plutocratic, one that was rooted in popular democracy and individual aspiration. Nixon, as a biographer described him, was "one of us," a commoner with tastes and attitudes to match and a finely tuned sense of what average Americans felt, thought, and dreamed.[25] He seemed to understand, in ways that elite liberals did not, that the United States was a nation with more small businessmen than large ones, more state college graduates than Ivy Leaguers, and more middle-income earners than rich or poor ones. Nixon also understood that as the leadership and knowledge classes in the metropolitan, cosmopolitan East began to back away from traditional American values—work, religion, community, materialism, mobility—most in the middle classes, including Catholics, suburbanites, Sun Belters, and southerners, were identifying with them all the more closely.

Nixon's classic articulation of those values came in his September 1952 Checkers speech, in which he fought for his political life after allegations of a slush fund paid for by wealthy Republican donors threatened to wreck his campaign for vice president. Using the crisis as an opportunity, Nixon constructed his nationally televised address as the story of a Republican without money whose outlook, lifestyle, and goals reflected those of the average American. He contrasted the "fur coats" worn by leading Democrats—bribery and corruption were major issues in the 1952 presidential campaign—with the more modest accouterments of Republicans. For the first time in at least two decades, a Republican and not a Democrat was an everyman. Nixon laid out his modest family finances, which were similar to those of millions of those watching him at home who also owed more than they owned.[26]

Nixon also pounced on a remark by Democratic national chair Stephen Mitchell that "if a fellow can't afford to be a senator, he shouldn't seek the office." Employing a quote commonly if mistakenly attributed to Abraham Lincoln—"God must have loved the common people, he made so many of them"—Nixon aligned himself and his party with the aspiring masses.[27] He noted that Adlai Stevenson, the Democratic presidential nominee in 1952, had "inherited a fortune from his father" and told his audience, "It is essential in this country of ours that a man of modest means can also run for president."[28] That man of modest means was now a Republican. In a final bow to populist democracy, Nixon closed by asking viewers to contact the Republican National Committee and "vote" on whether he should remain on the ticket, promising to abide by their verdict. The response was overwhelmingly favorable, and Nixon went on to be elected vice president alongside Dwight Eisenhower as president in November.[29]

In the aftermath of the Checkers speech, a newspaper columnist remarked in near amazement that "this time the common man was a Republican, for a change." Nixon "suddenly [had] placed the burden of old-style Republican aloofness on the Democrats."[30] Through Nixon the GOP could claim to be the party not of the distant rich but of the striving middle class. Not all Republicans had money. Not all Democrats lacked it. Furthermore, many Democrats possessed perhaps the most significant of all forms of capital: status and social power. A generation earlier the boss who was a son-of-a-bitch in the remark about Franklin Roosevelt's working-class empathy was undoubtedly an imperious businessman. By the time of Richard Nixon's election as vice president, that son-of-a-bitch may instead have been a supercilious Ivy Leaguer with a status-rich pedigree and ambivalence about traditional American values—someone, perhaps, like Alger Hiss.

Liberals could not comprehend the attraction of a Richard Nixon to traditional Democratic voters, men and women from average circumstances starting out in life with young families, mortgages, small-business loans, and G.I. Bill educations. Nixon seemed awkward, even gauche, wearing the insecurity of the newly arrived prominently on his sleeve. But his vulnerabilities were also his strengths. When he appeared on television— the newest marker of middle-class status—his audiences saw themselves. When they saw Hiss, they saw a different person entirely.

On February 9, 1950, a backbench Wisconsin senator, Joseph McCarthy, told a Republican women's club in Wheeling, West Virginia, that the U.S. State Department was infested with communists, security risks who kept their jobs thanks to the indifference of those in the highest reaches of the Truman administration. The initial furor over the exact number of "Reds" McCarthy mentioned—reports varied from 205 to 81 to 57—quickly gave way to the more important and lasting message of his speech: that Democratic Party elites, even if not personally disloyal themselves, had abetted disloyalty through their half-hearted investment in national values. "It is not the less fortunate, or members of minority groups who have been traitorous to this nation," McCarthy said, "but rather those who have had all the benefits the wealthiest nation on earth has to offer . . . the finest homes, the finest college educations, and the finest jobs in the government that we can give."[31] It was clear that the archetype of the class to which he referred was Dean Acheson. McCarthy took aim at Truman's secretary of state during his Wheeling speech, deriding him as "this pompous diplomat in striped pants, with a phony British accent," and he would attack him many times in the future.[32]

Acheson's background could not have been more different from that of the rough-edged McCarthy. A graduate of Yale College and Harvard Law School who was a Supreme Court clerk before becoming a partner in a prominent Washington law firm and serving in high-ranking positions in the Treasury and the State Department, Acheson was the establishment personified. Indeed, with his brisk mustache and clipped, superior air of an English gentleman, he was almost a caricature of the type. Had McCarthy, a Catholic midwesterner who received his law degree from Marquette University and ran a seat-of-his-pants practice in a nondescript small town, ever applied to Dean Acheson for a job, he would have been rejected on the spot. Both men instinctively knew this, and it fueled McCarthy's resentment of what Acheson represented. When McCarthy charged that Acheson had harbored communists in his department or had "lost" China to Mao Tse-tung or had tacitly encouraged North Korea's attack on its southern neighbor, he was also, in the words of conservative writer Peter Viereck, exacting "the revenge of the noses that for twenty years of fancy parties were pressed against the outside window pane."[33]

The hostility to Acheson and his kind emanating from these circles was rooted more in cultural resentments than material ones. "The resentment created by prosperity," wrote sociologist Seymour Martin Lipset, "is basically not against the economic power of Wall Street bankers, or

Yankees, but against their status power. An attack on their loyalty, on their Americanism, is clearly also an attack on their status."[34] The anger directed toward McCarthyism by liberals and especially the intellectual classes accentuated their anti-democratic tendencies and made it possible for Republicans such as McCarthy to assume the role of popular tribune. "Nobody Loves Joe but the People," the title of McCarthy's theme song, expressed the prevailing sentiment.

Public intellectuals like Richard Hofstadter could sneer at "the less educated members of the middle classes" whose exemplar "believes himself to be living in a world in which he is spied upon, plotted against, betrayed, and very likely destined for total ruin."[35] But whether he realized it or not, Hofstadter was describing what would come to be known as Middle Americans. During the New Deal, intellectuals celebrated them as American heroes. Supporters of Roosevelt's court-packing plan had sought to protect the rights of "the people" against an undemocratic judiciary. Liberal moviegoers had cheered at director John Ford's 1940 version of *The Grapes of Wrath* as Ma Joad proclaimed: "They can't wipe us out; they can't lick us. We'll go on forever . . . 'cause we're the people."[36] But by the early 1950s and the emergence of both McCarthy and McCarthyism, the idea of "the people" took on more sinister connotations. With the Wisconsin senator attracting so much support—from Catholics, suburbanites, southerners, small businessmen, even manual laborers—liberals began to question the virtues of unalloyed majoritarianism.[37] Perhaps the more rational, more educated, more intelligent class of Americans would have to step forward to protect the nation from itself.

In postwar America, where after the deep stresses of the Great Depression capitalism appeared to be "working," class and labor issues began to lose their sense of special urgency in comparison to those related to race and culture. This permitted citizens to shape their political views through values and outlooks as much as through wealth and income. It was not difficult to understand from this new perspective how a man with a high school education who had never voted for a Republican presidential candidate could nonetheless identify with Richard Nixon or Joe McCarthy. It could also explain how a man with a college education whose salary was many times that of the high school graduate could find these men vulgar and unappealing. The upper-income college graduate would likely have been a member of what Kevin Phillips identified as a new establishment class that was coming of age in the 1950s, composed of, among others, "research directors, associate professors, social workers, educational consultants, urbanologists, development planners, journalists, brotherhood executives, foundation staffers, communications specialists, culture vendors, pornography merchants, [and] poverty theorists."[38]

Missing from this admittedly subjective list of new elites were representatives of the traditional moneyed classes. The road to power in postwar America lay in control of culture as much as finance and commerce. It followed that if there were to be a new establishment class it would come from the ranks of the knowledge sector, where education and technological and administrative expertise would take the place of dollars and cents. It also followed that this class would identify with Dean Acheson or even Alger Hiss, whose innocence of any crime was widely accepted as fact, and would view Joseph McCarthy and Richard Nixon as alien spirits whose appeal was almost incomprehensible. But to a Catholic worried about communism, a southerner angry about civil rights, or a recently arrived suburbanite anxious about status, it was Democrats such as Acheson and Hiss who were the aliens. By the middle of the 1950s, the Democratic and Republican parties were reversing roles. The economic royalists of old were becoming cultural populists; the economic populists of the New Deal era were becoming cultural royalists and unelected gatekeepers. In a nation where middle-class cultural values of community and country, faith and family were beginning to matter as much as job security, and where Nixon and McCarthy could thus employ middle-class values as a means of redistributing political power, this was cause for Democratic concern.

On the surface, however, all seemed well. Even as Eisenhower followed up his resounding 1952 victory with an even more decisive one in 1956, the Democratic Party controlled both houses of Congress and in polls Americans affiliated with the party by a margin of 43 percent to 33 percent over the Republicans.[39] But Eisenhower was winning substantial support among traditionally Democratic Catholics. And in the new suburbs of American cities newcomers were taking on new identities as Republicans.[40] Installed in a Towson, Maryland, ranch-style home, immersed in the rituals and rhythms of suburban life, Spiro Agnew was one of them.

Throughout the remainder of the 1950s and into the next decade, liberalism became more and more associated with skepticism toward the conformism and materialism of mainstream American culture. That culture did not, however, lack for defenders. The great majority were Republicans. Richard Nixon became prominent among them when he traveled to Moscow in 1959 and engaged in an impromptu "kitchen debate" with USSR premier Nikita Khrushchev on the relative merits of the American and Soviet social and economic systems. When Khrushchev attempted to contrast his nation's "classless" society with the class-riven one in the United States, Nixon responded with a forceful defense of the American way of life calculated to resonate with potential voters back home. "The 67 million American wage earners are not the downtrodden masses," he told the Soviet leader. Rather, "the United States, the world's largest capitalist country, has from the standpoint of distribution of wealth come closest to the ideal of prosperity for all in a classless society."[41] Nixon argued that the average American's goal of material success, as exemplified by the ownership of private homes, automobiles, and consumer goods, was evidence of spiritual health and moral strength, not weakness and decadence.

Nixon thus positioned himself as a defender of the values of the average American; by comparison, his political opponents had a substantially smaller investment in them. Who, Nixon seemed to be asking, were the "real" Americans? Nixon thought he knew. They were like him. They came from the same places he did. They wanted the same things he did. They wanted success in conventional ways, in the system as it was. They were patriotic, loving America without apology.

Nixon had always been sensitive to the affronts of those he perceived as elites, whether they were eastern newspaper editors, Ivy League deans, or even coffeehouse comics, so many of whom, it seemed, identified as Democrats. Through them he could see a way to make millions of Americans who were like him, but who still were Democrats, into Republicans. They had resentments as well, he suspected. Like him, there was someone in their lives who had rejected them or patronized them or ridiculed them. In an America in which knowledge and education held the keys to advancement and success, it was more and more likely that the keepers of those keys were Democrats. For Republicans, an opportunity loomed. If enough people like Nixon—with his outlook, his values, even his resentments—could be convinced that the Democratic Party was no longer for them, the GOP could win the loyalty of voters who heretofore would never have thought to pull the lever for a Republican.

Culture and not economics would need to be the main engine of this transference of allegiance, since the pocketbook issue was still a Democratic province. But by the end of the 1950s, with the *Brown v. Board of Education* school desegregation decision settled in law, if not in practice, and the civil rights movement underway, any political argument based on culture carried powerful racial imputations. The Republican National Committee launched its "Operation Dixie" in 1957 in an effort to build strength for the party by capitalizing on growing anger among southern whites at the *Brown* decision and its implications. It made steady progress. In 1961 John Tower became the first Republican elected to the Senate from Texas since Reconstruction, and in 1964 Dixiecrat stalwart Strom Thurmond of South Carolina formally joined the GOP. The number of Republican votes for House of Representatives candidates in the eleven former Confederate states doubled between 1958 and 1962.[42]

As African Americans began to register and vote as Democrats in the outer South in the late 1950s and early 1960s, and as black Republican support dropped from 23 percent nationally in 1960 to 12 percent four years later, whites moved in the opposite direction.[43] Ironically, the "northernization" of the South after World War II had produced a suburbanizing white middle class with many of the attitudes and fears of its northern equivalent. It was a ripe target for Republicans. Symbolic was an episode during the 1960 presidential campaign when Martin Luther King Jr. was arrested in an Atlanta sit-in and sentenced to six months at hard labor. Candidates John F. Kennedy and Richard Nixon faced the question of whether to intervene on King's behalf.

The decision was fraught with political peril for both. For Kennedy, offering sympathy and assistance to King's wife would jeopardize already slipping Democratic support in the South. Nixon's dilemma lay in the

North. He had endorsed moderate civil rights measures in the past, but was wary of offending his party's emerging constituency among Catholics and suburbanizing northern whites by taking a public stand in support of a civil rights leader who was regarded in many quarters as a dangerous radical and lawbreaker. After some hesitation and soul-searching Kennedy made the call to Coretta King. Nixon did not. Kennedy's decision to help obtain King's release on bail has been credited with generating the black and liberal votes that gave him his narrow margin of victory in the presidential election, although that margin was so thin it is impossible to identify one source with certainty.

Nixon's inaction, which has received less historical attention, was equally significant. Three years after a Republican president committed troops to ensure compliance with a federal court order mandating public school integration in Little Rock, Arkansas, a Republican presidential candidate chose to align with northern whites who were increasingly fearful of and hostile to blacks, not to mention with segregationist whites in the South. Nixon did this not through overtly racialized language, and indeed, in the case of King, not through words at all. Instead, he let silence speak for him. His political calculus was straightforward. His party could have white suburbanites, Catholics, and southerners or it could have African Americans and northern liberals. It could not have both. There were more of the former than the latter. If the GOP ever wished to be known as the people's party—the majority party—it would be through their votes.

The nation's political center of gravity was moving southward and westward as jobs in defense, technology, and manufacturing migrated to Florida, Texas, Arizona, and California, with population shifts to match. The East was losing people and electoral college strength, as were urban areas in the Midwest. The new southerners and westerners were conventional folk with conventional ambitions and dreams. They were not racists in the manner of a brutal southern sheriff or a Ku Klux Klan member. But they had a sense of what was theirs and what belonged to them, and what civil rights activists appeared to threaten. It also seemed that everyone arrayed against them—professionals, professors, journalists, bureaucrats, and technocrats—identified as Democrat. Nixon, with his finely cultivated faculty for resentment, understood this instinctively.

Regardless of his personal feelings about the excessiveness and injustice of King's sentence to hard labor, he knew there was no electoral percentage for him or his party in a public display of support. The percentage, in fact, was in remaining silent. While Nixon lost the 1960 presidential election, he brought the Republican Party closer to those voters it would need to reach to change its image and win presidential elections in the future.

The dream of uniting black and white Americans in a working-class alliance has long been the squared circle of our nation's history. Nixon's unplaced telephone call to Coretta King in October 1960 epitomized its elusiveness. Yet long-term electoral hopes for Republicans depended on the call not being made. With the call, the GOP was an echo of the Democrats. Without it, another road opened, one that would traverse the darker corners of the American experience but that also offered the promise of rich electoral rewards.

Those rewards did not appear to be imminent during the Kennedy and early Johnson administrations. Kennedy took 78 percent of the Catholic vote in 1960, winning back substantial numbers of those who had supported Eisenhower in 1952 and 1956.[44] He appointed Republicans to his cabinet and advocated tax policies that were favorable to business, blunting some of the force of their criticisms.

Meanwhile the GOP, despite the rise of ordinary-guy leaders like Eisenhower and Nixon, warred with itself. The Democrats were not the only party with an Eastern Establishment. The Republican iteration was corporatist, bureaucratic, and internationalist in sentiment. It accepted the general philosophy of the New Deal, seeking merely to manage and contain its interventionist policies and institutions. It was also sympathetic to the goals of the civil rights movement. It replicated much of the top-bottom structure of the Democratic Party and mined for votes in many of the same places.

By the early 1960s the leading Eastern Republican was New York governor Nelson Rockefeller. First elected in 1958, Rockefeller was an advocate of activist government and civil rights. Almost from the moment he took office he was viewed as a potential presidential candidate. He had feinted at a run in 1960, only to back away and reach an accommodation with Nixon—dubbed the "Treaty of Fifth Avenue" for its genesis at a meeting in Rockefeller's luxury apartment—whereby the Republican platform would be amended to provide for interventionist economic policies, increased government spending, and strong support for civil rights.

To the conservative wing of the GOP the agreement encapsulated everything that was wrong with Eastern Republicanism. The Eastern wing was liberal in its political sensibilities, a softer version of the Democrats. It did not challenge the interventionist state. It was spendthrift, again mimicking the Democrats. It was insufficiently committed to the protection of individual rights and freedoms, especially in the area of civil rights, where it countenanced unwarranted interferences with personal choice and associational liberty. It favored coexistence and not confrontation with the Soviet Union, leaving communism's territorial and ideological advances in place. Finally, as exemplified by Rockefeller, its representatives were arrogantly self-entitled. They justified its control of the party apparatus by reason of their superior education, knowledge, financial resources, and even breeding. The Eastern Republican wing was merely an echo of the Democratic Party. Republican conservatives demanded a choice.

By 1960, with the publication of *The Conscience of a Conservative*, the leading articulator of that demand for choice and the most prominent anti–Eastern Republican was Arizona senator Barry Goldwater. While Goldwater represented western Republicans, he had potential that extended beyond his region. His book, a surprise best seller, was not an apologia for big business that evoked the image of economic royalism but a call for political, economic, and social freedom for the American citizen. Liberals wielded the power of big government. Business-oriented conservatives extolled the power of big capitalism. But what of everyday Americans? Who would speak for the small businessman, tradesman, farmer, or professional, or those who in turn worked for them? Goldwater argued that these citizens desired and deserved the freedom to make their own life decisions with as little interaction with the state as possible. In the nineteenth century these had been considered liberal freedoms. Now conservatives like Goldwater moved eagerly to capture them for their own cause.

Goldwater personally did not fit a classic racist profile. His family's

Phoenix department store had been one of the first integrated businesses in the city, and he had helped desegregate the Arizona Air National Guard. But it was not difficult to see how his philosophy would appeal to a white southerner who for his or her own reasons resented outside intrusions on behalf of civil rights, or to a northern white homeowner whose neighborhood had "gone bad," necessitating a move to the suburbs.

For these Americans the federal government had once been an instrument of benign power and upward mobility. For westerners it had provided their lifeblood—water—through irrigation projects and electricity-producing dams. For southerners it had subsidized and mechanized agriculture, transforming the region from an economic backwater. For easterners it had provided insured mortgages and loans that made mass suburbanization possible. But in its potential to coerce, especially in matters related to race, it now loomed as an enemy and even an oppressor. The lives that the federal government had helped build could now be uprooted by it.

Americans customarily want help from their government when they need it. After they receive it they want to be left alone. By the early 1960s the conservative wing of the Republican Party was poised to capitalize on this truism of American history. It was the government-driven policies of the Democratic Party—the New Deal and the Fair Deal—that had made mobility and security possible for millions of white Americans in all regions of the country. The Republican Party, and certainly the conservative wing of it, had little to do with those policies. Indeed, it had opposed them vigorously. Now, with material gains won, it argued to those same Americans that the federal government should stay out of their lives and not tell a free and independent people what to do. It should not tell them who to live with, or go to school with, or associate with, or hire. It should not force them to pay higher taxes to fund social programs—in his book Goldwater called them "welfarism"—that benefited the undeserving.[45] Conservative Republicanism may have had little to do with the educations, homes, jobs, and possessions that white Americans enjoyed by the 1960s, but it now promised to help them keep what they had.

The Democratic Party, seemingly more concerned with identity group politics than a continuation of the class politics that had attracted white working-class Americans in the first place, appeared less and less aware of what was occurring at the ground level in everyday lives. Democratic policies were affecting those lives, but it seemed that many Democrats were able to avoid the consequences of their policies in their own lives through a form of elitist status politics that relied less on moneyed wealth than on education, knowledge, position, and status. "Where do *you* live?" "Who are *your* neighbors?" "Where does *your* child go to school?" Those were the questions that hung over American politics, both national and local, in the early 1960s as whites to whom the Democratic Party had been a lifeline and a leg up began to look elsewhere for support and meaning— including to a faction of the Republican Party that in the 1930s and 1940s had seemed irrelevant to them and their concerns.

The most important question in American electoral politics is the one a voter asks a candidate or party: "Do you understand me and my life?" As long as the dominant issue in that voter's life was economic, as it was at least through the end of World War II, the Democratic Party could hold the allegiance of a young white voter because Franklin Roosevelt knew his boss was a son-of-a-bitch. But a quarter century after the New Deal, that voter had a steady job, a house in the suburbs, and children or perhaps even grandchildren in school. Economic issues never went away, of course, but they now had been joined by concerns over race, culture, and values. The Republicans could not help him in 1936, but they might be able to help him now.

First, however, the party would have to sort out its own ideological identity. The opposed figures—symbols, really—of Barry Goldwater and Nelson Rockefeller led the competing sections of the GOP. Rockefeller and Goldwater squared off not only for the 1964 Republican presidential nomination but for control of the party itself. Many intraparty struggles are about power, but this one was deeply invested in ideas and principles. At stake were the party's positions on civil rights and race, the Cold War, and the role of government in American political, social, and economic life. As the campaign unfolded it became clear that while Rockefeller had his family's legendary fortune, Goldwater possessed grassroots organization and support that his better-financed rival could not match.[46] By the end of the general election campaign in November Goldwater would receive 1.5 million individual contributions, three times as many as Lyndon Johnson even as Johnson won a landslide victory. In 1960 Nixon had brought in only fifty thousand.[47]

After narrowly winning the crucial California primary over Rockefeller, Goldwater went into the Republican National Convention in San Francisco with enough delegates to secure the nomination. Still, the convention was filled with acrimony. A proposed platform plank denouncing extremism, supported by the party's Eastern wing, was debated fiercely and ultimately defeated, but not before Rockefeller himself was booed and heckled by Goldwater supporters as he attempted to speak in its favor. "This is still a free country, ladies and gentlemen," Rockefeller lectured the hostile crowd before decrying the "communist and Nazi methods" of the Goldwater campaign.[48] The moment was symbolic as the ground shifted beneath the party's foundations. It would have been unthinkable as recently as four years earlier. But now, as the GOP prepared to nominate the first true representative of its new constituency, it turned against the man whose money, pedigree, politics, and culture made him the epitome of all that the Goldwaterites hated and feared.

Goldwater's acceptance speech on July 16 was a full-throated, unvarnished assault on the principles and premises of liberalism. It employed the words "freedom" and "free" more than thirty times and the word "equality" only twice.[49] He praised federalism, localism, self-reliance, economic incentive, private property, and individual responsibility. He attacked "the growing menace in our country tonight, to personal safety, to life, to limb and property," singling out "our great cities" for emphasis. He denounced "those who seek to live your lives for you" and who seek "a world in which earthly power can be substituted for divine will."[50]

Goldwater did not mention civil rights and race specifically, but he did not need to. His remarks were aimed not just at southern whites resisting integration but whites in other parts of the nation who were resisting it in more subtle ways. He was telling them that he would protect them in their homes and on their streets. But in a larger sense he was assuring them that he would protect the lives they had built over the preceding decades. Unlike liberals, he would leave them alone. Unlike liberals, he would not demand that they give up parts of their lives and redistribute some of their gains, with the implication they were unearned.

Less than a month before his convention acceptance speech Goldwater had voted against the Civil Rights Act of 1964, joining with southern Democrats in an unsuccessful effort to prevent its passage. While Goldwater's rationale was principled—an opposition to overreaching government initiatives—he was also justifying segregationist practices in the use and enjoyment of public facilities that had defined the South, and even parts of the North, for generations. Goldwater was telling whites in all regions that his party—at least his wing of it—would not disturb the patterns of everyday life that they had constructed over the years, whether it was the southerner who refused to share a restaurant meal with an African American or the northerner or westerner who did not wish to share a neighborhood with him. In contrast the national Democratic Party and the Eastern Republicans were committed to putting an end to those life patterns and to narrowing the scope of a freedom that justified the practices of formal or informal segregation. But to Goldwater "freedom" meant the right to be free *from* outside interference rather than the freedom *to* enjoy certain rights and entitlements. Thus formulated, it was a powerful appeal to millions of white Americans who instinctively viewed freedom in the same way.[51]

Goldwater, who had once half seriously remarked that "sometimes I think this country would be better off if we could just saw off the Eastern seaboard and let it float out to sea," was envisioning a "pure conservative" Republican Party shorn of its moderate-liberal wing.[52] In the short term this ideological consistency would likely lead to electoral defeat, as it did in the presidential contest of 1964. But if new constituencies could be attracted by the party's emphasis on individual rights, localism, and traditional culture and mores—a party of home, family, and faith—losses in the East and among moderate Republicans could be more than compensated for. Goldwater believed those new conservative votes were there for the taking. They might even be enough to turn the GOP into a majority party, or at least a presidential one. But the country would have to change along with the party.

Goldwater lost the 1964 presidential election to Lyndon Johnson by almost sixteen million votes, winning only one state—his own—outside the Deep South. The highlight of his campaign was not even generated by the candidate himself but by actor Ronald Reagan, a former Democrat whose politics had turned rightward during the 1950s and early 1960s. Reagan's televised "A Time for Choosing" address made an eloquent case for individual freedom and choice, decrying "a little intellectual elite in a far-distant capital" seeking to manage the lives of average Americans.[53] Reagan sought to portray himself, in words and demeanor, as an average citizen without airs or pretense, in contrast to entrenched and entitled liberal Democratic elites. Once again a Republican was speaking as "one of us."

In July 1964, as the Republican Convention took place, New York City erupted into racial violence after the shooting of an African American youth by a white patrolman. It was the first in a series of major civil disturbances that would roil American cities over the next four years. Although there was only one fatality in New York and property damage was relatively light in comparison to what was to come elsewhere, the riot was deeply unsettling to middle-class whites throughout the country. Violent crime was shooting up, especially in urban areas, with a 7 percent rise in the national murder rate over 1963, along with a 10 percent increase in robberies, 15 percent in aggravated assaults, and 20 percent in rapes.[54] The events in New York brought white fears of lawlessness and neighborhood destruction to the surface. The reaction could not help but cut against Democrats linked to the civil rights movement and favor those calling for order and stability. That more of the latter were Republicans boded well for their future political fortunes.

What also boded well was their fund-raising prowess. In 1964, 72 percent of individual contributions to the Republican Party were in amounts under five hundred dollars, an indication of the average-folks nature of much of its support.[55] In a reversal of traditional positions, between 1964 and 1966 the GOP received one million contributions, averaging ten dollars each, while more than 80 percent of Democratic donations during this period were in increments of one hundred dollars or more. Most of the latter, in fact, were over a thousand dollars.[56]

In 1964 many Americans still considered the GOP the party of economic royalism. Johnson's landslide presidential election victory and
continued Democratic dominance in both houses of Congress certainly
spoke to that. But the closer that changing race relations came to becoming the nation's preeminent domestic issue, the more opportunities presented themselves for Republicans to assure traditional white Democratic
voters that they were on their side and that their homes, families, and
communities were safe with them. It also gave Republicans the opportunity to paint certain Democrats—those who seemed to demand that
others expiate the nation's racial sins while paying no price themselves—
as ivory-tower idealists at best and elitist hypocrites at worst.

When Harry Truman described the Democrats as the people's party
in 1948, he was viewing it largely as an instrument of economic uplift
and mobility. Now the Democratic Party defined uplift and mobility in
cultural and racial terms. Much of its constituency, including the people
Truman had in mind when he gave his speech, was now viewed as an impediment to cultural and racial freedom. What would they do? Where
would they go? Segregationist Alabama governor George Wallace, running on a promise to leave white home and property owners alone, had
won a majority of white votes in the 1964 Maryland presidential primary,
but later that year, in the presidential election itself, LBJ won the state
easily.[57] How long would it take for these cognitively dissonant results
to resolve themselves? Could the Democratic Party continue to appeal
simultaneously to knowledge-class liberals and minority groups as well
as Catholics, suburbanites, and southerners? Could it keep the well-
situated, the white middle and working classes, and the minority poor in
a functioning electoral coalition? If not, the GOP would have the chance
to become what Harry Truman had said it never would be: the people's
party.

3

THE ROAD TO 1968

Middle America, Meet Spiro Agnew

The Democratic Party began 1965 in an enviable position. It held double the number of congressional seats and governorships as did the GOP.[1] But Lyndon Johnson, even in the wake of his massive reelection victory the previous November, knew better than to celebrate. "You've got to give it all you can, that first year," he told an aide. "Doesn't matter what kind of majority you come in with. You've got just one year when they treat you right."[2] The president could see that the Great Society programs he was planning for his elected term would divide the country. His urgency in obtaining passage of as many such measures as possible in 1965, including the War on Poverty legislation that lay at the Great Society's heart, was a result of this sense of unease as he contemplated the future of his party. "I think we just gave the South to the Republicans," LBJ had muttered six months earlier after signing the Civil Rights Act of 1964.[3] Now he would use what he called his honeymoon to push through his agenda before his congressional supporters started "worrying about themselves [and reelection]."[4]

Indeed, 1965 was a year of almost unprecedented legislative achievement for Johnson and the Democratic Party. That year saw the passage of Medicare, Medicaid, the Elementary and Secondary Education Act, the Voting Rights Act, and War on Poverty enactments that expanded job training, Social Security, urban redevelopment, community action, and welfare assistance. High costs and expanded bureaucracies inevitably accompanied them. One simultaneous development was a sharp escalation in troop levels for the Vietnam War, which Johnson ordered reluctantly in July, knowing that it would squeeze the Great Society budget as well as divide his party constituency and distract the nation from the domestic issues of equality, opportunity, and resource distribution that were closest to his heart.

American society itself began to fray and crack in 1965, making support for both the Great Society and the Vietnam War—the two great projects of the national Democratic Party—deeply problematic.[5] A nation at war, whether against a Marxist foe abroad or poverty and racism at home, requires a shared set of values and assumptions, a "unifying civic religion," in the words of sociologist Robert Bellah.[6] In 1965 these began to fragment. The war in Vietnam divided the political community. Disagreements over the efficacy and desirability of racial integration divided the civil rights movement. Young people increasingly challenged traditional forms of authority. Crime and civil disturbances and a burgeoning white backlash rent the social fabric. America's component parts spun in different directions. The divisions benefited the GOP as the out-of-power party. But the continuing association of the national Democrats with active government, centralism, racial equality, cultural openness, and educated-class elitism also allowed Republicans to position themselves as defenders of established custom and traditional values. These were the values of Americans who were neither black, young, nor poor—who in 1960s America represented two-thirds of the voting population.[7] The GOP was aligning with a powerful electoral force.

With the Watts riot of 1965 and the ongoing student unrest at Berkeley, by 1966 California had become a cultural maelstrom, the leading edge of the changes in dress, behavior, and lifestyle that represented a direct challenge to traditional centers of authority. Ronald Reagan's gubernatorial campaign spoke to those men and women who believed their values were under attack by forces they barely understood. Why the long hair? Why the jarring, dissonant music? Why the angry students? Why the disdain for parents? Reagan answered these questions with a soothing vision of a past world that could be revived through the vehicle of the Republican Party, the party of order, certainty, and security. Emphasizing individual freedom from government coercion, lowered taxation and spending, and insulation from the daily-life effects of the civil rights movement, Reagan took on the persona of a citizen-politician—an average man speaking to other average men and women about the threat that liberalism posed to their average lives.[8] On November 8 Reagan swept to an overwhelming victory, defeating incumbent Edmund "Pat" Brown by almost a million votes and carrying fifty-five of fifty-eight counties.[9]

Reagan's may have been the most prominent Republican electoral triumph of 1966 but it was far from the only one. The GOP won forty-seven House and three Senate seats nationally, gained eight governorships, and added some seven hundred state legislature seats.[10] In the South twenty-three Republicans were elected to the House of Representatives, giving the party its largest regional contingent since Reconstruction, when it was a very different entity. It also won 65 percent of the Catholic vote overall, cutting deeply into a long-standing Democratic base.[11]

Not all Republican victories were won by conservatives. Moderates Charles Percy of Illinois, Mark Hatfield of Oregon, and Edward Brooke of Massachusetts were elected to the Senate, along with Governors Winthrop Rockefeller in Arkansas and, of course, Spiro Agnew in Maryland. Nelson Rockefeller was reelected in New York.[12] But conservative Republicans were heavily represented in the victorious cohort in the House races, and while the Democrats continued to control Congress, overall GOP gains were further proof of the potency of white middle- and working-class anger as a motivating electoral force and the benefits that would accrue to the party that could capture and harness it.[13]

At the Democratic National Convention in August 1964, the Mississippi Freedom Democratic Party (MFDP), which had been formed by activists from the Student Nonviolent Coordinating Committee with the goal of integrating the all-white Mississippi delegation, offered powerful testimony on the systematic denial of voting rights to African Americans in that state. Nonetheless, on orders from Johnson, who was fearful of disruptions at what he hoped would be a triumphal nomination process, a compromise was offered in which the white Mississippi delegation would be seated, the MFDP was offered two honorary at-large seats, and a pledge made to choose all delegations on a nondiscriminatory basis beginning in 1968. MFDP delegates and SNCC workers rejected the compromise, left the convention, and soured on the possibilities of electoral politics generally. Despite their disillusionment, the changes set in motion at the 1964 convention would open the Democratic Party to African Americans in the years to follow as they took advantage of the opportunities offered by the Civil Rights Act of 1964 and Voting Rights Act of 1965 to elect public officials and move into positions of party leadership.

At roughly the same time the law and order issue was gathering political and emotional momentum. Between 1963 and 1968 the nation's murder rate almost doubled; by the latter year 35 percent of Americans polled and 50 percent of women said there were areas within one mile of their homes where they were afraid to walk at night.[14] Crime and race had become the primary domestic concerns for Americans beginning in 1963, and the mid-decade outbreak of civil disorders only reinforced the sentiment.[15]

Richard Nixon was also beginning to connect his own resentment of liberal elites to the frustration of average Americans with the pace and direction of social change. In 1967, after a fourth consecutive summer of urban disturbances, Nixon read a series of pieces by syndicated columnist Joseph Kraft on the "forgotten man" and the "disconnected middle."[16] Kraft described "ordinary whites" as discontented and marginalized. They represented, in his view, the key to future electoral success for the party that could attract and hold them. Kraft's formulation was strikingly similar to what would become Nixon's most potent rhetorical trope: the silent majority.

Nixon was still a political exile in 1967, but the Kraft columns represented both a distillation of his personal frustrations and a potential route out of the wilderness. He dropped his innate suspicion of the national press corps long enough to sit for an interview with Kraft. Nixon believed he understood something most liberal Democrats did not: one did not have to be a member of a minority group to feel marginalized in contemporary American life. Politics, to a pragmatist like Nixon, was not about reality so much as about perceived reality. Objectively, the "ordinary whites" of Kraft's formulation were much closer to the centers of power and influence in the United States than were impoverished African Americans and Latinos. Liberal Democrats expected whites to understand this fact and vote accordingly. Even if crime was rising in their

neighborhoods, they still had higher incomes, better access to education, housing, and employment, and more expansive life choices than did
members of minority groups. But by this time many white Americans
had internalized a narrative of victimization that may well have appeared
ludicrous to liberal Democrats but was nonetheless deeply emotional and
visceral. Nixon took this narrative on its own terms, because it spoke to
him in the same way.

But in 1967 few liberal Democrats seemed willing to take the law and
order issue seriously, often downplaying its magnitude and importance
and eliding or ignoring its statistical evidence or associating it exclusively
with racism. Their refusal to engage the issue was a product of their belief
that violent lawbreaking was the result of material want; indeed, Johnson's War on Poverty was justified as a crime prevention measure.[17] They
also feared alienating two of their core political constituencies, African
Americans and the urban professional classes, who reflexively recoiled
from the law and order issue's racial connotations. Liberals thus took
what could have been a Democratic or at the very least a bipartisan issue and made it a Republican one.[18] The sentiment behind law and order
now had a name: white backlash.

Nixon could see the interests of the Republican Party and the emerging white backlash vote converging. Capturing that vote was not only a
route to political power but also a means of saving the nation itself, he believed. As 1967 came to a close—a year marked by stalemate amid rising
casualty levels in Vietnam; another summer of civil disturbances, including uprisings in Detroit and Newark that were among the most destructive in the nation's history; the emergence of the Black Panthers; a sky-
rocketing crime rate; and student radical and countercultural movements
that challenged the foundations of American politics and culture—the
Democratic Party was presiding over what to many appeared to be a national disintegration.

As this chapter turns its focus more directly on Nixon and Agnew, it is
important to introduce a man whose career would intersect with both in
a significant way. Born in Washington, D.C., in 1938, Patrick Buchanan
grew up in a family of lapsed Democrats whose heroes included Francisco Franco and Joseph McCarthy. He cast his first presidential vote for

Richard Nixon in 1960.[19] After graduating from Georgetown University Buchanan joined the staff of the *St. Louis Globe-Democrat* as an editorial writer in 1962. Viscerally traditionalist and anticommunist, he viewed the civil rights movement, student protests, and the emerging counter-culture as threats to the values and ways of life with which he had grown up. He would spend the 1960s, and indeed the rest of his life, championing the interests of white working- and middle-class Americans who believed the Democratic Party, with its focus on minority rights and cultural liberation, had abandoned them.

Buchanan supported Goldwater in 1964 and by early 1966 was an assistant to Nixon in his New York law office, his only full-time staffer except for secretary Rose Mary Woods.[20] Buchanan, while to the right of Nixon politically—he was suspicious of internationalism and less committed to civil rights—shared his distrust of governing-class elites and his neo-populist sensibilities. In 1966 and 1967, as Nixon's campaign for the presidency began to take shape, no one was closer to the candidate than Buchanan, as speechwriter, traveling companion, and intellectual sounding board. A Catholic white ethnic disaffected with the cultural and racial shifts of the decade, Buchanan embodied the type of voter Nixon hoped to dislodge from the Democrats. Indeed, Nixon did not have to imagine how that voter would look and think; he was sitting across from him in hotel suites, at meals, and on airplanes.

As he guided Nixon toward his rendezvous with the silent majority, Buchanan advised him to pursue white Catholic votes in the North and white Protestant ones in the South. Write off black voters, Buchanan counseled, because they were "unreachable."[21] Still in the political wilderness but on the road to what Buchanan would call his "greatest comeback," Nixon now had an electoral strategy to go with his attitude and outlook.

Approaching the 1968 election the GOP had to chart its course carefully. The idea of rolling back the New Deal had failed miserably for Goldwater in 1964. Relitigating it in 1968 while asking for the votes of those launched into the middle class by New Deal programs would risk another electoral debacle. The economic royalist argument was still the most powerful political weapon at the Democratic Party's disposal. This meant that middle-class values and stability had to be at the core of the party's message, with economics only on the periphery. While the costs of the Vietnam War were ticking inflation upward, the mid- to late-1960s was still a prosperous time in America, with solid economic growth, relatively low unemployment, rising average personal income, and a poverty rate that by decade's end would be half of what it was in 1960.[22] Pocketbook issues thus favored the Democrats, and the political folly of running against the New Deal had been driven home by repeated electoral defeats.

Among the potential Republican presidential candidates, Nixon may have understood this best of all. The white middle- and working-class voters he hoped to convert to the GOP were uncomfortable with any tampering with the basic programs of the New Deal — Social Security, labor protections, wage and hour standards, and a basic social safety net. A successful campaign therefore would nibble around the edges of Democratic economic policies while making generalized promises of prosperity under a Republican administration. The more the election could be framed as being about cultural and social elites rather than economic elites, the better the Republican chances would be. Nixon was the perfect candidate to mount such a campaign. An economic pragmatist, he understood that if an effective argument could be made that the royalists were of the cultural and not the economic variety, his party could win in 1968.

The withdrawal of moderate Michigan governor George Romney from the Republican race in late February 1968 presented a clear opportunity for Nelson Rockefeller to enter. But the New York governor, so politically sure-footed in his home state, dithered and delayed his return to the national stage. Watching him with great interest from the State House in Annapolis was Agnew, who had been urging Rockefeller to declare his candidacy for the better part of two years and who had just become chair of his presidential campaign citizens' committee.[23] Rockefeller's hesitation was partially grounded in reluctance to subject himself and his new family — he had left his first wife to marry a younger woman and now had two young sons — to media scrutiny. But there was also the gnawing fear that he simply could not win, that the party had shifted too far to the right since 1964. In a bitter irony, he stood a better chance of winning the general election than the Republican nomination.

There was also Nixon to consider. By early 1968 he had positioned himself in the ideological sweet spot of the party, between Rockefeller to the left and a potential challenge from Ronald Reagan on the right. He was the only serious contender acceptable—or at least not unacceptable—to every party faction. Easily winning New Hampshire in March, Nixon cruised through the spring primaries, picking up delegates in the shadow of the more contested Democratic races. As he secured support from party establishment leaders in the nonprimary states, his road to the nomination was a relatively clear one.

Nixon's inevitability was made even clearer by the bumbling Rockefeller, who shocked his supporters on March 21 with the announcement that he would not run. Not seeing fit to inform Agnew of his decision in advance, Rockefeller embarrassed the governor, who watched the announcement in his office with newsmen and staff expecting it to propel him to a position as one of the most prominent Rockefeller supporters. A quietly furious Agnew would make Rockefeller pay a high price for his lack of political politesse. When Rockefeller reversed course and declared himself a candidate on April 30, Agnew had already moved toward the Nixon camp.

Nixon's greatest challenge and opportunity would come in the South. Goldwater's candidacy had made crucial inroads for the Republicans in 1964. Aside from the electoral outcomes themselves, the most important of these was Strom Thurmond's move to the GOP in September prior to the presidential election. Thurmond gave the Republican Party a figure around whom to build regional strength, and he also served as a dog whistler for Democratic white working-class voters. It was now acceptable for white southerners to identify with the Republican Party.

Nixon understood that capturing the white South on a permanent basis would shift the party irrevocably to the right. It would free conservatives from the obligation to compromise with moderate and liberal Republicans from other regions, especially the East. The party could present itself as unapologetically conservative on cultural and social issues and mine for votes among the non-Southern white working classes, turning them away from their traditional Democratic loyalties to create a powerful new electoral coalition and perhaps a new Republican national majority.

But in order to capture the white South, George Wallace's appeal had to be blunted or at least contained. For that, Nixon needed Strom Thurmond. To get him, Nixon would have to give him the respect he needed. Personal respect, yes, but respect for his region even more so. For the better part of a century the American South had been walled off from the rest of the United States by race, culture, and heritage, a nation within a nation. Thurmond's price for his support would be politically tangible, in the sense that Nixon would need to promise that as president he would do what he could to ease the impact of federal court desegregation orders and legislative mandates. But it would also be intangible: a reabsorption of the South into the national community.

Nixon's view of himself as an outsider, which drew him emotionally to the northern white ethnic working class, also attracted him to the South. He promised Thurmond and Texas senator John Tower that their region would cease to be a pariah if he became president.[24] In the words of a campaign journalist, Nixon believed that southerners were "just folks."[25] The idea that white southerners, regarded as a people apart for generations, could now be considered "like everybody else" was worth as much to Thurmond as the more concrete promises Nixon made in exchange for his backing.

By the spring Thurmond was Nixon's indispensable southern surrogate, assuring state party chairs throughout the region that Nixon favored voluntary compliance with federal court desegregation orders, opposed busing, would not insult them with his choice of a vice presidential nominee, and perhaps most important, would respect them. Aided by South Carolina Republican Party chair Harry Dent, Thurmond effectively played the unacceptable Rockefeller—the epitome of Republican civil rights liberalism—against the generally sympathetic Nixon to lock in support. Implicit was the argument that the delegates could essentially get what Wallace was offering on race without indulging his raw personality and harsh rhetoric.

Nixon was engaged in the process of what contemporary political observers would call triangulation. He was willing to accommodate white southern racial attitudes, but only through the use of euphemisms like "voluntarism" and "localism" that would not offend northern sensibilities. A campaign built around respect for law and constituted authority could not creditably advocate the type of overt resistance to federal court orders that Wallace himself had engaged in during the integration of the University of Alabama in 1963 and the Selma voting rights campaign of 1965. Yet it also needed to speak the language of the potentially Republican voters it hoped to peel away from Democratic candidates in the South and white working-class precincts in the North and Midwest.

The Nixon campaign would thus link social and cultural breakdown, exemplified by an upsurge in crime and civil disorder, to the policies of the Democratic Party, while simultaneously promising the South that federal edicts would be enforced with understanding and forbearance, a skillful piece of political legerdemain that would serve the Republican Party well in future national elections and ground its new majority status.

By June Nixon had four interrelated tasks before him as he prepared for the Republican Convention. He would need to defend his left flank against Rockefeller's declared candidacy and his right flank against Reagan's undeclared one. He would need to secure the support of the South. And he would need to choose a vice presidential nominee acceptable to both Republican flanks.

Of the four, fending off Rockefeller was the easiest. Since reentering the race in late April, Rockefeller had continued to stumble, offering a message that emphasized urban problems to a party base increasingly uninterested in solving big city issues. In a poll taken in the spring of 1968 "crime and social disorder" was cited as the nation's most pressing domestic issue.[26] Rockefeller's own poll earlier that year had ranked its reverse image, "rebuilding our cities," twenty-first and last among the most important issues facing the United States. "Reducing poverty" was ranked sixteenth and "Negro racial problems" seventeenth.[27]

In this inhospitable environment Rockefeller's campaign was politically tone-deaf, running a television ad that featured an African American veteran stepping out of the shadows ostensibly to illustrate the debt society owed to those who had served their country.[28] Instead, it inadvertently projected an image of menace and fear, one ill-suited to sway already skeptical Republican delegates, especially those outside the Northeast.

Rockefeller was reduced to arguing that he had a better chance in the general election against Hubert Humphrey than Nixon did, but his alleged superiority evaporated when polls released shortly before the convention were inconclusive. In the end he was not a serious threat to Nixon, receiving only 277 votes on the first and only convention ballot. Despite his entreaties and apologies Agnew never forgave Rockefeller for embarrassing him with his March 21 withdrawal announcement and never reinstated his endorsement.

Ronald Reagan presented Nixon with a more serious challenge. While Reagan's conservatism during his first year and a half as governor of California was expressed more in word than in deed—his attempts to rein in state spending were largely unsuccessful—he quickly established himself as a national figure in the Republican Party, a welcome light in the GOP's post-Goldwater darkness. Reagan had clung to his favorite son status in the months leading up to the 1968 convention, insisting he was not a candidate for the presidency. But it was clear that he harbored presidential ambitions and that he was considered the fresh new face of conservatism in the party, a vivid contrast to Nixon's pragmatism and decades-old familiarity. Nixon was most vulnerable to Reagan's advances in the South, where the California governor's states' rights localism appeared to justify the region's opposition to integration on grounds other than pure racism. Nixon knew that if Reagan decided to run, he would face a battle for southern delegates that he could not afford to lose.

Reagan announced his candidacy on August 5, the day the Republican Convention began in Miami Beach. While his bid was late and somewhat quixotic, it effectively forced Nixon, after a safety-first campaign that traded in inoffensiveness and vagueness, to reveal the kind of candidate he would be if nominated. Nixon made arrangements to speak directly to the southern delegations before balloting began, accompanied by Strom Thurmond. As had been the case when Nixon wooed the South Carolina senator earlier in the year, he emphasized respect and inclusion as much as any specific policy concessions. Nixon reiterated to the delegates what he had already told Thurmond. He opposed busing and wanted decisions about education—as well as those on housing and gun control—made on the local level. He stressed voluntary compliance with federal court decisions and attacked judicial activists and their "draconian" edicts. He also promised not to select a running mate who would divide the Republican Party, a veiled signal that he would not choose a northern liberal. Nixon's remarks were greeted with applause.[29]

The southern delegates were also applauding Nixon's implicit message: their racial attitudes were no longer considered aberrant and now had a place in the Republican mainstream. They did not need to support Reagan—or defect to Wallace, for that matter—to have their views accepted and respected within the culture of the GOP. Nixon was hinting that enough sympathetic non-southern Republicans existed to offer their region a permanent home in the party. This would not have been possible even four years earlier. The white South had moved from the margins to the middle, and Nixon was acknowledging it. The overt racism of the Ku Klux Klan and the White Citizens' Council had been replaced with a more indirect and euphemistic version rooted in principles most Republicans could acknowledge: localism, voluntarism, and community.

That the Republican and not the Democratic Party would be the vehicle of this reintegration into the national polity was perhaps the most fortuitous development in Nixon's political career. He reaped its benefits in the early morning of August 8, 1968, when, holding his southern support, he defeated Reagan on the first ballot with 692 votes to the Californian's 182.

Immediately after securing the nomination Nixon set to the task of choosing his running mate. While not familiar to most of the nation, Spiro Agnew was already well known to the former vice president. Nixon had kept his eye on him since Agnew's April 11 tongue-lashing of Baltimore's black leaders in the wake of the King assassination riots. Agnew's angry lecture articulated the entire Republican domestic campaign agenda in 1968. He had expounded the party's position on race: equality of opportunity but not result. He had come out strongly for law and order. He had alluded to what would become known as the silent majority. He had offered justifications for capitalist individualism. He had decried the nation's descent into cultural decay and chaos. Media coverage of Agnew's performance caught the attention of Pat Buchanan, who made sure that "the boss" saw the relevant clippings. "Here was a Republican with liberal credentials on domestic issues and a law-and-order temperament, a rare combination in those days," Buchanan recalled.[30] He was also impressed by the overwhelmingly positive popular response Agnew received; his mail ran in favor of his April 11 statements by a margin of 1,250 to 11.[31]

While Agnew's showdown with Baltimore's civil rights leadership did not by itself make him the Republican vice presidential nominee, it did put him on Nixon's radar screen. Thanks to Buchanan's promotional efforts Nixon became aware of how effective Agnew could be in spreading a Republican message that would resonate with the party's new targets in the upcoming election: white southerners, suburbanites, Sun Belters, and workers. "I've stood still while the rest of the country, led by the press, has rushed headlong to the left," Agnew asserted in the aftermath of his April 11 remarks.[32] He uttered these words proudly and without apology. Agnew considered himself a supporter of civil rights, as difficult as it was to believe for the black leaders he had berated. But for Agnew and the many northern whites for whom he spoke, there was no contradiction whatsoever. He had endorsed the civil rights movement, however cautiously, when its goals included the constitutional rights guaranteed every American—when, for example, activists attempted to desegregate an amusement park like Gwynn Oak.

But when the movement broadened the scope of its demands to include economic and social redistribution, as it had after 1965, Agnew had defiantly stood still. These objectives did not constitute civil rights to him, nor did they to the thousands of men and women whose views he represented. They believed there once had been a consensus on the meaning of racial equality in America, and it was a simple one: race-blind treatment under the law. Now that consensus was gone—broken, they believed, by African Americans and their elite white supporters who had taken that definition in harmful and destructive directions, to places they would not and could not go.

The King riots and their angry rhetorical aftermath had radicalized Agnew. They metastasized the impulses that had been building inside him for years—the feeling that blacks had gone too far, that respect for traditional forms of authority was breaking down, that new and unwelcome understandings of equality and freedom were afoot, and that hard work and merit were no longer being rewarded. Agnew's words to Baltimore's black leaders were expressions of smoldering resentments that finally burst to the surface. It is impossible to know with certainty if Agnew understood at that moment that millions of Americans shared his feelings. But they did, and the fact that they did would make him Nixon's running mate and vice president. As man met moment, they would complete the GOP's journey from economic elitism to what its members believed was the people's party that had been thirty years in the making.

In the months following April 11 Agnew reinforced his growing reputation as the voice of the white everyman and boosted his chances to become a legitimate contender to join Nixon on the national ticket. His confrontation with the Baltimore black leadership had been personal as well as political. Many politicians are capable of putting even the bitterest disputes behind them, separating business instincts from human ones. Agnew, whose experience in the political world was relatively limited and who possessed a strong sense of moral sanctimony, was not one of them. In many ways he resembled the people whose lives he embodied, simultaneously proud and defensive. Like them, his resentments were visceral.

Only a week after his contretemps in Baltimore, Agnew was asked during a press conference if he agreed with the conclusion of the National Commission on Civil Disorders that white racism was the primary cause of urban riots. "I think that black racism is another contributing cause," he snapped, an indication that he had no plans to put the firestorm he had ignited to rest.[33] The next month he told a Republican women's club, "We must confront evil conditions and the evil men that exploit them. Too often and too long our nation's intellectual, spiritual, and political leaders have countenanced, condoned, and even counseled with such men."[34]

Here Agnew was clearly referring to the educated elites, who in his mind—and doubtless those of his audience—were liberal Democrats. The problem, in Agnew's view, was not with average Democrats but with their leaders, who now scoffed at the nation's essential rightness and goodness. And if Democratic elites had lost faith in America, where should the rest—southern Democrats, working-class Democrats, ethnic Democrats—go? To Agnew the answer was obvious. Their true home was with him and with Richard Nixon in the new Republican Party.

The GOP could thus pry a crucial element of the Democratic Party constituency away in the easiest possible manner, by arguing they could become Republicans without altering their belief systems or lifestyles. Democratic elites demanded that they change. The GOP would accept them as they were. To the elites they were racial bigots. To Republicans they were law-abiding citizens justifiably concerned about crime and disorder. In the Democratic Party they were reactionaries. In the GOP they were champions of the virtues and verities that had defined national greatness in the past and could do so yet again.

Agnew's approach to race relations was designed to dovetail with the color blindness that emerged from the pre-1965 phase of the civil rights movement and with which his audiences were comfortable. He combined this with an attack on the excesses of black militants that was calculated to resonate with those who like Agnew reacted to civil rights activism in emotional terms. Doubtless his constituency could recall conflicts and confrontations that had hardened their own racial attitudes. Agnew spoke for them. On June 20 he told a press audience:

> The biggest race questions that are arising today come, I submit to you, from the civil rights militants who are trying to create an unhealthy black racism in this country. And we've got to do something about that. I've always thought that the whole purpose of civil rights was one thing—that eventually, if everything goes the way we'd like it to go, I can sit down with a man of any color or creed and talk to him and not even think of the fact that he is a Negro or a white. . . . I can appraise him as an individual based on his individual work. That's what this is all about.[35]

By linking race relations to culture and not economics, Agnew also came down squarely on the side of those in the white community who believed that black people were primarily responsible for their own difficulties and that their values and lifestyles were flawed. Agnew never stated directly that the black community lacked respect for traditional cultural mores, but he did not have to. For his intended audience the implication was enough. Also, by denouncing lawbreaking as "socially acceptable" and "stylish," condoned by the press, Agnew could bring in, again by implication, his three bête noirs: black radicals, who justified criminal activity

as a form of political expression; Democratic-leaning elites, who roman-
ticized it; and the liberal media, which rationalized it.[36]

Agnew hammered home his critique of what he considered a decadent
governing class in a June address to a Republican urban affairs task force,
reminding his audience that "great nations collapse only when their foundations decay. Today, the foundations of America are rotting while most
of us stand fretfully by, watching with morbid curiosity. The disease of our
times is an artificial and masochistic sophistication—a vague uneasiness
that our values are corny. That there is something wrong with being patriotic, honest, moral, or hard working. The sneer of the nonconformist
has become an effective weapon for those who cannot achieve within the
framework of our society and therefore seek to destroy it."[37] He returned
to this theme a month later when he warned that "an acceptance of mass
guilt coupled with an abrogation of individual responsibility could be
disastrous for this great country of ours."[38]

By late July Nixon was well aware of Agnew's potential to connect with
the Democrats he hoped to turn into Republican voters. Agnew had not
backed down in the wake of his April 11 remarks. On the contrary, he had
underscored and amplified them. Nixon appreciated this. In Buchanan's
words, "The boss thought this guy was a very tough guy."[39] And toughness
was what Nixon prized. Having undergone his own personal tests—the
Hiss case, the Checkers speech, the 1960 and 1962 campaigns—he sought
a running mate who was also strong in a crisis. Agnew had not flinched,
even as most of his black audience on April 11 walked out on him and labeled him a racist. Nixon liked what he saw.

As the governor of a border state, Agnew could help the GOP in the
outer South. As an ethnic, he could attract white working- and middle-
class voters with similar outlooks, fears, and resentments. As a suburbanite, he could speak for those who had taken similar journeys over the past
two decades. Agnew was thus in the enviable position of acceptability to
all stripes of Republicans. In fact, as Nixon aide Stephen Hess observed,
"if you put all the conflicting Republican elements into a computer and
programmed it to produce a Vice President who would do least harm to
party unity, the tape would be punched SPIRO T. AGNEW."[40]

Nonetheless Agnew's name was only one of a number of possibilities being floated as the convention opened on August 5. That Agnew had been asked to give one of the nominating speeches was a positive sign, but it did not signal an inevitability about his elevation to the No. 2 spot. Although one historian has argued that Nixon decided on Agnew ten days before the convention, others have surmised that the decision may have been made as early as June. It is more likely that Nixon had put him on his internal wish list in the late spring without placing him front and center.[41] He did not, however, ask that Agnew's conduct in office be thoroughly vetted, an omission that would prove costly to both. Had Agnew's pattern of bribe-taking been discovered at this point, history might have taken a different turn.

In conversation with staff and political allies during the convention Nixon praised Agnew's nominating speech, perhaps hoping for a positive reaction, to little effect.[42] It was only in the early morning hours of August 8, after Nixon had officially secured the nomination, that the discussion of the vice presidential choice began in earnest. Nixon had already promised southern delegates that he would not choose a party divider, which eliminated Rockefeller-style candidates, notably Mayor John Lindsay of New York City.[43] But the dangers of choosing a "real" conservative like Reagan were also clear.

Nixon conducted four separate meetings with party leaders and close aides that morning. By the end five possibilities remained: Massachusetts governor John Volpe, Tennessee senator Howard Baker, Maryland congressman Rogers Morton, California lieutenant governor Robert Finch, and Agnew. One by one they were eliminated or eliminated themselves. Finch, a close friend of Nixon's, said he did not want the job.[44] Morton, Nixon's convention floor manager, was a nuts-and-bolts political operative but would not add much to a national ticket. Baker was only forty-two years old and in his second year in the Senate. Volpe's Italian background was a plus, but he was a northerner who would be of little help in other regions. Agnew, whom Goldwater had endorsed earlier that morning, appeared to make more sense.[45] He was a down-to-earth everyman, a border stater, a defender of law and order, an exponent of traditional cultural values, and a blunt-spoken anti-elitist. Having run a county and a state, he had executive experience. And as a more palatable echo of George Wallace, he could play on the Alabaman's populist themes while avoiding his taint of overt racism. So Nixon made the decision: Agnew it would be. In the early afternoon of August 8 he telephoned Agnew's suite at Miami's Eden Roc Hotel and gave him the news.

At a press conference a few minutes later Nixon announced Agnew as his choice, to retorts of "Spiro who?" from the media.[46] In his own meeting with the press Agnew acknowledged his lack of a household name.[47] He had risen as quickly as any candidate in modern American political history—from the last of five candidates in a Baltimore County circuit court judge election in 1960 to a place on a major party ticket in eight years—and his reference to "the improbability of this moment" in his acceptance speech that same day, after being nominated on the first ballot, was a testament to his rapid ascent.[48] He would now get the chance to prove his worth to a Nixon campaign that was banking on the existence of millions of Spiro Agnews.

Most accounts of Agnew's 1968 campaign for the vice presidency focus on a series of gaffes committed by the candidate at various stops on the trail. They included using the word "Polack" to refer to Polish-Americans and calling a reporter a "fat Jap," as well as informing an interviewer, "If you've seen one city slum you've seen them all."[49] The incidents received outsized amounts of media coverage and made Agnew the butt of innumerable jokes on late-night talk shows and among stand-up comedians. A widely viewed Democratic television campaign ad featured the sound of laughter over the words "Agnew for Vice President?" followed by a warning: "This would be funny if it weren't so serious."[50]

But in reality Agnew offered a powerful articulation of Republican principles grounded in cultural traditionalism and populist egalitarianism. He helped to both rebrand the GOP and saddle the Democratic Party with what would become enduring political liabilities as the party of elitism, racial favoritism, and liberalism. Nixon understood this and therefore gave less weight to Agnew's verbal slips than did the media and his Democratic opponents. While opinion makers saw a bumbling, malaprop-prone candidate, Nixon saw one whose message resonated among the middle—and middle-minded—Americans he needed in order to be elected president. Nixon could sense the vote-getting potential in a man he described admiringly as "a hanging judge."[51]

The Republicans received a political gift in August in the form of the disastrous Democratic National Convention in Chicago. The proceedings included a bitter floor fight over the Vietnam platform plank. Chicago mayor Richard Daley kept war opponents at bay on the convention floor, often with heavy-handed tactics. The image of Daley screaming anti-Semitic obscenities at the antiwar senator Abraham Ribicoff of Connecticut, captured live on television, epitomized the angry, despairing mood of the party. Humphrey was duly nominated on the first ballot on August 29, with Senator Edmund Muskie of Maine as his running mate. Few rejoiced.

What took place outside the convention hall hurt the Democrats most. An alliance of New Left groups led by members of Students for a Democratic Society and the Youth International Party, or Yippies, descended on Chicago determined to mount a massive and disruptive demonstration against the war. Aided by the city's gratuitously brutal police force, they succeeded. To chants of "the whole world is watching," protesters were beaten, clubbed, and tear-gassed. Even members of the media and some delegates fell victim to the strong-arm tactics of Daley's finest. Television brought the chaos into the nation's living rooms.

As damaging as the scenes of mayhem were, the confrontations between the police and demonstrators harmed the Democratic Party in a broader sense by vivifying the elites-versus-the-people divisions that were being put to such good political use by Republicans, including Spiro Agnew. When in the aftermath of the convention Tom Wicker of the *New York Times* lamented, "These were our children in the streets and the Chicago police beat them up," he was only confirming the existence of the divide and betraying his class's ignorance of its implications.[52] The Chicago police epitomized the image of more-conservative, white working-class Democrats. Wicker's "children," cursing and baiting them in the streets and parks surrounding the Conrad Hilton Hotel, may not have been registered Democrats, but as leftists they were associated with them in the public mind. It was the worst possible public face for the left and, by extension, liberal Democrats.

At the beginning of September the newly nominated Humphrey trailed Nixon in the Gallup Poll 43 to 31 percent, with Wallace at 19 percent. However, the Democrat from Minnesota had the backing of most organized labor leaders, notably AFL-CIO president George Meany, and he could tap into a well of union support with roots stretching back to the New Deal.[53] The historic image of the GOP as the foe of the working-man was never far from the surface; it was, realistically, the only chance the Democrats had to win. But if Agnew and Nixon could make the campaign about middle-class values and order, not money and the pocketbook, they could turn the national debate to their advantage. They succeeded, with Nixon building a bland, cliché-ridden effort around staged media appearances and ad agency–massaged television spots and Agnew making use of his everyman status to connect with the legions of voters who resembled and identified with him. "There is in this country a creeping paralysis of our national purpose, and we've got to do something about that," he told a San Francisco audience shortly after his nomination.[54] Over the weeks that followed he set out to do just that.

As the national press focused almost obsessively on his bloopers, Agnew crafted a bluntly worded defense of the moral virtues of Middle America, one calculated to arouse the emotions and sensibilities of his almost exclusively white audiences. He echoed many of Wallace's themes, but without his raw edge and his heavy racial baggage. Agnew also skillfully connected Humphrey and Democrats in general to the loss of respect for authority in America, more political catnip for his fearful, angry listeners. In contrast to his new image as an inarticulate bumbler, Agnew on the stump was a crisp, stinging, and precise rhetorician, honed in on his intended targets. His effectiveness permitted the Nixon campaign to look past Agnew's references to Japs and Polacks to the more immediate task of bringing those to whom Nixon had referred during his nomination acceptance speech as "the forgotten Americans—the non-shouters; the non-demonstrators" into the Republican fold.[55] Agnew knew how to reach them.

Speaking in Michigan as the Democratic Convention began, Agnew took note of the "dull" Republican Convention earlier that month and turned its lack of drama into a virtue:

After all . . . we didn't have a march on the convention by the hippies or the yippies. . . . And when we win, we're just liable to bring back into American life a lot of things that the devotees of the so-called "New Politics" consider dull. Dull things like patriotism. Dull things like incentive. Dull things like a respect for law and a concern for a greater justice for all Americans. In fact, things could become so dull, that some little old ladies who wear sneakers to get a fast start on criminals on city streets might go back to wearing high heels. And some of the fellows hanging around street corners might want to go to work again just to block out the boredom from their lives.[56]

On September 18, in the midst of a controversy over his use of the word "soft" to describe Humphrey's positions on communism and crime, Agnew spoke in Casper, Wyoming, about the nation's need for a "new moral climate": "When I read and I hear from some of the most sophisticated observers of the public media, that law and order has no place in this national campaign, I'm astounded. . . . The primary right of every American is the protection of himself and his family. The primary responsibility of every American is to conduct himself so others will be protected."[57] Agnew was interrupted by applause twenty-two times in eighteen minutes.[58]

If the national media was obsessed with Agnew's linguistic stumbles, his audiences on the ground lapped up his rhetoric of resentment and his vision of restoration. Agnew sensed what they yearned for: a defense of what to them seemed a simpler time, when the rules were unquestioned and the lines of authority were clear. In an environment where the terrain seemed to be shifting under their feet, Agnew offered stability and certainty. To a Democratic Party that appeared ambivalent about the value of American institutions, Agnew gave a blunt retort: "Everything's right with our system."[59]

Nine days later in Milwaukee, a racially divided city in a state that had given a third of its Democratic primary vote to Wallace four years earlier, Agnew used a top-and-bottom-against-the-middle formulation to identify his and his audience's enemies. Speaking to a virtually all-white crowd on the city's heavily ethnic South Side, he said: "There is now emerging something called a social criminal class; a group of self-appointed elitists who feel their instincts or educations give them the right to decide which laws to obey and which they are entitled to disregard."[60]

Agnew understood the hostility of his audience, in Milwaukee and nationally, toward elites and African Americans. He skillfully wove the two targets together, associating both with a Democratic Party represented by a parasitic class of idlers, taking what did not belong to them and enjoying the benefits of the hard work of others. Is this the America you want? Agnew asked his crowds, implying that Democratic leaders did. Most of his listeners in South Milwaukee had voted Democratic for generations. But now a Republican was speaking to them in ways to which they could relate, presenting a vision of their country that they shared. Under these circumstances, his mislabeling of Polish Americans—and South Milwaukee was filled with them—mattered less than the connection Agnew forged with voters whose aspirations and fears he articulated.

It did not take Agnew long to draw the attention of hecklers, perhaps a sign of his candidacy's growing importance. Their presence served only to increase sympathy for him, as did his sharp and often witty retorts to their provocations. After a group of demonstrators shouted "No more war!" and were ejected during a speech in Portland, Oregon, in early October, Agnew quipped, "Now if the delegation from Hanoi has left, perhaps we can conclude," to loud applause.[61] He then transitioned seamlessly to a discussion of the limits of responsible protest, remarking that it was "an appropriate moment, my friends, that that little demonstration took place because I was just about to begin speaking in terms of the violence that strikes our cities, about what is permissible dissent."[62] After disposing of yet another antiwar heckler—"Yes, yes, children are unfortunately killed but the Viet Cong kills children too"—he told the crowd: "If we allow anyone to take the law into his own hands, to make the judgments, we're heading for a society that's disrupted by constant attempts at anarchy. And this country hasn't come all that way for this."[63]

Turning prior remarks by Humphrey against him, Agnew charged that "when the Vice President of the United States who seeks the presidency says, while the fires are still burning in Cleveland, that he could lead a pretty good riot under those conditions—I say to you he's not creating the proper atmosphere for this country."[64] Agnew thus combined attacks on criminal activity, cultural breakdown, class privilege, and weak-willed Democratic politicians to make a compelling case for a Republican presidential vote in 1968. He was casting himself in the image of his audiences, telling their stories through his own and reflecting his life through theirs.

There still remained the challenge of Wallace, of course. The former Alabama governor had peaked in the national polls at 21 percent in late September, and a concerned Nixon campaign had begun to train its rhetorical fire on him, warning off potential Republican voters, especially in the border states and upper South, from their "wasted" vote.[65] Agnew was well suited for this task. He articulated Wallace's anger but without his jagged edges. For example, Agnew criticized demonstrators who blocked intersections for going beyond the boundaries of acceptable dissent. "The right to demonstrate peacefully . . . does not mean lying down in the streets to disrupt traffic," he told a Midland, Texas, audience in October. However, he did not threaten, as did Wallace, to run them over.[66] Without Wallace's racial baggage, and with a civil rights record that was better than that of most border state governors, Agnew could describe "police brutality" as "one of the most overworked phrases in the country today."[67]

Wallace's disastrous announcement of retired U.S. Air Force general Curtis LeMay as his running mate on October 3 made Agnew's job much easier. LeMay, the architect of the massive conventional bombing campaign against Japan during World War II that killed even more civilians than the atomic blasts at Hiroshima and Nagasaki, was a notoriously aggressive Cold War hawk. He used his introductory press conference to raise the possibility of using nuclear weapons in the Vietnam conflict.[68] This presented Agnew with an opportunity to feint toward the center, leavening his own hawkish Vietnam position with what in comparison appeared to be calm good sense. "Mr. LeMay's very casual statements about atomic warfare frighten me a great deal," he told a hometown audience in Towson a week after the LeMay announcement. "And I'm sure they do you, too. He has a distinguished war record but obviously we can't have a man who treats the awesome power of nuclear catastrophe so casually as Mr. LeMay does."[69]

Agnew then shifted to his strongest argument against Wallace—that he could not win. "Please urge your friends that no matter how much they dislike Hubert Humphrey, no matter how much they'd like to react [to Humphrey], to be diametrically opposed, don't waste a vote on a man you can't elect, because a vote for George Wallace is a vote for Hubert Humphrey."[70]

By October the national media was comparing Agnew unfavorably with his Democratic rival, Senator Edmund Muskie. A deliberate, thoughtful Mainer, Muskie soon became known for his calm responses to hecklers and demonstrators, whom he allowed to state their cases and sometimes even invited onto the speaker's platform. In contrast to the emotional, frenetic Humphrey, Muskie cut a more presidential—some observers called it Lincolnesque—figure.[71] Agnew already had a tense relationship with the media. He avoided back-of-the-plane bonhomie with journalists; indeed, his "fat Jap" remark, a rare attempt at campaign informality, had been directed at a reporter for the *Baltimore Sun* whom he knew from his days in Annapolis. It was thus almost inevitable that Muskie's media image would be burnished at the expense of Agnew's. But when he came before the voters on the level of retail politics Agnew was able to exploit their differences for his own benefit. His responses to hecklers were much harsher than Muskie's—"They've never done a productive thing in their lives; they take their tactics from Castro and their money from daddy," he spat contemptuously during his Towson speech in October—and more appreciated by his audiences.[72]

Agnew also used Muskie's civility against him. At one of his campaign appearances Muskie had watched a group of war opponents burn their draft cards, commenting only that while they had the right to free expression they also had to be prepared to face the legal consequences of their actions. When confronted with his own hecklers, Agnew lambasted Muskie's weak response. In Towson, he charged: "There's little doubt that this sort of thing is encouraged by the very type of candidate that you're here to make certain doesn't get elected to the vice presidency. . . .

The kind of candidate who sits and grins sheepishly while a few protesters burn their draft cards in front of him. And that's the big difference between Senator Muskie and me."[73] Agnew would go on to hammer Muskie for this instance of softness on crime for the remainder of the campaign, leveraging the very attribute that drew praise from the national media into a powerful point of rebuttal on the grassroots level.

As the campaign moved into its concluding weeks, the fact that Agnew had become an object of derision for the press, elites, and liberal Democrats began to work in his favor with the constituencies the Republicans needed. These were profitable enemies to have in a nation in which, according to a Harris poll in September, more than 50 percent of respondents agreed with the statement "Liberals, intellectuals, and long-hairs have run the country for too long."[74] The journalists Lewis Chester, Godfrey Hodgson, and Bruce Page, writing in their perceptive account of the 1968 campaign, *An American Melodrama*, observed, "What Agnew was doing was giving the Democratic elite—who knew exactly who he was—someone to hate and someone to organize against."[75] But the reverse was also true. By October Agnew's supporters loved him for the enemies he had made. They were their enemies too.

Agnew may have captured the essence of the average American's resentments of those who appeared to live comfortably in a nation whose values they rejected. In another section of his Towson speech, as he fenced verbally with demonstrators from the local college chapter of Students for a Democratic Society, he remarked, "There must be some peculiar significance to the fact that one half of the total crime that's committed in this country of a violent nature is committed by people under 21 years of age." He continued: "And I think it's because the permissible limits of dissent are blurred—blurred by the New Left. Blurred by . . . the Abby [sic] Hoffmans and the Jerry Rubins and all the people who expect when they turn the faucet the water is [going] to run and when they turn the thermostat the heat is going to come up and when they get in a car it's supposed to run."[76] Agnew concluded the speech with the warning that his hecklers "represent what you're going to get more and more of if you put Hubert H. Humphrey in the presidency."[77] Neither Humphrey, Muskie, nor members of the Democratic Party establishment approved of violent protest or the disruption of campaign speeches, nor did they view America as morally irredeemable. But they were trapped by events and by history. It had taken some thirty years, but Hubert Humphrey, a Democrat who had spent his life fighting for labor rights and racial equality, and Spiro Agnew, a business-class suburban Republican, had reversed roles. The Democrats were now seen as the self-appointed mandarins of American culture. Agnew and the Republicans represented "the rest of us," the "forgotten Americans," "the people." What had appeared implausible only a few years earlier was now real.

Still, the Democrats could summon up old allegiances to get them back into the race. Humphrey jump-started his moribund campaign on September 30 by breaking with Johnson and calling for a halt to bombing in Vietnam. Many of his erstwhile adversaries in the McCarthy, Kennedy, and McGovern camps began edging toward him, and McCarthy himself offered an endorsement in late October. As Nixon sought to get through October with his fifteen-point lead in the polls intact, he became more and more cautious in his strategy, limiting his live appearances and unscripted exposure. Humphrey's longtime allies in the labor movement began to deploy their financial and organizational muscle on his behalf. Big Labor had always viewed Nixon with suspicion, and the candidacy of Wallace, a product of the most anti-union region in the United States and a deeply divisive racial figure, was ominous in its implications. Humphrey finally found his voice, demanding of his heavily unionized audiences, "What has Richard Nixon ever done for workingmen?" "Nothing!" came the answer. "So what are you going to do for Richard Nixon?" "Nothing!"[78]

As Humphrey's economic arguments gained traction, traditional working-class Democratic voters started to trickle back home, enough of them to tighten the race as the month progressed. By October 12 Nixon led Humphrey 43 percent to 31 percent in the Gallup Poll; a few days earlier, the Democratic-leaning Harris Poll had showed Humphrey trailing by only five percentage points.[79] On October 21 Gallup reported that Nixon's lead had shrunk to eight points—44 to 36 percent.[80]

With pocketbook issues beginning to work for the Democrats, it was more important than ever for Agnew to press the issue of middle-class values under threat, but without veering into expressions of overt racism. One means toward this goal was citing the enormous waste in Great Society antipoverty and jobs programs. Agnew told a Woodbridge, New Jersey, crowd on October 14 of "a woman from Watts" hired by the Office of Economic Opportunity "at $19,000 a year who's been indicted for embezzling another $22,000." "This particular woman has never held a job a year in her life—she's had 6 or 7 very recently," he continued, ". . . and the one she has held she's held under 6 separate aliases. Now isn't that a great person to hire to administer poverty funds? Are we going to put up with this?"[81] Agnew then described "an Office of Economic Opportunity grant given to two Chicago street gangs where they were provided with $927,000 supposedly to do something constructive. Constructive to them I assume means stockpiling weapons to use in riots. . . . Are you going to put up with that?" The crowd shouted its response: "No!"[82] Later in the speech Agnew took aim at the Democratic elites who planned and administered the programs that had gone awry, referring to them as "a group of phony intellectuals who don't understand what we mean by hard work and patriotism."[83] Agnew's speech transcriber noted marginally: "What a *friendly*, interruptive crowd!!!"[84]

At Nixon's behest Pat Buchanan began traveling with and writing speeches for Agnew in October. While he did not stay for the length of the campaign, those speeches bore the mark of Buchanan's populist conservatism.[85] Buchanan helped ensure that Agnew's remarks during the campaign's final weeks were more substantive than those of his running mate.

Agnew continued to defend a political and economic system in which he said Democrats had lost faith. In Midland, Texas, in late October, he recounted: "I used to see my father sit down and talk politics with some of the other first generation Americans, who came to this country and loved it so dearly because of the opportunity it gave them—I just get a little sick and tired of hearing people run the country down, because they've been too lazy and too inefficient to make anything of themselves."[86] He continued, speaking to his middle-class audience's concerns about the future in a nation that was changing in confusing and threatening ways: "There is no such thing as . . . welfare rights in this country. The Constitution doesn't guarantee everyone makes a certain amount of money. The Constitution doesn't guarantee you instantaneous economic equality or success. It guarantees you, however, the opportunity, and it's our obligation to provide that opportunity for everyone in this country, regardless of race, creed, or color. But let's not confuse the providing of an opportunity with the giveaway program that takes from the majority."[87]

Agnew's use of the word "majority" was deliberate. It reflected a growing confidence that he and the Republican Party were reaching the kinds of voters—not the black, the poor, or the young, but "the rest of us"— who could not only carry the election but also create a new popular base for the GOP. Still, the race continued to tighten as Wallace's support dropped and traditional Democrats returned to Humphrey. During the last two weeks of the campaign Agnew visited border states as well as southern states in which Nixon had a chance to edge out Wallace, including Kentucky, Tennessee, Virginia, Florida, and South Carolina.[88] Over the final weekend the Gallup Poll had Nixon ahead 42 percent to 40 percent. Louis Harris's last official poll showed Humphrey leading 43 percent to 40 percent.[89] But within forty-eight hours of Election Day, and once the public had the chance to absorb the news of a failed Vietnam peace initiative, Harris detected a small shift back to Nixon. In the end he rated the race a toss-up.[90]

At the beginning of his telethon from Los Angeles on the eve of the election, Nixon went out of his way to praise Agnew's campaign work on his and the GOP's behalf. He had reason to be grateful. Agnew had denounced Democrats as elitists and apologists for crime and disorder who were hostile to traditional American mores and values. At the same time he had played a major role in identifying the Republican Party with "the people," the average Americans who had given the Democratic Party majorities for decades. Many Republicans had helped facilitate the political role reversal that was now at hand—Joseph McCarthy, Dwight Eisenhower, Barry Goldwater, Ronald Reagan, and Richard Nixon himself— but Spiro Agnew was also its instrument. A joke to opinion makers and knowledge-class elites, Agnew was deadly serious to the men and women who counted on Election Day. In a campaign where the ratio of anti- to pro-Nixon words on the three national television networks was disproportionately high, Agnew succeeded in going over the heads of the anchors and commenters to meet the "plain people" of America where they stood.[91] He made it possible for a transformed Republican Party to face the nation's voters on November 5, 1968.

That night Agnew followed the returns from the Governor's Mansion in Annapolis. Early on, Humphrey took New York, Pennsylvania, and Michigan, and his chances appeared promising. But Nixon carried New Jersey narrowly and then Ohio, Indiana, and Wisconsin, sweeping the nation to the West Coast. The following morning Illinois and California were officially called for Nixon, giving him the presidency with 302 electoral votes to Humphrey's 191 and Wallace's 46.

It was the outer South and border states that had meant the most to Nixon's victory. Wallace held his Deep South base—Alabama, Mississippi, Louisiana, Georgia, and Arkansas. Humphrey carried Lyndon Johnson's home state of Texas. But Nixon had won the rest—Virginia, Kentucky, Tennessee, and North Carolina in the upper South, as well as Oklahoma on the border. Nixon also won Florida and, thanks to his ally Strom Thurmond, South Carolina.[92] Together these states represented seventy-five electoral votes. All were historically Democratic. Agnew had been placed on the ticket in order to help Republicans win them, and win them they did.

How much did Agnew contribute to these victories? Quite a bit, argued Louis Harris, who in an analysis immediately following the election linked every one of them to his efforts.[93] Agnew had spent time in almost all of these states in the closing weeks of the campaign.[94] In another election postmortem, *New York Daily News* Washington reporter Ted Lewis wrote, "Not even a pseudointellectual could imagine Nixon having a prayer in Wallace country" had he selected a northern liberal running mate instead of Agnew.[95] The *Dallas Morning News* in its breakdown of the results argued that if Nixon wished to win over the voters of the upper South and border states from longstanding Democratic allegiances as well as the rightward siren call of George Wallace, "he had to offer a running mate who spoke their language."[96] Nixon did, and Agnew had paid off for him. Lyndon Johnson told Nixon on Inauguration Day that while "the press had slobbered over Muskie . . . when it came down to votes Muskie had delivered Maine with 4 votes, whereas Agnew could take credit or at least a great deal of the credit on South Carolina, North Carolina, Virginia, Tennessee, and Kentucky."[97]

Spiro Agnew, an average man from an average background with an average family, an average intellect, and an average sensibility, had moved millions of average men and women who had taken him as one of their own. He was now a symbol of that averageness, a very good place for a Republican to be, and a place the party had sought to occupy for three decades.

4

BECOMING THE SPOKESMAN
FOR THE SILENT MAJORITY

Spiro Agnew came to Washington in 1969 with little national stature despite his higher profile during the campaign. Four years later, he would be reelected vice president in a landslide, backed by a political base that personally identified with him. He had the admiration of a growing number of the Republican faithful, particularly in the South and the Midwest, an understanding of international affairs, four years of experience as the No. 2, and was considered by journalists and party insiders to be a formidable front-runner for the 1976 Republican presidential nomination.

Much of the fascination with Agnew's unlikely popularity centered on the question, "How did this happen?" The short answer is that Agnew, with a big assist from Nixon staffer Pat Buchanan, chose his targets and his method of political combat well. His use of public speeches to make skillful attacks on network television news, the *New York Times*, and the *Washington Post* endeared him to many Americans who felt marginalized by some notion of "the elite." Chip-on-the-shoulder Republicans—who didn't want to be talked down to by the *Post's* Ben Bradlee, or the Sulzbergers of the *Times*, or Ivy Leaguers generally—thrilled to Agnew's rhetoric. In addition to being a harbinger of things to come (see Donald Trump's "failing *New York Times*"), his ongoing verbal assaults on students, faculty, and college presidents helped further the tribalism of "us" (hard-working, straight-talking Americans) versus "them" (Vietnam War–protesting, over-indulged, ivory-towered slackers). Agnew dug even deeper, challenging affirmative action and quotas at a time when the Republican Party wasn't yet ready to cede that position to the Democrats.

He barnstormed around the country in the midterm elections of 1970 taking no prisoners, disparaging radical-liberals or "radiclibs" (coarsened in today's parlance to "libtards") and those who would later be dubbed Republicans in Name Only (RiNOs). He became a sought-after Lincoln Day speaker to the faithful in the heartland, a top fund-raiser, and a fixture on news programs.

Remarkably, Agnew became a force despite his poor relationship with Nixon, who sought to minimize his role, particularly in policymaking, at almost every turn. Nixon talked behind Agnew's back, diminishing him repeatedly behind closed doors, and actively tried to replace him on the 1972 ticket with Treasury Secretary John Connally. At the end of four years, however, Agnew's newfound national political power forced Nixon to keep him on as vice president. This chapter will explore Agnew's journey during the first term of the Nixon administration and trace his rise from political obscurity to potential powerbroker.

Less than three years removed from his position as Baltimore County executive in Towson, Agnew had improbably ascended to the second-most important political position in the country. Sworn in by Senate Minority Leader Everett Dirksen on January 20, 1969, the new veep wore a conservative steel-blue tie and looked the part, but he already felt isolated from the new administration. He perceived, correctly, that Nixon's people viewed him as "the dumb rookie who said the wrong things."[1]

Agnew's lack of understanding about the ways of Washington was particularly acute when compared to that of his new boss, who had spent his entire adult life wrapped up in the intricacies of elected politics and domestic and international affairs. To compound matters Nixon stocked his new cabinet and inner circle with well-educated and more-experienced Washington hands, including William Rogers (State), George Shultz (Labor), Mel Laird (Defense), Henry Kissinger (National Security Council), and Daniel Patrick Moynihan (special advisor for urban affairs), among others. Like many presidents Nixon also had a tight circle of political advisors that he had brought with him to Washington and who knew him from his many years in politics. This group included John Mitchell (attorney general), Maurice Stans (Commerce), Robert Finch (Health, Education, and Welfare), H. R. Haldeman (chief of staff), and

John Ehrlichman (domestic policy advisor). Agnew, with just six years of elected state and local political experience and only a cursory relationship with Nixon, struggled to find his place. He had particular difficulty finding allies or relevance within the cabinet.

It was an unexpected turn for Agnew because the first few weeks after the election had looked promising. Nixon invited Agnew and his wife, Judy, to his winter getaway in Key Biscayne, Florida, prior to the January inauguration to discuss his responsibilities. He asked Agnew to take on policymaking tasks and flattered him by suggesting that he locate his office in the West Wing of the White House, a first for a vice president. Nixon also asked him to draw on his experience as a governor by taking on "the major responsibility" for federal/state relations and urged him to get to know Congress and its members so that he might serve as their primary liaison to the White House.[2] It seemed like a positive start to the working political relationship between the two men, and it boded well for Agnew's own standing within the administration. But whether Nixon then had a change of heart or, more likely, this was classic Nixon disingenuousness, their relationship remained distant.

The new vice president also didn't make matters easy for himself, bringing in aides whose experience did not extend much beyond Maryland.[3] His first chief of staff, Stanley Blair, had been a member of the Maryland House of Delegates from rural Harford County for a single term and then served a short stint as Agnew's secretary of state during his truncated governorship. Art Sohmer, who had run Agnew's successful campaigns for Baltimore County executive and later was his appointments secretary in Annapolis, followed Blair as chief of staff within Agnew's first year in office.[4] His first press secretary, Herb Thompson, had been the Annapolis bureau chief for the Associated Press, and his chief speechwriter, Cynthia "Cynnie" Rosenwald, was a "Baltimore housewife" whose primary experience was that she had written drafts of Agnew's speeches when he was governor.[5]

With his inexperienced staff and his own naïveté about the ways of the capital, Agnew tried to find his early footing outside of Washington. In his first few weeks as vice president he gave perfunctory speeches to organizations with little political value or visibility. The banality of his early public addresses, in light of his later use of high-profile speechmaking, is striking. His remarks in those first weeks were often delivered as prepared, with few notes in the margins. Agnew employed a standard script: a welcome, followed by a joke, a little substance, maybe a quick political shot, and then a succinct conclusion.[6] Memos from Rosenwald in the first months displayed an abundance of deference toward Nixon's staffers and publicists, even seeking approval for the use of jokes.[7] In preparation notes for his speech at the March 1969 Gridiron Dinner, the light-hearted Washington event for political journalists, Agnew solicited ideas from comedian Bob Hope. Among the quips Agnew chose not to use: "I hope that the next time the President goes on a trip, he will see fit to ask me to go. It is a little embarrassing following him around all day singing, 'Take Me Along.'" But Agnew did take Hope up on a one-liner: "And when I go to the White House, I don't have to use the back door. I go right in with the regular tour."[8]

At least at the outset of his term Agnew seemed destined to play the traditional role of the forgotten vice president, constantly tugging on the president's sleeve. The job of keeping the increasingly disgruntled and bored Agnew away from Nixon fell to White House chief of staff H. R. Haldeman.[9] There are numerous references to "the Agnew problem" in Haldeman's diaries between 1969 and 1972. Nixon and his aides spent an inordinate amount of time figuring out how to cope with, and sufficiently occupy, the vice president. Keeping Agnew at arm's length from Nixon was also a priority for White House staffers. An early entry in Haldeman's diary, just a couple of weeks into the term, showed how flummoxed Nixon's people were: "Strange problem with Agnew, who has hired LBJ's top advance man as an administrative assistant. No one seems to be able to dissuade him, the guy has turned out to be a total spy."[10] In April Haldeman noted that Nixon had "decided [Arthur] Burns [a counselor to Nixon] should explain to Agnew how the Vice Presidency works."[11] Agnew quickly felt shut out; he wrote in his memoirs that he soon learned that "everything was run as a closed corporation. Haldeman and Ehrlichman didn't tell me what they were doing. There was a lot of secrecy and jealousy and vying for the President's attention among senior people. I finally got disgusted and started spending more time with my own staff across the street in the Old Executive Office Building."[12] Agnew soon gave up his West Wing office. Ehrlichman, the domestic policy advisor, would later recall that relations between Nixon and Agnew were very poor, both personally and professionally: "[Agnew] was continually badgering Nixon to give him more to do, and Nixon—and frankly all of us—lacked the confidence in Agnew to give him much substantive stuff to do."[13]

As the spring progressed, however, it was clear that Agnew saw his public speeches as a pathway to relevance both inside the administration and on the national stage. He became the Republican Party's point man in an emerging cultural war on issues of class, race, and morality that would become a staple of American politics for the next half century. While the slashing rhetoric of his public crusades and speeches made him a household name, he also put forward a bold, more populist vision for the party. In a speech to the College Republican National Committee at Yale in April 1969, he pushed aside the old royalist image of the GOP: "We must now set about selling the case for Republicanism, and with a new image, to the American public. But first we must do some unselling. We must lay to permanent rest the notion that our party is a partner to special privilege, wealth and parochialism. We must unsell the idea that we are more concerned with the public ledgers than we are with the public good."[14] It wasn't just what Agnew stood for but, more important, who and what he was against. In time the list grew: the ivory-tower universities with their snooty intellectuals and their long-haired student radicals, the condescending media, the free-love, unpatriotic Vietnam War protesters, and anyone else who tolerated the lack of law and order in the streets and on college campuses as "free assembly" and "free speech."

Asked to deliver two commencement addresses on successive days in June at Ohio State (where he was filling in for Nixon) and Loyola University in Maryland, Agnew tasked Rosenwald with writing the first drafts. A memo from her to the vice president confessed that "while you may be calm—I am prepared to panic since both must be fresh and important."[15] Agnew's handwritten notes back to Rosenwald asked for a "new opening—more interest more punch" and suggested that she include his idea that "those who would destroy [our system] for the sake of change" ought to be called out.[16] It was clear that if Agnew intended to use speeches as the engine that drove his political persona, he was also going to need more intellectual firepower to help make his points heard by a larger audience. But while Nixon speechwriters Pat Buchanan and William Safire received much of the credit for Agnew's later speechmaking, these drafts reveal that he brought to the vice presidency the sharp-elbowed rhetorical style he had developed in Maryland in the early 1960s.

In the Ohio State speech Agnew showed more signs that he had begun to hit his stride, finding his silent majority voice that would propel him to national prominence in the months ahead. Echoing the accusations of over-emotionalism and over-indulgence he had used in his Maryland speeches, Agnew charged that "a society which comes to fear its children is effete. A sniveling, hand wringing power structure deserves the violent rebellion it encourages. If my generation doesn't stop cringing, yours will inherit a lawless society where emotion and muscle displace reason. . . . We have a choice. Will we treat all that is wrong with America as a challenge or as an indictment? Will we condemn our institutions or correct them? Will we repudiate democracy because it moves slowly, or revitalize it so its pace quickens?" Cited by Ohio State administrators as a "talented lawyer, public servant, administrator and statesman," Agnew received a standing ovation from the crowd of forty thousand as he accepted his honorary doctorate of laws degree.[17]

Bob Hope, another honoree that day, once again cast Agnew as a political no-name with intellectual pretensions. Hope opened with "I am happy that Vice President Agnew is here today . . . and that you recognize him." He went on to poke fun at Agnew's intellect by quipping, "They said the Agnew Library burned down and destroyed both his books. One of them, he hadn't even colored yet."[18] Hope's teasing, while good-natured and well received, presented Agnew with an odd dichotomy. He had something to say, but he also had a public reputation as a nobody from nowhere. As he would soon discover, this could also be played to his advantage. Hope may have painted him as an average guy with average intelligence, struggling for recognition and a voice, but wasn't that just like the majority of Americans? If he was also trying to say something important about people like him across the nation, wouldn't his voice be more powerful because the opinion makers and the establishment didn't take him seriously? Agnew therefore was on the one hand a football-watching Kiwanian and the father of a son serving in Vietnam whose connection with the midwestern moms and dads in the Ohio State audience and elsewhere was real. But he also happened to be vice president of the United States, and all of Bob Hope's lame jokes could not change that fact.[19]

Even as Agnew began to find his voice on the hustings, he continued to struggle to find relevance inside the White House. He was largely marginalized at National Security Council meetings, where, he would later say, "it was a sad thing" for him to see "a dove at each elbow" of the president, referring to Secretary of State Bill Rogers and Secretary of Defense Mel Laird.[20] Agnew criticized both men in his memoirs, not just for their policy positions on the Vietnam War ("they believed the war was already lost and they both had a fixed idea of getting out as fast as possible") but also as the embodiment of an establishment that he felt was crippling the country.[21] Since Agnew had already surmised that he was not going to be a major player in the Nixon cabinet, he was going to have to find his influence elsewhere.

The fall of 1969 was the pivotal moment in Agnew's vice presidency. A group of White House staffers, including Pat Buchanan, anointed themselves the Middle America Committee, with the charge of finding ways to better connect Nixon and the Republican Party with "the large and politically powerful white middle class [that] is deeply troubled, primarily over the erosion of what they consider to be their values."[22] In Agnew the group found its ultimate avatar. He cemented his place in history in a series of speeches over a six-week period in October and November. By making his political importance too valuable to ignore or replace, Agnew also established his brand of conservative populism that has echoed through the Republican Party for the last half century and that culminated in the 2016 election of Donald Trump.

At a speech at the Citizens' Testimonial Dinner in New Orleans on October 19 Agnew bluntly went after the new campus culture that was flowering across the land. Administrators, faculty, and students were calling for curricular and campus-life changes that reflected the social upheavals of the decade, such as the free speech movement, new black studies programs, coed dormitories, and antiwar protests. Agnew saw an opening to speak to the silent majority of Americans looking in from outside the debate. Again reviving the stern Agnew from his Maryland days, he complained: "The student now goes to college to proclaim rather than to learn. The lessons of the past are ignored or obliterated in a contemporary antagonism known as the generation gap. A spirit of national masochism prevails, encouraged by an effete corps of impudent snobs who characterize themselves as intellectuals." In one fell swoop Agnew gave voice to those Americans who looked upon Berkeley, Madison, and Ann Arbor as taxpayer-funded hotbeds of radicalism where students took classes from leftist professors on subjects that seemed to have little practical value. In Agnew's world, college and universities in 1969 were filled with marijuana-smoking, jeans-wearing pseudo-intellectuals who were using draft deferments to dodge service in Vietnam. This group couldn't be more foreign to Agnew's constituency. In addition to being radicals they were also weak and spoiled, and "effete corps of impudent snobs" soon became a catchphrase.[23]

The night after the New Orleans speech, at the Mississippi Republican Dinner in Jackson, Agnew tied this picture of campus radicalism directly to the Democratic Party to show how out of step the party was with white culture below the Mason-Dixon line in the civil rights era. The South, he proclaimed, was "the punching bag for those who characterize themselves as liberal intellectuals." Many white southerners had remained in the Democratic fold after the Kennedy-Johnson years, but just barely. A rising tide of changing party identification continued throughout the 1960s and early 1970s, and Agnew helped egg it on. Meanwhile, he had identified the emerging base of a new Republican Party: suburban, white, southern, and up until this point largely voiceless in the mainstream political debate.

Locally, GOP leaders saw Agnew's value instantly. Pennsylvania governor Raymond Shafer said, "Agnew had become a big gun in the political arsenal. He's going to be no end of help next year [in the midterm elections]." Governor Louie Nunn of Kentucky said, "Popular in my state? Hell, yes. I'd say he's more popular than Nixon." Governor David Cargo of New Mexico said that Agnew was saying "exactly what the majority of the people in my state want to hear." And freshman senator Bob Dole of Kansas told Nixon that Agnew was "the one Republican who can get money for us without carrying a gun."[24]

Agnew received letters of support from around the country. In response to David Johnson of Bowie, Maryland, he ruminated on his newfound role: "One of the most gratifying aspects of my recent speeches is the favorable public response which they have evoked. This office has been flooded with virtually thousands of endorsements from what President Nixon has described as 'the silent majority.' This indicates that many long-silent, long-suffering Americans have at last decided to launch an active defense of their values. As you so accurately noted, one of the fallacies of both the new and old Left is their unnecessary negativism."[25]

But complaints also started coming in from the more moderate wing of the party. House Republican leaders like Michigan's Gerald Ford and Pennsylvania's Hugh Scott met with White House aides to try to get them to quiet Agnew down. His rhetoric was viewed as counterproductive to the legislative agenda on the Hill, where the Democrats still controlled both houses of Congress.[26] Republican senator Charles Goodell of New York publicly condemned the vice president's "inflammatory rhetoric" and "baseless charges against the anti-war demonstrators."[27] Some prominent Democrats, however, exacerbated the situation, playing right into Agnew's hands. Senator Albert Gore Sr. of Tennessee backhanded loyal Americans serving in harm's way and those who still felt Vietnam was a worthy cause by saying, "The Vice President is the greatest disaster this country has suffered since Vietnam."[28] Hubert Humphrey compared him to Joe McCarthy: "I personally doubt that our country has seen in 20 years such a calculated appeal to our nastier interests."[29] The criticism was like catnip to Agnew and to Pat Buchanan, who had suddenly found a willing spokesman. But the cherry on top of Agnew's public speech offensive was still to come.

Agnew developed a close relationship with Buchanan and William Safire, two of Nixon's most prolific speechwriters and big thinkers. Buchanan in particular had long admired the vice president and was instrumental in drawing Nixon's attention to the then obscure governor's response to the rioting in Baltimore following the assassination of Martin Luther King Jr. in April 1968. Buchanan had studied Agnew's "effete corps of impudent snobs" speech in New Orleans and noted the audience response and the media's attention.[30] The young conservative, who had been an editorial writer at the *St. Louis Globe-Democrat* prior to signing on with Nixon, saw an opening with Agnew and a way to connect the administration to key voting blocs.

On November 3, 1969, Nixon delivered his so-called "silent majority speech" to the nation, which outlined the "Vietnamization" of the war and asked citizens to accept a continued American military presence in Southeast Asia while rejecting "an immediate, precipitate withdrawal of all Americans."[31] The speech predictably dominated the news cycle. Even though bad news from Vietnam had struggled to find its way into American newspapers and broadcasts for much of the 1960s, setbacks were increasingly being reported now, especially in light of the Tet Offensive, the Viet Cong's surprise attack on U.S. forces in January 1968 that changed the dynamic of the war. Nixon was unhappy with the way television news covered his speech.[32] Buchanan played directly to the president's instincts by unleashing a memo to him that he would later call "among the most consequential I ever wrote." It outlined an anti-media strategy that would guide Agnew's next steps: "If we can put together a three-week offensive on this one subject—the result will be to terrify the networks; and to discredit their reporting in the minds of millions of people. But it ought to be concerted, coordinated, and it ought to be done in the public arena. While the commentators talk to tens of millions, we normally make one-on-one phone calls of complaint." Haldeman's reply to Buchanan's memo: "Pat, let's go! P[resident] is all for it."[33]

Agnew came late to the game in the editing and writing of what would become his most famous speech, delivered at the Midwestern Regional Republican Conference in Des Moines, Iowa, on November 13, 1969. Buchanan wrote the first draft and went over it line by line with Nixon, who told him, "This really flicks the scab off, doesn't it?"[34] Remembering the drafting process a half century later, Buchanan marveled that the speech was "a sustained polemic indicting the networks for biased and irresponsible stewardship of their power over American public opinion."[35] According to Safire and Buchanan, Nixon edited the speech carefully, toughening it up, but only three drafts were written.[36] The young speechwriters had clearly found a willing vessel in Agnew, who touched up what they wrote but left the core of their words and arguments intact. Buchanan remembered that Nixon would "go through draft after draft until it was hard to find anything of mine left in his rhetoric. . . . [But] with Agnew it was different. I could spend days crafting speeches on subjects on which we agreed, and he would deliver them with only modest changes."[37]

In the week leading up to the Des Moines speech the drafting process was held unusually close within an already compartmentalized White House. Buchanan realized that he was playing with political dynamite because "[the White House staff] would have been appalled at the idea of an attack on the networks by a vice president they thought should never have been selected and should be put on a short leash. They would have gone to Nixon to kill the speech."[38] Buchanan's fears were correct. When Agnew's own staff saw a final draft of the speech the day before it was to be delivered, they were horrified. Not only had Buchanan stepped all over their professional turf, but they worried that he had appropriated their boss's political future. Staff members were concerned that if Agnew delivered the speech as written, he would be crossing a point of no return with the national media. A memorandum for Agnew's speechwriter Cynthia Rosenwald from the vice president's chief of staff, Stanley Blair, sounded the alarm: "This refers to the draft DeMoines [sic] speech. I have great respect and affection for Pat Buchanan and you. Neither of these, however, can keep me from saying that I think the Demoines [sic] is basically unsound, not in its idea, but its development. I won't cite illustrations, but I think it is rife with them. . . . I realize the time is late and that it is easier to criticize than to construct, but I feel that we are far from winning the round if we stick to the speech as presently developed." Blair wanted Agnew to leave out the broadsides on the media. Rosenwald's handwritten reply, penciled in the margin, echoed Blair's concerns: "Stan—I agree. What is more I would play it even more conservatively than you."[39]

Agnew did not listen to his staff. He later wrote: "For Pat Buchanan and me, the crafting and polish of that speech was a labor of love."[40] The vice president had found his muse. In the Des Moines speech he went after the networks, their executives, and the journalists who presented the news with a bluntness that was unprecedented in 1969 and a precursor to Republican attacks on television programs and newspapers over the next half century.[41] He blasted away at the New York/Washington clubbiness of the media: "What do Americans know of these men? . . . [They] read the same newspapers and draw their political views from the same sources. Worse, they talk constantly to one another, thereby providing artificial reinforcement to their shared viewpoints. . . . A monopoly sanctioned and licensed by the government. . . . Perhaps it is time that the networks were made more responsive to the views of the nation and more responsible to the people they serve."

The speech would have the desired effect and then some. With an audience of fifty million watching on live television, Agnew broke free of his provincial boundaries and became a national political phenomenon with his own independent following. He was on the covers of *Newsweek* and *Time.* The networks reacted indignantly. Eric Severeid of CBS accused Agnew of using "patriotism as a club to try to silence his critics."[42] David Brinkley at NBC said he wasn't "going to get down in the gutter with this guy."[43] Writing in the *Washington Post*, Frank Mankiewicz and Tom Braden said that they had detected an implicit anti-Semitic argument that Jews in New York and Washington controlled America's press and television networks.[44] Not unlike the reaction to Agnew's attack on Baltimore's civil rights community in 1968, his supporters let the networks know they were ready to stand up for the vice president. ABC News received 29,709 cards, letters, and wires in the two months following the speech, and more than 25,000 of them were considered pro-Agnew. Oppressed and angry, resentful of the East Coast educated elite and the news media, viewers were fierce in their reactions: "I think the judgment of the American people has spoken! And their verdict is that you are guilty of bias and prejudice." Others replied to a form letter ABC News sent in response to their initial comments, tying the networks, in one writer's words, to "today's left wing liberals, many words expounded and not an ounce of sense, much less truth in the whole letter."[45]

The speech also had the desired effect of earning Agnew some rare plaudits from inside the White House. Haldeman's diary entries the day before and after the speech highlighted Nixon's glee that the response "said what people think." The president now believed that Agnew had "become a really good property and we should keep building him and using him," Haldeman wrote.[46] Nixon also liked that South Dakota senator and Democratic presidential hopeful George McGovern thought the speech was "the most frightening single statement ever to come from a high government official in my public career."[47] According to Buchanan, when Agnew boarded Air Force Two for a trip to Florida the day after the speech, "he walked back to my seat, reached out his hand, and with a huge grin, boomed, 'Gangbusters!' He was rhapsodic about the Des Moines speech."[48]

Not all Republicans were cheering. Echoing the reaction to Agnew's inflammatory speeches in New Orleans and Jackson, Mississippi, a month earlier, the more moderate and establishment wing of the party thought Des Moines was a serious mistake. As Gerald Ford wrote later, "Nixon may have had some valid complaints about the way the media had treated him in the past. Since his election, however, the press had been fair to him, and it was stupid to reopen old wounds. But this was only a harbinger of things to come."[49] Criticism from moderate Republicans on the Hill wasn't Nixon's most important concern, however. Buchanan and Agnew, meanwhile, gleefully readied for round two.

In the original draft of a second speech to be delivered in Montgomery, Alabama, on November 20, the vice president and Buchanan wanted to go after the print media, specifically the *New York Times* and the *Washington Post*. Buchanan took pains again to keep the draft on the downlow, arguing in a memo to Agnew's chief of staff that "no one in the West Wing or my floor—with the exception of two people on my staff—know I worked on this draft. Maybe we can do better with security this time."[50] But the White House balked at the first draft, and a fierce internal debate broke out about whether and how Agnew should follow up on the Des Moines speech. While the White House was tickled that the Iowa speech had garnered national attention, Haldeman noted that the Alabama draft was "a real blast, not just at TV, now he takes on newspapers, a lot of individuals and the [college] kids again. Pretty rough, and really does go too far. Problem is Agnew is determined to give it."[51] Haldeman wanted the follow-up speech spiked, but Buchanan argued that Agnew's failure to deliver a rejoinder to the first speech would show "weakness and cowardice." As he later wrote, "The press would say the White House had shut down Agnew. . . . This would be taken as a White House admission that we thought Agnew had gone too far, that Des Moines had been a blunder, that we had gotten cold feet."[52] Haldeman decided to bring the president into the discussion, and Nixon agreed that the speech was over the top. After working with Buchanan, Haldeman thought the final draft still hit "very hard, especially at the *New York Times*," but that he had helped make the speech less personal and defensive.[53]

The Montgomery speech called out the *Post* and the *Times* for being monopolistic and accused them of "lacking the vigor of competition" and having grown "fat and irresponsible." Moreover, Agnew took on the role of victim, saying that the critics of his Des Moines speech were thin-skinned and had overreacted. The vice president, claiming to speak on behalf of his entire generation, charged that the *Times* had slurred all those who served in World War II by comparing the young people of the 1960s favorably to those of the 1940s: "But whatever freedom exists today in Western Europe and Japan exists because hundreds of thousands of young men in my generation are lying in graves in North Africa and France and Korea and a score of islands in the Western Pacific. This might not be considered enough of a 'sense of service' for the *New York Times*, but it's good enough for me." Agnew's comparison of those who had served in the military to members of the media who implicitly criticized and hadn't served stoked the flames of those watching across the country. The speech was carried live on public television and excerpted everywhere. The *Washington Post* ran the text in its entirety the next day.

In a series of four speeches over the course of a month Agnew had exploded into the public's consciousness. The Gallup organization took a poll at the end of the fall that identified the vice president as the third-most admired man in the world, behind Nixon and Billy Graham. Within days the International Press Institute in Zurich juxtaposed the Gallup results by proclaiming that Agnew's attacks on the media were the "most serious threat to the freedom of information in the Western world."[54] A Harris poll taken at the end of November presented Nixon with a clear conundrum: Agnew was both popular and unpopular. Forty percent of Americans thought he was doing an "excellent" or "pretty good" job, and 42 percent thought he was doing a "poor" job.[55]

In the midst of Agnew's rise, Nixon decided to shut his vice president down for a while and sent him on a classic goodwill tour of eleven nations in Asia, including an appearance at the inauguration of Ferdinand Marcos of the Philippines.[56] The timing of the hastily planned trip was curious, and Agnew later thought that Nixon's inherent distrust of anyone who had an independent political identity may have been a reason for his quick dispatch.[57] Nevertheless, while in Vietnam Agnew again attacked the media and linked his criticism by the popular press to antiwar protesters and the denigration of the rank and file serviceman.[58]

Despite public disavowals by Nixon and White House press secretary Ron Ziegler, the president really did want Agnew to pipe down.[59] Haldeman noted in a diary entry for November 25, 1969, that Nixon wanted it conveyed to Agnew that he should "stop talking about the media except for some light quips, and [he] said the Vice President could now talk about all those things he had been talking about before but no one was listening, and now they'll listen because he's become a national figure. Sort of a backhanded compliment, not intended that way."[60] But had the anti-media speeches helped Agnew and the Republican Party's political fortunes?

The attention launched Agnew's political ascendency, and he became a sought-after speaker across the nation. Invitations came pouring in for his 1970 calendar, and not just as a fill-in for the president. Agnew was now a main attraction in his own right.[61] But he was also a polarizing figure who by taking on the media may have dulled some of his future electability. The 1964 Republican vice presidential nominee, Congressman William Miller of New York, said, "No one who has presidential ambitions would do what he did in his Des Moines speech. For years people have said those things in private but no one in politics would dare say them out loud. . . . No one with national political ambitions would tackle the networks. It is political suicide."[62]

Agnew faced a stark choice: would he revert to the forgotten vice president of Bob Hope's jokes, endlessly marginalized to international goodwill tours and ribbon-cutting fill-ins for his boss, or would he continue to try to carve out his own identity? He chose the latter. He now had a political future, and whether it might catapult him to the presidency was another matter. While Agnew would get a chance to test his popularity during the 1970 midterms, Buchanan saw the media speeches as a watershed in the history of political/press relations, a "first Manassas of that epic battle."[63] Agnew's speech helped trigger changes in the way the news media covered politics and the way many Americans consumed politics through the media. Agnew and Buchanan successfully planted the seeds of doubt about the basic fairness and objectivity of the media. As Buchanan would later conclude, the Des Moines speech opened the door to a new way of looking at network and East Coast press. "Their reportage and commentary were fair game for critical analysis and counter-attack. . . . Op-ed pages blossomed in the establishment press. CBS and the other networks began to bring forward conservatives to do commentary. 'Instant analysis' after presidential speeches became more balanced. Talk would begin of creating a conservative network."[64] Agnew had finally arrived on the national stage as a player. The question was how Nixon and the Republican Party would make the best use of him.

As Agnew's second year in office began it was clear he would have to pivot away from the media issue, if only to placate the president. Nixon was of two minds on Agnew's role. On the one hand he asked his speechwriters to study his vice president's newfound popularity and ordered a January 13, 1970, *Wall Street Journal* editorial titled "Assaulting the Aristocracy" to be copied and distributed throughout the White House. The opinion spelled out in stark terms "the heart of the Agnew phenomenon" that Nixon wanted to harness:

> A class has sprung up in this nation that considers itself uniquely qualified ("the thinking people") and is quite willing to dismiss the ordinary Americans with utter contempt ("the rednecks"). Mr. Agnew's targets—the media, war protestors, rebellious youth—are representatives of a class that has enjoyed unusual moral and cultural authority through the 1960s. Seldom before has such wide influence been wielded by the highbrows, the intellectual beautiful people—Eastern liberal elite. Yet how well have the

members of this elite discharged this authority? Has the economy been well managed? Have the cities prospered?[65]

But according to Buchanan, Nixon was worried that Agnew was becoming too popular and might eclipse the ever-insecure president.[66] Nixon slapped down an Agnew-Buchanan speech that was to be given in Atlanta in February that would have called for the end of the desegregation movement in the public schools. Nixon explained weakly to Haldeman that while he agreed with the thesis, he didn't want Agnew to "get out beyond his own position," and that he was "afraid to dilute or waste the great asset he has become."[67] Agnew and Buchanan instead turned the speech into a diatribe against the anti–Vietnam War movement and those in the media who would abet the cause, imploring the audience to "never be persuaded that the vicious reactionaries of our society are more than a small minority."

Agnew had found a new hot-button issue, and he pressed it inside the White House as well. While often quiet in National Security Council and cabinet meetings, the vice president emerged as a leading hawk on Vietnam. He accused those who would equivocate about going after the Viet Cong hamlets in Cambodia of "pussyfooting" and said that Nixon ought to decide whether the sanctuaries were a danger or not. The task, in Agnew's mind, was to make Nixon's Vietnamization policy succeed. National Security Advisor Henry Kissinger would later say that "Agnew's intervention accelerated Nixon's decision to order an attack on all the [Cambodian] sanctuaries and use American forces.'"[68] Nixon, who believed the vice president's role was to always support the president, was not pleased with Agnew's foray into foreign policy and let Kissinger know about the misstep.[69]

As unrest on college and university campuses reached a boiling point in the spring of 1970, Agnew again went on the rhetorical offensive. In April, with the help of Buchanan's wordsmithing, he attacked higher education in several blistering speeches in which he resumed his accusations that students of the day were lazy, over-emotional, and over-indulged. College administrators and faculty enabled this permissive culture, Agnew charged, and they were now letting in even more undeserving students through open enrollments and affirmative action. What university leaders saw as reforms to democratize higher education and begin to address past wrongs such as segregation, Agnew and the silent majority saw as out-of-touch, do-gooder elitism.

At the Iowa Republican Statewide Fundraising Dinner in Des Moines, Agnew began his talk by saying that while the U.S. educational system was the envy of the world, it was already in sharp decline. He then launched into a blunt critique of affirmative action policies with an argument that would presage the Republican Party's platform for the next fifty years. In doing so, he aimed his remarks at the GOP's emerging constituency: lower- and middle-class white voters and disaffected southern Democrats:

> Now there are two methods by which unqualified students are being swept into college on the wave of the new socialism. One is called the quota system, and the other an open admissions policy. They may be equally bad. . . . For each youth unprepared for a college curriculum who is brought in under the quota system, some better-prepared student is denied entrance. Admitting the obligation to compensate for past deprivation and discrimination, it just does not make sense to atone by discriminating against and depriving someone else.

Agnew had put his finger on another ideological divide that would help brand Republican populism in future elections.[70]

Agnew kept after the sacred cows of colleges and universities, even beyond their anti–Vietnam War postures. In the second Des Moines speech he called out the University of Michigan in particular for weak leadership and an open admissions policy that had led to a degradation of the value of a diploma. He concluded by saying that while education should be affordable, not everyone should go to college. Too many undergraduates arrived on campus "restless, purposeless, bored and rebellious. College, at one time considered a privilege, is considered to be a right today—and is less valued because of that."[71]

The response from leaders in higher education and the media was swift but, surprisingly, not entirely negative. Agnew's press secretary, Herb Thompson, had adroitly sent the speech out in advance to three thousand reporters, as well as to targeted leaders at lesser known institutions such as Gulf Coast Bible College in Houston, Texas; Our Lady of Angels College in Glen Riddle, Pennsylvania; Southern Baptist College in Walnut Ridge, Arkansas; and Fort Hays Kansas State College, all deep within silent majority country.[72] A handwritten note from a dean at Platte Valley Bible College in Scottsbluff, Nebraska, showed how successful the ploy was in certain circles: "We were indeed interested in the copy of the Vice President's speech at Des Moines, Iowa. I have read it, and placed it in our faculty lounge."[73] By simply paying these colleges the courtesy of sending a special copy from the vice president, Agnew scored political points in Middle America. Not all reactions were as positive. Orville Johnston, president of Alfred University in New York, wrote that he was "returning the speech that you sent to me made by the Vice President. . . . Until the Vice President has something significant to say and can exercise freedom of speech responsibly I do not care to receive his speeches."[74] The Candlelight Club at the University of Wisconsin-Oshkosh even debated the issue: "Resolved: Spiro T. Agnew is a Public Menace."[75]

Agnew by now made good copy, and the text of the entire speech appeared in the April 20 edition of the *Chronicle of Higher Education*, with Agnew's photo on page one.[76] The president of the University of Michigan, Robben Wright Fleming, told the *Associated Press*, "The Vice President is badly misinformed about the commitment the university's regents, faculty and administration have made to provide educational opportunity to disadvantaged young people, particularly blacks."[77] But what did it matter to Agnew what Fleming and the readers of the *Chronicle of Higher Education* thought? The more they disliked the speech, the more he scored points with the very constituencies he was trying to reach.

The outlets in silent majority country seemed more positively inclined. The *Birmingham (Alabama) News* said, "The questions the Vice President has raised are legitimate ones which deserve public consideration."[78] The *Detroit News* concurred: "The questions raised by the Agnew speech will not disappear; they will insist on answers from our universities. And those answers will preserve or destroy quality education."[79] The *Boston Globe* countered that "Agnew overlooks the tradition that the best possible education is the right of every American youth."[80] The *New York*

Post's editorial board commented, "Agnew's remarks on quotas form a coded message to those who want to keep unacceptable people in their place, wherever that is."[81]

The split reaction toward the speech was mimicked inside the White House. The April 15 memo that Nixon's special assistant, Jeb Magruder, wrote to Haldeman was indicative of the nervousness among moderate Republicans about Agnew's offensive against higher education. Magruder argued that in trying to win the hearts and minds of the silent majority, the vice president was distancing the administration from "those people who are alienated by Middle America: the young, the poor and the black. And perhaps we have also alienated . . . the under-40-college[-]educated-urban[-]dwelling business and professional people who enjoy art, attend the symphony, read the *New York Times Book Review.*"[82] Of course these were exactly the kinds of people Agnew wanted to antagonize in the emerging political debate, even if some offended Republicans were in the mix. Not everyone in the White House objected to the vice president's line of attack against universities. Agnew's words allowed Nixon to reap the political benefits of a riled-up Middle America without having to do much to stoke the flames himself.[83] The voters Nixon needed the most in his new coalition agreed with Agnew.

Emboldened by the response of those who liked what they were hearing, Agnew took the gloves off again on April 28 in Fort Lauderdale. Again he went going after the moral degradation of campus culture and the lack of accountability among faculty and administrators. Campuses "spiced with rock music, acid and pot" were places where "the old Marxist idea of regulated equality without effort becomes exciting, and [where universities] assail the institutions of the free enterprise system without beginning to understand them." Agnew singled out Yale University and its president, the outspoken Kingman Brewster, who had been particularly critical of the Nixon administration's Vietnam War policies. Agnew minced no words in calling for Brewster to be replaced, saying, "It is clearly time for the alumni of that fine old college to demand that it be headed by a more mature and responsible person."[84] The Yale student body and trustees rallied behind Brewster. William Horowitz, chair of the Connecticut State Board of Education, sent Agnew a sniffy response saying that he did not believe Agnew's "experience as a President of a PTA chapter qualifies you to evaluate the contributions to education by the most distinguished university president in the United States."[85] It was just what Agnew and Buchanan wanted. The speechwriter would soon boast in a private memo to Agnew that "the bread we put upon the waters after the Des Moines speech seems to be coming through a bit."[86]

The exhilarating effect of Agnew's rhetoric came crashing down just a few days after the Fort Lauderdale speech when Ohio National Guardsmen at Kent State killed four students protesting U.S. bombings in Cambodia. Secretary of the Interior Walter Hickel criticized Agnew, his fellow cabinet member, by name in a letter to Nixon soon after the incident. Hickel wrote that Agnew's attack on the young and their motives "can serve little purpose other than to further cement those attitudes to a solidity impossible to penetrate with reason."[87] Nixon also heard from college and university leaders and his own staff about how Agnew's speeches directly linked the administration to the violence at Kent State. Nathan Pusey of Harvard and seven other university presidents met with Nixon at the White House on May 8 and told him how unpopular Agnew was on their campuses. The vice president's public comments hindered their attempts to keep the peace, they said.[88] Health, Education, and Welfare secretary Robert Finch, when asked what had led to the shootings, blamed a series of things but explicitly cited the speeches as having contributed to the climate.[89]

Nixon once again shut Agnew down. A few days after Kent State Haldeman recorded in his diary: "Nixon wants VP to stop saying anything about students . . . [even though the] Vice President strongly disagrees. I passed the word. The VP said he would act only on order of the President. . . . The whole university community is now politicized, and there's no way to turn it off. All blame Agnew primarily."[90]

Even before Agnew's higher education speeches, campuses in early 1970 were seething over the Vietnam War and racial division. But a study by a special commission of the American Council on Education reported that "political exploitation of campus problems by some public figures" had become one of the most divisive elements at colleges and universities.

Agnew and California governor Ronald Reagan were specifically cited as examples.[91]

Whether or not Agnew helped incite the violence at Kent State, he had again touched a nerve. He had excited the same segment of the American voting population that lined up with his earlier attacks on the media. To Agnew and his supporters, what was wrong with America were the long-haired, draft-dodging protesters and their college professor/administrator enablers. They were the radicals, outside the mainstream, and if the media would take a more critical look at their actions, it would become clear that the roots of the country's moral decay lay not only among the powerful press in New York and Washington but also in New Haven, Austin, and Ann Arbor. And Agnew, a suburbanite with his own humble roots, wasn't just talking trash from the John Birch fringes of the American political debate. He was doing it in a sophisticated, calmly delivered voice and from behind a podium affixed with the seal of the vice president of the United States.

Nixon's dilemma about how to use Agnew was now acute. After a year of national attention and his emergence as a galvanizing force of the new Republican base, the vice president could not simply be returned to obscurity and mundane tasks. As the midterms neared, it was time to focus on winning elections instead of taunting eggheads.

In the summer of 1970 Arthur Schlesinger Jr., the historian and former aide to John F. Kennedy, penned a seventy-five-hundred-word essay in the *New York Times Book Review* that tried to answer the question of why Agnew had become such a sudden political success story with an almost cult-like following. Schlesinger argued that for Agnew it was never about public policy. His words were "perfunctory and banal." Rather, Schlesinger maintained, it was all about "cultural politics," where Agnew had "emerged as hero, or villain, not in the battle of programs but in the battle of life styles."[92] After much hemming and hawing, Nixon finally came around to a similar view.[93]

In the weeks that followed Kent State Nixon struggled to find value and purpose for his newly popular vice president. Haldeman noted in his diary in June that Nixon wondered aloud if Agnew was doing more harm than good, even though he was convinced that he was a major asset.[94] Nixon ended up tasking his senior staff, now more than a year and a half into his administration, to come up with a "basic recommendation . . . as to [the] exact role of Agnew and how to implement it."[95]

Buchanan, Haldeman, and other senior aides had the perfect idea: Agnew would serve as the "bayonet of the party" during the upcoming midterm congressional elections, raising money for the GOP, defining the Democrats into a corner, and stirring up the faithful.[96] The White House wanted Agnew to chase the Democrats so "far into left field" that the Republicans would appear to be sensible moderates by default. Journalists Rowland Evans and Robert Novak explained the scorched earth strategy as one where Democrats would be blamed "for the cost of bread to the housewife, for failing to vote Nixon's law and order crime bills into law, for a permissiveness that was ruining America's children, for pornography and drugs, for being ready to sell out to Communism abroad."[97] Worried that Agnew would need political tutelage for the campaign, Nixon assigned an old political hand, the Oklahoma Democrat-turned-Republican Bryce Harlow, along with Buchanan and Safire, to travel with the vice president during the fall electioneering season.[98]

As the campaign kicked off in earnest after Labor Day 1970, Nixon sat down with Buchanan and others assigned to Agnew's fall offensive. The president emphasized that he wanted Agnew to stress that "our opponents are not bad men, they are sincere, dedicated radicals. They honestly believe in the liberal left. And force them on the defensive, to deny it, as they did to us about the Birchers in '62."[99] As Buchanan explained with glee a half century later, "Thus began the Seven Weeks War against the radical liberals."[100]

In his kickoff speech at the State Republican Dinner in Springfield, Illinois, on September 10, Agnew went after Adlai Stevenson III, who was running to fill the seat that had been left vacant by the death of Everett Dirksen. While never referring to Stevenson by name, Agnew tied him to the violence in Chicago during the Democratic National Convention in 1968. Making use of a term that Buchanan and Safire had coined, he dubbed Stevenson a radical-liberal or radiclib, as in "How do you fathom the thinking of these radical-liberals who work themselves into a lather over an alleged shortage of nutriments in a child's box of Wheaties—but who cannot get exercised at all over that same child's constant exposure to a flood of hard core pornography that could warp his moral outlook for a lifetime?" Stevenson would go on to defeat Ralph Tyler Smith in November, but other Democratic incumbents would not be so fortunate.

As Agnew and his team of handlers began to skip around the country, they set their sights on particularly vulnerable incumbents. One of their prime targets was Senator Albert Gore Sr. of Tennessee. In preparation for a vice presidential visit to the state, Roy Goodearle, a close Agnew aide who served as a liaison to the Republican National Committee, outlined how the strategy would be put into practice. Nixon had carried Tennessee in the 1968 election, and if the Nixon vote had combined with George Wallace's count, the Republicans would have had 70 percent of the state's vote. Gore was vulnerable to being portrayed as out of step with voters on law and order, spending, and his dovish stand on Vietnam. "Care should be taken," Goodearle wrote, "not to attack Gore so vehemently as to cause a sympathy sentiment to develop, but to attack the elements of society that [he] has represented such as the peaceniks, campus dissidents, anarchists, big spenders and those who opposed the President's [failed] southern nominees for the Supreme Court."[101] Gore lost to Republican Bill Brock in a nasty election that would lead his son, Al Gore Jr., the future vice president, to decide to become a newspaper reporter because he "didn't want to swim in the whirlpool that was left by the election of 1970."[102]

Out on the trail Agnew and his speechwriters were having a rollicking good time and, at least initially, getting more media attention than they knew what do with. The vice president decided to use the gimmick of alliteration to draw even more attention to his addresses and asked Safire and Buchanan to come up with a version of Adlai Stevenson's "prophets of doom and gloom." Agnew unleashed "hopeless, hysterical hypochondriacs of history" and "nattering nabobs of negativism" in the same speech in San Diego in mid-September. Two weeks later in South Dakota he described a recent report on campus unrest as "pabulum for the permissivists." Safire later said he was able to talk the vice president out of using "he mounted the moment with the relish of a randy rogue."[103] But the alliteration caught on and became synonymous with Agnew's persona and his style, so much so that Safire described racing home to Washington, D.C., before sundown for Yom Kippur services only to hear his rabbi admonish the congregation to not let the country "be divided and polarized by those who use the technique of alliteration." As Safire recounted, "That was all I needed; the 'nattering nabobs of negativism' was not a sin I had come to atone for."[104]

Agnew's visit to Wilmington, Delaware, was typical of a campaign stop during the 1970 campaign. He arrived in the afternoon on Air Force Two, delivered a speech to the faithful, raised some money, and bolstered the candidacies of the Republican nominees for the Senate, William Roth, and the House, Pierre du Pont.[105] The October 15 edition of the local newspaper led with a banner headline on page one: "GOP Hears Agnew Roast Elite Snobs." The accompanying article quoted liberally from the speech, in which the vice president "hurled barbed darts at 'paralyzing elitism,' snobs and intellectuals who support militant minorities and denounce Middle America as morally inferior." Even more column inches were devoted to the text of the speech and Agnew's ten-question test to uncover elitism:

1. Do you walk about with an expression on your face that seems to say that the whole world smells a bit funny?
2. Do you wish those great masses of people would stop questioning your right to determine public morals and public policy?
3. Do you think that a college education makes you not only intellectually superior, but morally superior as well to those who did not have your opportunity?
4. Do you think that blue-collar work — like fixing an automobile or driving a truck — is not nearly as dignified or significant as pushing a pencil at a tax-exempt foundation?
5. Does the very thought of a silent majority fill you with revulsion, while a phrase like "power to the people" appears to you as the essence of revealed wisdom?
6. Does it make you feel warm and snugly protected to read the *New York Review of Books?*

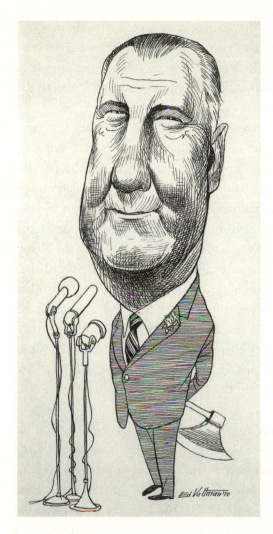

Fig. 1. Early in his vice presidency Spiro Agnew emerged as a voice for the silent majority through his slashing attacks on protestors, professors, and the press. (Library of Congress, Prints and Photographs Division, drawing by Edmund S. Valtman [LC-DIG-ppmsc-07953])

7. Do you think it is awkward and demeaning for U.S. senators to have to submit themselves for re-election to a group you call the great unwashed?

8. Do you tune in a presidential speech at the end just to get your opinions from the instant analysis?

9. Did you ever go to sleep and dream of J. William Fulbright becoming Secretary of State—without waking up screaming?

10. Do you support a constitutional amendment to abolish the office of Vice President of the United States?

Agnew concluded this part of his Wilmington speech with a scorecard: "My friends, if your answer even to two or three of these questions is 'yes,' you may regard yourself as a full-fledged elitist. . . . But if your answer to each of these questions is a ringing, indignant no—then welcome to the silent majority."[106]

The most controversial intervention by Agnew during the 1970 campaign came in New York, where he went after one of his own, Republican senator Charles Goodell, who was locked in a three-way battle with Democratic congressman Richard Ottinger and Conservative Party nominee James Buckley. Goodell had been appointed by Governor Nelson Rockefeller to fill out the term of Robert Kennedy, who was assassinated in June 1968. Goodell had been particularly outspoken against the Nixon administration's policies in Vietnam and had also been a behind-the-scenes opponent of Agnew's nomination in 1968.[107] Agnew went after Goodell in personal terms, comparing his political transformation on Vietnam policy to the physical transformation of Christine Jorgensen, the first person to undergo a sex change operation. At an October 5 luncheon speech Agnew went all out on his fellow Republican, calling him a radiclib "dead set on frustrating the President" and a "waffler on civil disruption."[108]

More-moderate Republicans openly rebelled at Agnew's attack on Goodell, wondering if they were next and whether this was the purge of the moderates that they had feared since Nixon's surprise selection of Agnew at the Republican National Convention in 1968. In California, where incumbent Republican senator George Murphy would eventually lose to his Democratic challenger, John Tunney, state party officials asked Agnew not to make a second visit.[109] Nelson Rockefeller called the White House and made a similar request.[110] After Agnew's old Maryland political friend, Republican National Committee chair Rogers Morton, reiterated his strong support for Goodell, Agnew dismissed Morton as a mere "party functionary."[111] Even inside the White House, aides such as Jeb Magruder, who thought Agnew had peaked too soon with his rhetoric, had mixed feelings about the vice president's performance on the campaign trail: "We enjoyed what he was saying, but we sensed that he might be going too far. Agnew, of course, was having the time of his life.

He'd been frozen out by Nixon for almost two years, but now the eyes of the nation were upon him and he gloried in the attention. He was getting tremendous publicity as our cutting edge, the spokesman for the Silent Majority."[112]

The results of Election Day 1970 brought a glass half empty or half full, depending on one's point of view, to Agnew's efforts. The Republicans lost nine seats in the House and two in the Senate. On the plus side for the Republicans, in addition to Gore's loss in Tennessee, incumbent Democrat Joe Tydings of Maryland lost to Republican J. Glenn Beall Jr., whose brother George, the soon-to-be U.S. attorney in Baltimore, would later figure prominently in the legal predicament that would lead to Agnew's downfall. Goodell lost as well, splitting the moderate vote with the Democratic nominee and thus allowing the independent conservative candidate to prevail. The results were pretty much on par for the party in power in the White House,[113] but there was a palpable sense of disappointment.[114] The discontent wasn't so much because of the outcome but because it was hard to tell whether Agnew had made much of a difference. But if 1970 had any long-lasting impact, it was that social issues resonated in close general elections with Democrats.[115] If need be Agnew could be called upon to reprise his role in the 1972 presidential election.

Nixon believed that in the immediate post-election period Agnew "should de-escalate the rhetoric. . . . He should be shown fighting for something, rather than just railing against everything."[116] And he thought that Agnew should be given (yet again) a new set of responsibilities. Predictably, Nixon's inner circle struggled to define a portfolio that would be perceived as essential enough to assuage Agnew's ego but still far enough from the president's main agenda that he would be out of Nixon's hair. Initially it was thought that Agnew might work on environmental or health issues. Congressional and labor/union relations were also floated, as were various political issues that might emerge during the 1972 campaign.[117] In the end Nixon settled on federal/state relations, relaying the news to Agnew via Haldeman just before Christmas 1970.[118] The assignment was explicitly designed to "keep the Vice President out of substantive policy development."[119]

The White House also tried to keep Agnew busy in the summer of 1971 by sending him on an aggressive thirty-two-day tour of world capitals for meetings with key Cold War allies that had particularly unsavory histories. The purpose was in part to keep Agnew in the dark about Nixon's ongoing overtures to China. Agnew wanted to go to Peking, but Nixon quashed the request.[120] Instead he met with a retinue of tin-pot dictators: Singapore's Lee Kuan Yew, Ethiopia's Haile Selassie, Kenya's Jomo Kenyatta, the Congo's Joseph Mobutu, Spain's Francisco Franco, and strongmen in South Korea, Kuwait, Saudi Arabia, Morocco, and Portugal.[121] In October Agnew even made an awkward visit to his ancestral home in Greece and broke bread with the military junta and President Georgios Papadopoulos, who had been shunned by all the major western democracies after a 1967 military coup overthrew the popularly elected government.[122] The trip was largely ceremonial. Agnew traveled to his father's birthplace in the Peloponnese and received the Grand Cross of George I from the junta. Although Congress had recently cut back military aid to Greece over the Nixon administration's objections, Agnew told the press upon his departure that he was convinced that Papadopoulos "intends to return his country to representative government." One observer noted that "Agnew was not only a tool of the regime, he was a willing tool."[123] The English-language *Athens News* printed photographs of Lincoln, Washington, and Jefferson with the caption, "Would he have visited Greece today?"[124]

Nixon thought Agnew failed miserably on these foreign trips and mercilessly critiqued his vice president's work ethic in private.[125] By the middle of 1971 it was clear that the two were on parallel tracks and neither man was happy with the other. Nixon aide Murray Chotiner had spoken with Agnew in Spain during his world tour and reported back to Nixon that Agnew "had pulled him aside and unloaded his troubles to him. He had launched into a tirade . . . and complained that they don't give him anything to do, and no responsibility, they don't ask for his advice, and pay no attention to him. [He] said he was annoyed by low-level people calling him. The clerks call and tell him to do things."[126] Completely out of the loop on Nixon's opening to China, he stewed on the sidelines of the debate.[127] Despite Agnew's spike in popularity among the emerging GOP base, Nixon had made up his mind that he was simply not up to the task of being a heartbeat away from the presidency. On the White House tapes Nixon groused that "taking on the press is fine, doing his political chores are fine, alliteration's fine. But goddamn it [pounding the desk], if he can't run a staff, he cannot be in this office."[128]

If Nixon hoped that by exiling and talking down his vice president he could force Agnew to withdraw from the ticket before the 1972 race began, he was mistaken. The rumor mill within the White House may have stoked Nixon's optimism that Agnew was going to step aside on his own accord, but the vice president had visions of the 1976 presidential race dancing in his head. He told biographer Theo Lippman in August 1971: "I'm not ready to concede that anybody else should get the [1976 presidential] mantle. There are three questions you would have to answer. First, do I have a chance of winning the nomination? My answer would be heavily in the affirmative. Second, could I win the election? I have to think I would have a good chance. Third, what does the presidency do to a man and to his family, and is it worth it?"[129]

Nixon wanted to replace Agnew on the 1972 ticket with his treasury secretary, John Connally. The Agnew versus Connally debate turned out to be a skirmish on the direction of the party that would be replayed in Republican primaries for years to come. Would the GOP turn to a moderate who embraced the New Deal/Great Society consensus or to a law and order cultural conservative who spoke directly to the silent majority?

While Connolly was still a Democrat in the run-up to the 1972 election, he was moving toward the Republican Party. And Nixon had a political crush on him, arguing in his memoirs that he was "the only man in either party who clearly had the potential to be a great President. He had the necessary political 'fire in the belly,' the energy to win, and the vision to lead.[130] Agnew, slow to recognize Nixon's desire to replace him, recalled that the president "became more remote towards me as his attachment to Connally grew." He started seriously thinking about his future life outside of politics, perhaps as a columnist or television personality, if he was bumped out of the No. 2 spot.[131]

Connally never clearly signaled to Nixon that he would definitely accept the vice presidency in 1972.[132] Nixon and Attorney General John Mitchell approached the Texan about the possibility of becoming the nominee late in 1971 and again in the summer of 1972 prior to the Republican National Convention. Perhaps playing coy, Connally said that he did in fact want to be president one day, but that he didn't see the vice presidency as a stepping-stone to power.[133] But Nixon and his political team had an even more important internal question to answer. Had Agnew become too politically important within the Republican Party to jettison for a more moderate replacement? Mitchell told Nixon that naming Connally would "backfire with the conservative new majority Republicans and Democrats, particularly in the South, among whom Agnew had become almost a folk hero."[134] Nixon, as Agnew biographer Theo Lippman concluded, was now "a hostage to the creature he had helped to create, the Agnew-loving silent majority."[135]

The left-right factions within the GOP were split on Agnew's future. The liberal Ripon Society called for his replacement, while the more conservative Young Americans for Freedom enthusiastically mock-nominated Agnew for president in 1972.[136] Liberal Republicans led by New York senator Jacob Javits openly campaigned at the 1972 national convention to change the convention's voting rules. They wanted to make Agnew's possible presidential run in 1976 more difficult by allowing more urban and liberal states to gain representation and creating quotas for female and minority delegates who presumably would be against his candidacy.[137] But Agnew had the strong support of Barry Goldwater, the champion of the more conservative wing of the party. Goldwater told Agnew in private that he should remain on the ticket because many Republicans had more faith in him than in Nixon.[138] Agnew's aide David Keene recalled that he and others took steps to make sure conservative activists expressed their support for the vice president.[139] During his first term Nixon had clearly tacked leftward on important domestic and international issues— affirmative action, urban policy, the environment, a basic defense of LBJ's Great Society programs, a perceived softness in Vietnam, détente with the Soviets, and the opening to China—and his right political flank was exposed. A conservative Ohio congressman, John Ashbrook, announced a long-shot candidacy for the 1972 Republican presidential nomination.[140] Agnew was the antidote to what ailed Nixon with conservatives and the members of the party's right wing, and they let him know that the vice president should not be pulled off the national ticket.

Several of the South's emerging state Republican leaders publicly declared that Agnew was more popular than Nixon in their regions and that replacing him might open the door for George Wallace in 1972. The American Conservative Union editorialized: "The time has come to say what should not have to be said at all: The dumping of Vice President Agnew from the 1972 Republican ticket would be unacceptable to American conservatives."[141] Agnew's support ran deep in the Senate as well, where Texas's John Tower, Bob Dole of Kansas, and upset winner James Buckley of the Conservative Party of New York openly supported the re-nomination. Perhaps most important, however, Goldwater went on the record at a crucial juncture prior to the Republican National Convention in July 1972 and said that it was an "absolute necessity" to keep Agnew in the vice presidency because he had "built himself into a national figure with courage enough to say things that should be said. Any suggestion about dumping him at this time will alienate Republican workers across this country. Agnew's popularity equals that of the President."[142] Nixon asked Agnew to formally run with him again on the eve of the Republican National Convention.

The Democratic and Republican National Conventions both took place in Miami Beach in 1972. The Democrats met in July and it turned out to be a disaster, heralding their landslide loss to come in November. They adopted a platform that "was probably the most liberal one ever adopted by a major party in the United States," advocating among other things for an immediate withdrawal from Vietnam, amnesty for war resisters, guaranteed jobs for all Americans, and a minimum income for poor families.[143] They also nominated U.S. senator George McGovern of South Dakota, who famously gave his acceptance speech after 2 a.m., thus missing the prime time television audience. McGovern had well-documented problems finding a running mate. Prior to the convention, he had asked U.S. senators Edmund Muskie of Maine and Hubert Humphrey of Minnesota and they both turned him down. As McGovern later explained, "I met with my staff in my hotel room on Thursday, the day after I was nominated. We had until 4 p.m. to find a vice-presidential nominee." McGovern then asked Senators Ted Kennedy of Massachusetts, Walter Mondale of Minnesota, Abe Ribicoff of Connecticut, and Gaylord Nelson of Wisconsin. All turned him down as well. Boston mayor Kevin White's name was floated and then withdrawn. At 3:45 p.m., McGovern asked Senator Tom Eagleton of Missouri, who accepted, telling McGovern that there was nothing problematic in his background. As McGovern would remember after Eagleton's death, "History would render a different judgment."[144] Two weeks later McGovern asked Eagleton to withdraw because of the revelation that he had been treated with electroshock therapy for clinical depression in the 1960s. Former Peace Corps director Sargent Shriver, Kennedy's brother-in-law, became the new running mate.

The Republicans were brimming with confidence when they held their own convention in August. A pre-convention memo from Agnew's press secretary, Herb Thompson, outlined a shift toward a more "statesmanlike tone" and urged that Agnew's acceptance speech "reflect the warmth and compassion that those close to you know you possess but that seldom comes through in the media."[145]

Introduced at the convention by his eventual successor, Congressman Gerald Ford of Michigan, Agnew gave a twenty-minute acceptance speech that was all smiles. As his family joined him onstage prior to the address for the obligatory Sousa march and hand waves, his long-haired and mustachioed son, Randy, was the only visual exception to an otherwise Brady Bunch–scripted, early-1970s picture of the perfect Middle American family. Agnew, speaking from a teleprompter, was subdued, and his speech barely drew a response from the audience. His words were carefully chosen to let supporters know that his politics were subordinate to Nixon's views. Agnew emphasized that he saw two primary functions of the vice presidency: "to serve the President and to learn from the President" because "the Vice President is the President's man and not a competing political entity." Democratic nominee George McGovern was mentioned twice, almost in passing, and Shriver wasn't mentioned at all.[146] Somewhat bizarrely, Agnew wanted to have psychologist Joyce

Brothers second his nomination for vice president, but the White House knocked the idea down. Nixon had to intervene personally, viewing it as a disaster in the making in that it would look like Agnew had used a psychologist "to prove he isn't nuts like Eagleton is."[147]

At the conclusion of Agnew's speech, the vice president introduced Nixon and the two walked arm in arm around the stage for the cameras and the crowd until a visibly relieved Nixon traded Agnew's arm for that of his wife, Pat. Nixon had scripted the entire sequence and specifically requested that the two families not be onstage at the same time, nor did he want "hands over the head type shots" of the running mates together.[148]

Well before the Republican Convention, and even before Eagleton's withdrawal, Nixon had decided to micromanage and limit Agnew's role in the upcoming campaign, telling Haldeman that "we should put him in the South, the small states. No important duties."[149] Subdued after the convention, Agnew adopted a new tone. He steered clear of direct attacks on McGovern and worked for Republicans down the ticket, thus earning points for a possible 1976 presidential run. Nixon told journalist Theodore White in September 1972 that Agnew was going to circulate around the country in support of Republican congressional candidates because "that's his job. That's a Vice President's job. I did it in 1956 [when Nixon was the sitting vice president running for reelection with Eisenhower]."[150] Nixon for his part avoided personal contact with Agnew on the trail and used intermediaries instead of speaking directly with him. But with the McGovern campaign imploding and Nixon far ahead in the polls, the president let Agnew do more than his fair share of stumping. Nixon attended to foreign policy issues and left Washington sporadically during the fall. McGovern castigated Nixon, to no avail, for letting the vice president do his bidding, warning that the Republicans were preparing for eight years of an Agnew presidency. McGovern emphasized, "If that isn't enough to make you tremble, I don't know what is."[151] But in reality Agnew's role in the fall campaign lacked much passion or controversy. As Timothy Crouse wrote in his classic campaign diary *The Boys on the Bus*, "Agnew spent most afternoons in his hotel room. When he was not being an ogre, it became clear, Agnew was a bore. . . . Agnew was calm and conciliatory. The President was Presidential. Peace was at hand. The press had become too weak, frightened, and demoralized to try to dent the Administration's handsome veneer."[152]

Nixon and Agnew were reelected with 520 electoral votes, the most recorded at the time with the exception of Franklin Roosevelt's 1936 landslide.[153] On election night at the Shoreham Hotel in Washington, D.C., Nixon praised Agnew publicly as having kept his cool during the campaign and noted that "he can take it and he can dish it out."[154] Agnew partied with pals Sammy Davis Jr. and Frank Sinatra, and in his written remarks he crowed that "the American people voted as a Nation unified in concern for its future. They voted to affirm their belief in the essential rightness and goodness of our system."[155]

Agnew had helped boost the Republican Party to a lofty national position that no one could have imagined forty years earlier. He could take partial credit for making the party of Lincoln dominant in Dixie and competitive for white working-class voters across the country. But the judiciary and the press were about to change the trajectory of Agnew's career, the party, and the presidency.

5

DIXIE'S FAVORITE

Agnew and the Southern Strategy

In April 1972, as the presidential election season was kicking into gear, Congressman William Dickinson, a Republican from Alabama, invited Spiro Agnew to attend the upcoming Independence Day celebration in Montgomery. Dickinson's election to Congress in 1964, when he defeated a long-standing Democratic incumbent, was part of the growing success of the Republican Party in encouraging conservative white southerners to abandon the party of their ancestors.[1] Dickinson made headlines his first year in office when he accused the organizers of the famous march from Selma to Montgomery of engaging in biracial sex parties. "Drunkenness and sex orgies were the order of the day," he proclaimed. A collection of "human flotsam—adventurers, beatniks, prostitutes, and similar rabble . . . engaged in an all-night session of debauchery within the church itself," Dickinson charged, adding, "Only by the ultimate sex act with one of another color can they demonstrate they have no prejudice."[2] Now in 1972, as part of the effort to transform the white south into the Republican Party's conservative base, Dickinson knew that Agnew could help the cause. Therefore it was not just the usual political flattery when Dickinson wrote, "Mr. Vice President, Alabamians love Spiro Agnew."[3]

By 1969 the national press had already recognized Agnew's strength in growing the GOP in the southern states. In December the *New York Times* reported that an Arkansas Democrat had conceded, "It used to be that at a Democratic meeting of any kind, you were safe to lead off with a Spiro Agnew joke. But no longer." The vice president, the article continued, "is one of the most popular men in the South" and "the new leader in the drive to expand Republican strength in the South."[4] By 1971 Agnew was being hailed as "Dixie's favorite."[5] Harry Dent, Strom Thurmond's right-hand man, recalled that "Agnew became not only a beloved household name in the South, but even to many he became 'Spiro, Is My Hero.'"[6] By the end of his first term some southern conservatives even voiced a preference for Agnew over Richard Nixon. Political analysts Richard Scammon and Ben Wattenberg relayed the sentiments of one southern politician who said "he was voting for Agnew in 1972, and if that means voting for Nixon, so be it."[7]

That Agnew would emerge as a key figure in the transformation of the white South into a Republican bastion would have come as a great surprise to the political pundits of just a few years earlier. Agnew, after all, came out forcefully against George Wallace when the Alabama governor campaigned in Maryland during the 1964 Democratic primary. Kevin Phillips didn't mention Agnew in his sweeping analysis of the 1968 election, *The Emerging Republican Majority*, which includes an examination of the party's success in the South. Agnew's nomination as Nixon's vice presidential candidate was largely seen as a compromise to placate competing regional and ideological factions, although it is significant that the leading southern Republican of the day, South Carolina's Thurmond, played a key role in the final selection. In describing the fight over the vice presidential choice, journalists Rowland Evans and Robert Novak referred to "the South's new power in the Party." Nixon, according to their report, instructed the party leaders that the candidate would "have to be acceptable to all sections—in effect, bestowing veto power on the South."[8] Of the candidates mentioned in the Evans and Novak article, Agnew was the only one with even geographic proximity to the South. The others—John Lindsay of New York, Charles Percy of Illinois, Mark Hatfield of Oregon, and John Volpe of Massachusetts—were for one reason or another deemed unacceptable by the southerners.

Yet from this convoluted process Agnew rose to be one of Nixon's best weapons in building the Republican Party's presence in the South. Agnew's style and message resonated with a white southern constituency that felt abandoned by the increasingly liberal Democratic Party and that welcomed tougher talk on law and order. He also shared their resentment of "the elites," as when he told a predominantly white Alabama audience that he understood what it was like to "wake up each morning to learn that some prominent man or institution has implied that you are a bigot, a racist, or a fool."[9] As Phillips pointed out, although it seemed unlikely that either party in 1968 would nominate a presidential candidate able to "pre-empt Wallace's impetus" in the South, it turned out there was a vice presidential candidate up to the challenge.[10]

By the time the Civil Rights Act of 1964 and the Voting Rights Act of 1965 became law, the old Jim Crow, Democratic, so-called "Solid South" had already begun to crack. Nixon knew from his time as vice president in the 1950s that the Republican Party had made inroads. Dwight Eisenhower won Virginia, Texas, Tennessee, Florida, and Maryland in 1952 and then grew the map for the GOP in 1956 by adding Kentucky and Louisiana. Still, Strom Thurmond's switch to the Republican Party in 1964 was both big news and a harbinger of things to come. Thurmond did not mince words in his televised announcement on September 16. Through its support of civil rights, he said, the Democratic Party had "abandoned the people" and "repudiated the Constitution of the United States." Democrats were "leading the evolution of our nation to a socialistic dictatorship"—a prediction that some conservatives have continued to echo over the past half century.[11] Immediate reaction to the announcement focused on the short term: could Thurmond help GOP nominee Barry Goldwater take South Carolina? Yes, handily, as it turned out. However, other instant analyses mistook the long-term significance of Thurmond's switch. A *New York Times* editorial posited that it "underscores the extent to which the Republican party in the South is now being built as a 'lily-white' party." Should that happen, the editorial continued, there could be "no future for the Republican party."[12]

Four years later it was clear from the beginning that 1968 was not going to be a normal election year. Nixon announced his candidacy in early February; Wallace followed a week later on his newly created American Independent Party ticket, thus creating an unusual three-party race for the presidency. On the Democratic side Eugene McCarthy's grassroots challenge, Robert Kennedy's dramatic entrance, and then Lyndon Johnson's stunning withdrawal added to the drama of the political season.

The letters that poured into Thurmond's office as the year began provide ample evidence of the potential that Nixon's eventual law and order campaign held for furthering the Republican reach into the South. They also explain why a tough-talking Agnew would come to be a folk hero for so many white southerners. Their hostile tone—laced, not surprisingly, with racism—reflected a wider sense of alienation from the perceived direction of the nation and a growing conviction that white southerners had become, in the words of one Thurmond supporter, an "oppressed majority."[13]

By 1968 Thurmond had become a focal point for those southerners who linked their desire for law and order with their belief that civil rights legislation and an over-indulgent federal government had contributed to the recurring unrest. J. A. Arrouet echoed the feelings of many of the correspondents. "For many months, my reaction to violent demonstrations and rioting has progressed from shock to outright anger," Arrouet began. "Needless to say, I have plenty of company in this opinion."[14] Colie Fox shared a letter he sent to Attorney General Ramsey Clark lamenting the "flouting of our laws daily, increasing rebelliousness, degeneration of our moral fibers and apathy on the part of our people and officials to cope with it." Instead, the "concept of what is right or wrong has faded so far into obscurity until it is no longer a reckoning factor. . . . Entirely to [sic] much concern is directed toward the minorities and not enough to the wishes of the majority. If a sample of the feelings were taken on the matter I am sure the majority would say 'put a silencer on them or deport them.'"[15] Similarly, Peter Stabovitz Jr. wanted to know, "Why is the Government forcing and pushing all this Civil rights stuff down our throats?"[16]

Some letter writers mixed expressions of racism with conspiracy theories. In February highway patrol officers fired into a crowd of African American students protesting at South Carolina State University in Orangeburg, killing three and injuring twenty-seven. The combination of the deadly unrest at Orangeburg and Congress's debate on fair housing legislation set off Charleston attorney David Stack, who cast a wide net of fear and conspiracy in his rant. Stack first congratulated Thurmond for trying to "filibuster to death that damnable so-called Civil Rights [Fair

Housing] bill . . . which the left-wing Radicals and Commies up there are trying to foist upon the decent citizens of this country." Next up, Orangeburg: "No doubt you have heard about the black savages rioting in Orangeburg, S.C., the last few days." Stack warned that the "country was going to have trouble with these savages . . . until we get somebody to stop them cold. They won't be satisfied, no matter what you do for them, because that is what they have been taught." He forecast imminent trouble: "I predict a general war between the decent citizens of this country on the one hand and the black savages on the other, because the decent citizens of this country are not going to stand for this outrageous stuff much longer." And, Stack wanted to know, "Who is it that keeps putting that ugly mug of Martin Lucifer King on television? It seems like every time he opens his ugly mouth, someone is right there to take his picture. I become nauseated . . . and rush to the bathroom."[17]

William Jones, a Kentuckian serving in Vietnam, had a more direct solution to the unrest in mind. "Why doesn't our Government organize a reaction force made up entirely of Viet Nam Combat Vets. It would require at least 4 Bns [battalions] in case there were 4 different riots going on at the same time. These reaction forces could be air lifted to any place in the States in a matter of hours. Once they reach their destinations, helicopters would be ready to air lift them to any part of the city they were needed. Curfews would go into effect and anyone found on the streets, or engaged in looting would be subject to be shot on sight." Jones acknowledged that "these are drastic measures" but said they were necessary to save "our beautiful cities."[18] Even Thurmond agreed that the idea was "perhaps a little drastic."[19]

While Martin Luther King Jr.'s assassination in April dealt a terrible blow to what cohesion was left in the civil rights movement, it also unsettled those who would soon identify with the silent majority. R. B. Ward described himself as a "deeply troubled, very much concerned, and frightened American citizen." The "U.S. Government can no longer maintain law and order and can no longer guarantee the safety of its citizens," Ward wrote. "Anarchy prevails."[20] C. B. Lashar urged Thurmond "in the name of sanity help stop this martyrdom of King. This country is in real trouble."[21] Sumter Lowry painted a frightening picture from his home in

Tampa, Florida: "Tuesday night I looked out of my window just as it got dark and my next door neighbor was passing through my yard accompanied by a young eighteen year old girl. He had a rifle in his hand. This girl had been over to my neighbor's house to see his daughter and he was taking her back to her own home. It was the day of Martin Luther King's funeral." The scene that took place outside his window "made me realize that our dear country is truly in desperate shape." If "our government does not take the necessary *firm action* to put down this insurrection which is in full progress at the moment we won't have any country left."[22]

Writing from the small South Carolina town of Latta, Margaret White noted: "Tonight, for the first time in my forty-four years, I am afraid to walk the streets of nearby towns by day and of my own town by night. I do not feel safe in my own home." White said her mother, who lived alone, "was afraid to attend church because it was not safe to return home alone. Of course, we know our small business, the work of a life time, may be maliciously destroyed at any time." She asked desperately, "Senator Thurmond, what can be done? What can you do? What can I, an average U.S. citizen do? What can the people of Latta do? What can South Carolinians with your help do?" The "people of Latta are uneasy," she added. "Today more firearms and ammunition were bought by decent people than would have been bought over a period of a year ordinarily."[23]

Walter Leneau's letter demonstrated how thoroughly blended were the calls for law and order with white resentment against civil rights progress for African Americans. "Truly decent Americans," Leneau proclaimed, "must be sick with disgust and fear as they witness the worsening violence, all of which is taking place in an age of unprecedented civil rights legislation and programs to aid the Negro. . . . Law and order have become almost non-existent while the Federal Government has devoted undue attention to Negro rights." Leneau then landed on what has since become a core belief of conservative southerners like him: that the federal government had been so long "in favor of Negroes" that white people were "fast becoming an oppressed majority."[24]

Many of Thurmond's constituents were enraged further by the order to honor King by lowering the U.S. flag to half-staff on federal buildings. James White Jr. shared his "resentment of the use of the flag of the United

States to honor a communistic, revolutionary, rabble-rousing civil rights proponent."[25] Mr. and Mrs. Don Harvey complained that King had been "praised and made a martyr through the efforts of our federal government and news media." The Harveys contended that King had "caused more *violence* and hatred between the two races than any other one individual on the face of this earth." As for the flag, "*What* about the *men;* both *white* and black who have died *for* our country in Viet Nam? How many days did we have the flag at half-staff? How many national days of mourning for these 19 and 20 year old men who gave their *precious* life for us?" They concluded, "If God had intended for all races to mix, he would not have made 'races' to begin with."[26] Similarly, Hugh Fenzel had recently attended the funeral of Allen Kohn, killed in Vietnam and the son of a friend: "No flags were flown at half mast for him. No day of morning [*sic*] was ordered for him." And now Lyndon Johnson was going to "ask for more civil rights legislation. If Congress gives in to this blackmail effort induced by the Negroes then I think it would be an insult to the American people—America's forgotten man, the ordinary decent man. Too much has been given away already in the name of civil rights."[27]

Thurmond's supporters wrote next to complain about the Poor People's Campaign, the large protest camp in Washington, D.C., aimed at bringing attention to the plight of the poor. King had been in the process of launching the effort when he was killed. The Poor People's Campaign gave critics an opportunity to be even more blunt about the civil rights movement without having to dance around the issue of King's murder. Mattie Seegars wrote that she was "sick, sick, sick of paying taxes to support these sorry good for nothing people marching all over the country demanding this and that. . . . Are we, the majority, going to sit by and let 11 percent of the population of the U.S. take over?"[28]

Clear patterns of grievances emerge in these letters: the black community was undeserving of federal aid, the federal government was too accommodating of protesters, and the rights of everyday Americans were being forgotten or sacrificed in the process. Mary Neary complained: "If these people have time and money to leave their jobs for the purpose of demonstrating they do not come in the category of 'poor' people." She was, meanwhile, "an average housewife, tired of being manipulated by pseudo-intellectuals who are trying to appease and buy decent behavior by handouts."[29] Katharine Adams also criticized what she saw as the federal government's complicity in the disturbing sight of the encampment: "Let them go home and do honest labor like the rest of us." She concluded, "I for one am sick of hearing and reading the term 'angry young Negro.' . . . If the angry white taxpayers ever throw restraint to the winds, the angry young Negro punks now indulging in arson, looting, and blackmail will most certainly be heavy losers."[30]

Similarly aggrieved, Gladys Walker wrote, "We the people of the South (White folks) wonder when we get rights too." "Why," she asked, "do you have to be black to get by with the rotten things they do. . . . [It] burns me up. We are all tired of such rot." Walker urged Thurmond to "Remember the Whites please."[31] Annelle Davis's assessment, meanwhile, surely was music to the ears of a conservative like Thurmond: "Since my skin isn't black and I don't belong to a union, I have become today's forgotten man; a real political liability."[32] And A. A. Richards concluded that it was "time to stop threats and co-ercions of these dam [*sic*] Communist-negroes and violence peddling (by threats) opportunists before their violence becomes real." How to prevent that violence? "Shoot them between the eyes, the dam [*sic*] anarchists."[33]

The 1968 campaign unfolded in the South against this backdrop. As Nixon's main southern ally, Thurmond was as concerned with George Wallace as he was with whoever would end up with the Democratic nomination. With good reason: data compiled later showed that in 1968 Wallace supporters polled higher — in some instances significantly higher — than either Nixon or Humphrey voters on the following issues: "Disapprove of permitting protest marches," "Federal government getting too powerful," "Federal government wastes a lot of money," "Against federal push to school integration," "Civil rights people pushing too fast," "Black actions seen as mostly violent," "In favor of strict segregation."[34]

The letters to Thurmond attest to the groundswell of support for Wallace based on these issues. A group letter from "The Very Concerned" anticipated perfectly Wallace's message. "What in heaven's name has happened to law and order in the land?" the writers asked, without a trace of irony. "Is one race so important that other's rights are sacrificed on the altar of vote-getting? Are the rest of us expendable?" It was time that leaders "cleaned house" and "started following the constitution again. . . . It seems that George Wallace just might be our only hope for constitutional, local government." "Please don't get us wrong," the letter writers continued, "we're not against the Negro. We believe in giving due recognition to *anyone* who deserves it and is willing to work—after all, isn't that supposed to be the American Way?" This flickering of color-blind merit passed, however: "How can you change a condition overnight that took at least one hundred and fifty years to form?" The writers insisted they were "just plain citizens who are just plain tired of all the shenanigans and bowing and scraping and licking and rioting and demonstrating that's been going on. How long are we the plain, ordinary, hard-working citizens going to have to wait for sanity to return to our 'leaders' or are there no statesmen left?"[35]

Similarly, John Kennemur, a retired marine master sergeant, wondered reluctantly if Wallace was the only alternative for those as angry as he had become. Kennemur described himself as a "political independent" who had voted for Thurmond in the past. But, he wrote, "I can assure you that neither the Republican nor Democratic Party will receive my vote this year unless their presidential candidate takes a firm stand for law and order." Moreover, the candidate "must not merely indicate that he is for law and order, but he has to be positive and dynamic in his actions and statements, willing to call a spade a spade, and demand that the police be unshackled." Kennemur warned, "I don't want to cast a protest vote but like Governor Wallace—I am sick and tired of what's going on."[36]

Wallace's popularity complicated Nixon's chances in the South and in the electoral college. Should Wallace win enough electoral votes to prevent either Nixon or Hubert Humphrey from going over the top, the election would go to the House of Representatives, where a Democratic majority was sure to vote Humphrey president. Thurmond, safe in his Senate seat from an easy 1966 reelection, became Nixon's southern broker. The letters he received in 1968 indicated that many southern voters were ready to leave the Democratic Party. But, with Wallace in the race on a third-party ticket, would they automatically join the GOP?

While both ran on law and order campaigns, Wallace had a knack for putting Nixon on the defensive by speaking bluntly against more civil rights legislation, especially with busing on the near horizon. And the fact remained that Nixon was not an especially easy sell to conservative southerners. As a Wallace "Presidential Quiz" flyer pointed out, Nixon's time as vice president included the appointment of Chief Justice Earl Warren, he of the *Brown v. Board of Education* decision in 1954. These years also saw the passage of the 1957 Civil Rights Act, "the first civil rights bill in eighty-two years." Nixon, the flyer noted, was part of a Republican administration that "sent Federal troops into Little Rock to enforce school integration." The Department of Health, Education, and Welfare, "whose agents have been for some time and are now harassing school administrations throughout the South" over desegregation, was created during the Eisenhower-Nixon years. Even during the current campaign, the flyer added, Nixon had reiterated that he would "support and invoke when necessary Title VI of the Civil Rights Act of 1964, which empowers federal agencies to withhold funds from school districts that refuse to desegregate."[37] A Wallace campaign letter reminded voters that the "Eisenhower-Nixon Administration . . . passed the first 'Civil Rights' Bill since Reconstruction, and sent Federal troops to coerce the children of Little Rock." Nixon, it continued, "this year described himself as 'a liberal on the race issue' and has supported every 'Civil Rights' Bill."[38]

Thurmond, in coordination with the Nixon campaign, sent out a "Presidential Scorecard" for prospective voters to complete to show their support. It featured a picture of a smiling Nixon, with smaller pictures of Thurmond and Nixon supporters General Mark Clark and baseball hero Bobby Richardson. Dozens of Wallace supporters gleefully sent the scorecard back to Thurmond's office with various commentaries. One respondent added the words "Born Loser" near Nixon's face, and another wrote simply "HA!! HA!!" Another mocked the "Nixon's the ONE!" slogan by writing "Wallace is the Only One!" Another added: "My vote will count for Wallace. . . . You may take your junk & do whatever you please with it. I don't want it." After scrawling "VOTE FOR WALLACE. HE'S OUR MAN," one supporter added, "Send me another one, and I'll fix it for you, too." Not surprisingly, several scorecards received the artist's touch, the favorites being blacking out one or two of Nixon's teeth or drawing devil's horns on his head.[39]

The Nixon team had to think carefully about how to push back against Wallace without alienating these voters. The answer they hit upon was brilliant: as Thurmond's chief aide, Harry Dent, recalled later, the message to Wallace voters was simply "He can't win." A vote for Wallace and not for Nixon would help Humphrey and the party that, presumably, these more conservative voters were increasingly willing to leave. In addition, Nixon had the messenger he needed. Wallace campaign director Tom Turnipseed later told Dent that just on the issues "the Wallace effort could succeed except for the one most vital ingredient, Thurmond." Turnipseed was referring to the message of the television ads flooding the southern markets: "All Thurmond had to do was point up . . . the futility of the Wallace campaign—'George can't win.' . . . Wallace could only succeed in throwing the 1968 presidential election into the Democratic House where the 'evil' Humphrey would surely win over the 'OK' Nixon."[40]

Despite giving a speech on law and order at the Southern GOP Governors' Conference the year before, Agnew had little reputation in the South heading into the 1968 election. As Ari Berman noted, the Republican National Convention itself was carefully choreographed to appeal to its white base of support. A tiny 3.5 percent of the delegates were African American, and the convention featured only one prominent black speaker. (A former Nixon supporter, baseball legend Jackie Robinson, was sickened that Nixon had "prostituted himself to get the Southern vote.") But the staging worked; in the "air conditioned halls of the Miami Beach Convention Center, it was as if the civil rights movement had never happened."[41] During the backroom political machinations, however, the movement was very much on the minds of the GOP operatives.

Dent recalled that heading into the convention, "Thurmond and I did not know much about Agnew." As the wheeling and dealing for the vice presidential pick began, Agnew landed only in Thurmond's "no objections" column. But Thurmond and Dent began to warm to Agnew almost immediately, not necessarily for who he was but for the reactions he produced—a lesson the Nixon team learned quickly and never forgot. Having Agnew on the ticket "looked even better for the southern strategy after a group of liberals blasted the selection and staged a brief effort to defeat Agnew with liberal Mayor John Lindsay of New York City." This delightful turn of events, from Thurmond and Dent's perspective, "made the Agnew selection more salable in Dixie."[42]

Despite the stories that Agnew was a disaster on the campaign trail (Scammon and Wattenberg asserted that he "almost lost" the election for Nixon[43]), Dent recalled that "Agnew was a big favorite for southern audiences."[44] His role was to make Wallace-like appeals to disgruntled and anxious white southerners, like those who wrote to Thurmond during this time. His campaign in the South combined Nixon's law and order theme with Thurmond's "George can't win" message. In October Agnew targeted Florida and North Carolina, both seen as potential Wallace states. (Wallace picked up one electoral vote from North Carolina, despite finishing second, but the states otherwise went for Nixon.) Agnew's foray into the South was to extend "an invitation to 'protest' voters supporting George C. Wallace to make their protests count by voting Republican." His speeches "sounded not unlike Wallace texts." Meanwhile, Agnew asserted that "Mr. Wallace may not realize it, but he is the only man in America who can pull Hubert Humphrey's chestnuts from the fire." He added, "I say let them roast."[45]

Typical of his campaign stops in the South, before a crowd in Jacksonville, Florida, Agnew blamed Democrats for "allowing a climate to grow in the country in which 'flag burnings are more newsworthy than flag raisings.'" With a refrain of "there's something wrong," he attacked the usual suspects. Referring to the recent resignation of Columbia University president Grayson Kirk after protesters called for his ouster, Agnew lamented, "When the president of one of our greatest universities is chased from his job by a small group of student radicals, there's something wrong with the way we're doing things." He referenced a recent study showing that "the people who participated in [the Poor People's Campaign] were typically between 23 and 24 years old, single and quite able-bodied." Echoing a line he had used previously, he continued, "And when little old ladies have to wear tennis shoes so they can outleg the criminals

on city streets, there's something wrong with the way we're doing things."
He ended with a flourish: "When arson and larceny and the murder of
law enforcement officials become stylish forms of dissent in this country, then there's something very wrong with what's going on." Just a few
whirlwind months after his controversial appearance before Baltimore's
black leaders, Agnew promised that a Nixon presidency would not give
public funds to "people whose slogan is give us the money or we'll burn
your city down."[46]

As the campaign neared the finish line, Agnew launched another tour
of the "Old Confederacy," targeting those "areas susceptible to the appeal of George C. Wallace."[47] Even Thurmond's South Carolina appeared
to be in jeopardy. In early October Gallup polls showed Wallace with a
38 percent to 31 percent lead over Nixon in the South, with Humphrey
trailing at 24 percent.[48] By the end of the month "local observers feared
that South Carolina was a three-way tossup."[49] Agnew's successful appearance in Charleston on October 29 helped shore up South Carolina as
he again "echoed the theme that Mr. Wallace was 'not electable.' If you
split the protest vote you will be guaranteeing four more years of Hubert
Humphrey."[50] "Give serious thought to this election—the most serious
that you've ever given to any election," Agnew urged. "Vote as if your life
depended on it, because it very well may."[51]

The victorious Nixon-Agnew team relished the fact that even though
the final outcome in the popular vote was razor thin, they had done very
well in the South. As Kevin Phillips described it, Humphrey was "an-
nihilated below the Mason-Dixon line." Nixon won South Carolina,
North Carolina, Virginia, Tennessee, Kentucky, Arkansas, and Florida,
while Wallace took the rest of the South. Together they combined to
win 80 percent of the white southern popular vote.[52] As a result Nixon
expanded Agnew's efforts to recruit disaffected white southerners—or
"the switchovers," as Harry Dent called them. Dent played a key role in
this project because he recognized earlier than most that Agnew was "the
South's friend."[53] After the election Dent joined Nixon's staff, where he
functioned as the political advisor "in charge of all things southern."[54]
Dent was at the intersection between the Nixon White House, Agnew's
office, and the ongoing effort to grow the GOP in the South. By Novem-

ber 1969 he already was able to report that southerners were "ecstatic over the Vice President's recent series of speeches, particularly the one on TV commentators." Dent urged Nixon to continue deploying Agnew to the South to "take full advantage of the current atmosphere" and to "try to get more switchovers."[55]

The Agnew-to-the-South strategy worked spectacularly well. For one, it put southern Democrats on the defensive, especially if they had the temerity to question the administration on such vital issues as Vietnam. Arkansas senator J. William Fulbright, a war critic and a veritable institution in Washington, D.C., claimed in November 1969 that Agnew's speeches had led to "extreme emotionalism" among the vice president's supporters. Agnew's base flooded Fulbright's office "with the most threatening and meanest letters I've received since the days of Joe McCarthy," the senator said. He revealed that the letters branded him a traitor, urged him to leave the country, and vowed political retaliation. And, Fulbright made clear, they "began shortly after Agnew opened a campaign of rhetoric against anti-war protesters, their leaders and those politicians who have shared their doubts about the Nixon administration's conduct of the war."[56]

Having rocketed onto the scene with blistering speeches in New Orleans, Des Moines, and Montgomery, as discussed in the previous chapter, Agnew in December 1969 was suddenly "one of the most popular men in Dixie . . . his prestige perhaps surpassing that of Alabama's George Wallace."[57] Harold Fyle, editor of the *Houston Tribune*, reported the results of a recent poll his paper had taken on Agnew's attacks on the networks: "707 readers back your position while only 4 disagreed with you." Fyle conceded that the "lopsided result can be accounted for, in large part, by the fact that the TRIBUNE is a conservative newspaper with primarily conservative readers. Still, we are confident that in Texas as a whole your position is favored by an overwhelming majority."[58] A typical letter of southern support came from A. L. Pecorado, president of the Community State Bank of Independence, Louisiana, who congratulated Agnew—"Your stock has gone up considerably"—and decried the "ignoramuses that are prone to drag our wonderful nation into the mire. The silent voice will want you to continue the attack because you are in a position to offset the terrible situation brought about by this element.

I, as well as the majority, am yelling to continue to give it to them, Mr. Vice President."[59] Congressman L. Mendel Rivers of South Carolina sent a joyful telegram to Agnew urging him to "keep pouring it on. God bless you."[60] And Congressman James Collins of Texas congratulated Agnew on his New Orleans speech and its special appeal to southerners: "As you could tell when you were in New Orleans—your message really comes through loud and clear in the South. You are doing a tremendous service for the Country as the Spokesman for the Silent Majority."[61] In August Jim Allison Jr., deputy chair of the Republican National Committee, wrote a "very confidential" memo to Dent asking him to send Agnew to other parts of the country as well. If Agnew went to GOP conferences in the West and Midwest, Allison said, "this would be a good move." If he went only to that year's Southern GOP Conference, however, "I think the press would rap us for that." The problem, as Allison indicated, was that "we are just getting beaten over the head daily with all this southern strategy stuff."[62]

Indeed, the publication of Kevin Phillips's *The Emerging Republican Majority* and the popularization of the term "southern strategy" created some problems in the Nixon White House. The president's advisors feared that Phillips had been a little too candid in describing the likelihood that the white southern vote would continue to move into the Republican Party in the aftermath of the Civil Rights and Voting Rights Acts. Phillips explained that already in 1966 white voters of the Deep South were "angrier than ever" over enforcement of the Voting Rights Act.[63] His description of the GOP's calculation of the region's racial politics did not even attempt nuance: he concluded bluntly that "maintenance of Negro voting rights was essential to the GOP" in the South.[64] As the national Democratic Party continued to embrace black civil rights, white southerners would likely follow "their opinion-molding classes into the Republican Party."[65]

While the Nixon team was delighted with the results of Agnew's speeches, members remained concerned about potentially alienating Republicans from outside the South. The solution was purely Nixonian: deny there was such a strategy. In a summary memo on "The White Reaction," Dent suggested, "We should disavow Phillips' book as party policy." Instead, he said, the Nixon White House and the GOP should describe their growing strength as a product of "the soundness of our philosophy . . . the sanctity of individual freedom, the evils of centralism, the importance of efficient fiscally sound government."[66] In another memo to Nixon, and in conjunction with Agnew's recent appearance at the Southern GOP Conference in New Orleans on December 4, 1969, Dent reported that in answer to media questions, "we are responding (and so are all Southern Chairmen) that this Administration has no Southern strategy but rather a national strategy that, for the first time in modern times, *includes* the South, rather than *excludes* the South from full and equal participation in national affairs." It was, Dent said, the Democrats who by their appeal to the black vote "seem to have written the South out of the Union."[67] Nixon liked that approach: a White House memo back to Dent assured him that "the President feels that this is a good line to hit continually. He requested that you arrange to get this out to the Democratic districts throughout the South."[68] Agnew continued to employ this message the next year in South Carolina when he "denied the existence of a 'Southern strategy' on the part of the Administration. 'That's just the opposition trying to create an illusion,' the Vice President remarked."[69]

Agnew's visit to the Montgomery, Alabama, home of George Wallace, in late November and the Southern GOP Conference in New Orleans in early December 1969 marked a new level of his and the party's popularity in the South. His strength in the region was undeniable, as the *New York Times* reported, and it was "evident that if President Nixon is pursuing his much-discussed Southern strategy . . . he is making much headway."[70] As Dent reported back to Nixon, the conference drew an enormous crowd: "More than 1000 Southern Republicans gathered . . . to put on the biggest Regional Conference we have had this year . . . at least two to three times as large as any other of the conferences." The audience gave Agnew "long and sustained applause which I have only seen exceeded by the President's acceptance speech in Miami," Dent said, adding, "By the way, the Vice President liked every minute of it."[71]

The *New York Times* observed that at the New Orleans conference, "the hottest item in the handout packet was not the blue-and-white sticker saying, 'Back the President,' but the red, white, and blue one proclaiming the heroism of Mr. Agnew." Agnew had both the Wallacites and the national Democrats on the back foot: "For Mr. Wallace the Agnew threat is awesome. The Vice President is cutting seriously into Mr. Wallace's base of strength in the South. Many observers believe that Mr. Agnew's Southern popularity may have surpassed Mr. Wallace's." With impressive foresight, *Times* writer Roy Reed noted that "loyalist Democrats" feared that "the Vice President is the cutting edge of the Republican threat that could eventually cause the once solidly Democratic South to become not just a two-party region, but predominantly Republican." In response, southern Democrats "now speak out against Mr. Agnew at their peril," and some "speak openly for him." His southern fans were "buying what Agnew's saying and think it's about time somebody in Washington spoke out in blunt terms." There was even some "growing suspicion" that Agnew was more popular than Nixon in the South. One Mississippi man proclaimed, "I'm going to vote for Agnew." When asked about Nixon, he replied, "Well, I've got to vote for him to vote for Agnew."[72]

Despite the momentum, however, the efforts to grow southern support did not always run smoothly. Officials from the Department of Health, Education, and Welfare such as Leon Panetta were determined to keep the pace of school desegregation going.[73] Nixon put forward two conservative southerners for the Supreme Court, Clement Haynsworth and G. Harrold Carswell. Both failed. (Agnew, in by-now vintage style, blamed the court rejections on the "most nebulous set of trumped-up charges ever contrived by the labor and civil rights lobbies and their allies in the news profession" and "the flimsy, subjective excuses of 'insensitivity' and 'mediocrity.'"[74]) Also, Nixon's Family Assistance Plan, which guaranteed an income for all American families, was anathema to southern conservatives who viewed this as an appalling thing for the federal government to get into.

Heading into the 1970 midterm election, Agnew's role was to continue to attract disgruntled white southerners away from the Democratic Party and to shore up conservative support for Nixon from those who were already in the Republican Party. That included voters such as Paul McCoy of New Hill, North Carolina, who assured Agnew that "you have the support of the great silent majority that has been silent and patient way too long." McCoy urged him: "In the months ahead *please come to the Raleigh, Durham, Chapel Hill area* and help stiffen the backbones of the great majority here that can not be heard because of the great noise that the pointed headed liberals around here generate."[75] A Kentucky Republican congressional candidate wondered why the party was not helping Agnew more in the South. Herbert Myers asked: "Do you people in Washington really want the Republican Congressional candidates to win or [are] we just spinning our wheels and spending our money and time for a lost cause?" It was "high time for some of the other Republicans VIPS . . . to help the candidates instead of letting Vice-President Agnew do it all."[76]

Agnew meanwhile continued his outreach to the South. Before a "roaring crowd" in Columbia he headlined the "largest fund-raising gathering ever held in South Carolina" in late April 1970. Strom Thurmond proclaimed that "South Carolinians now know for sure they have a strong and capable ally in Spiro T. Agnew."[77] In his remarks Agnew proclaimed it was time to "forthrightly declare our rejection and contempt for those who practice subversion, lawlessness, and violence."[78] He stoked the crowd by warning that should another Supreme Court nominee be rejected by the "learned idiocy" of the Senate, "the public will arise in wrath."[79] Columnist Ernest Furgurson of the *Baltimore Sun* drew attention to the pointedly southern appeal of Agnew's appearance in South Carolina and his support of the unreconstructed Albert Watson as the Republican nominee for governor. "The southern strategy he keeps saying doesn't exist has got Mr. Agnew into bed with yet another ex-Democrat who would be flattered to be compared with George Wallace," Furgurson wrote. "By the time Agnew left," he added, "the South Carolina contingent was deliriously in love with him and confident about Watson's chances."[80]

In the immediate aftermath of the Kent State shootings in early May 1970, Agnew replaced Nixon at the dedication of the memorial to Confederate heroes carved into the side of Stone Mountain, just outside Atlanta. Nixon was under mounting pressure to reel Agnew in, given the extraordinarily volatile climate on college campuses. H. R. Haldeman, as mentioned, recorded that at the ceremony Nixon wanted Agnew "to avoid any remarks about students, etc. VP strongly disagrees. I passed the word. VP said he would act only on order of P[resident]." Nixon responded by meeting with a select group of university presidents who, Haldeman noted, "all blame Agnew primarily."[81] The word evidently got to Agnew. In a speech that the *New York Times* described as "subdued and nonpartisan," Agnew hailed the "new" South as a region that "rejects the old grievances and the old political appeals to the worst in all. The new South embraces the future, and presses forward with a robust economy fueled by industrial development."[82]

The *Times* reporter, Jon Nordheimer, did relay the feelings of one Agnew supporter who planned to boycott the dedication ceremony. James Venable, a sixty-five-year-old attorney, hailed from the family that originally leased Stone Mountain to the United Daughters of the Confederacy in 1916 for the purpose of creating the memorial. Venable, who described himself as the Imperial Wizard of the National Knights of the Ku Klux Klan, was sitting out the ceremony because of the inclusion of a black minister. William Holmes Border's presence was, Venable said, an "'offense' to the memory of General Lee, General Jackson, and Mr. Davis." However, he "had no objection to the invitation of a Republican, Mr. Agnew, to deliver the main dedication talk." Agnew, Venable explained, "is even a better man suited for this occasion than the President. . . . I share his views on college students and professors running amok and all that communistic, socialistic, stuff."[83]

Even though the *Times* described Agnew's speech at Stone Mountain as "non-partisan," the Nixon White House understood the power of the Lost Cause to help the GOP in the South. When Stanley Pottinger of the Department of Health, Education, and Welfare, searching for ways to ease tensions in newly integrated southern schools, suggested that "something might have to be done about Confederate statues and the playing of Dixie," Dent's response was unequivocal: "We better not do anything against Dixie. This is real explosive." Instead, Dent suggested that Agnew continue to reach out to white southerners because they liked the "tough talk about student demonstrations, law and order, strong foreign policy, and the way the Vice President is working on the radical liberals."[84]

Letter writers during this time urged Agnew to buck up the Nixon administration and keep it on a more conservative course. A particularly sore subject was the fact that Health, Education, and Welfare continued to push for school integration. Bernice Morten of Florence, South Carolina, wrote that white southerners' confidence in Nixon had already been "shattered by the Health, Integration, and Welfare board (where there are no educators, only integrationists)." The government "noodleheads, [Robert] Finch and [James] Allen [Jr.], who are promoting this mess, care not a whit for the chaos created at the local level. Their sole purpose is to mix up the schools at any cost." So Morten was appealing to Agnew: "Truly, Sir, this situation now in South Carolina has done severe damage to the GOP. The party is *not* well established. It is slipping fast—and sending people to a third party movement in droves. Disillusioned with our party (I've been a Republican all my life—50 years), they turn to something else. I find this so distressing that I don't know what to do, or where to turn, because the local Republicans can give me no answers. They, too, are dismayed and unhappy. Do you have an answer? We were so proud to have you visit our State recently. Please, Mr. Agnew, don't let the bureaucrats ruin our schools. They don't care. We do."[85]

Despite the heat from his right, Nixon was also being criticized for going too far in the direction of his conservative southern supporters. A report issued by the moderate Ripon Society concluded that Republicans "who try to out-segregate the Democrats seldom win. . . . Those who await the mass conversions of racist Democrats to Republicanism have a long wait indeed." The main problem heading toward 1972 was the fact that George Wallace was still very much in the national picture, having won back the governor's seat in Alabama. Minus Wallace, "Nixon could look forward to sweeping the entire South, the Great Plains, and the Rockies." But a now-likely Wallace candidacy could "be expected to take about fifty electoral votes [he took forty-six in 1968] and put Texas in the doubtful column. This reduces Nixon's hard core to a mere 115 electoral votes; in order to win, he would need both California and Illinois; and then *every* remaining state of any size—Ohio, New Jersey, Indiana, Missouri, Wisconsin, and Kentucky—that he took in 1968. In short, Mr. Nixon is in trouble." The solution was "an election year approach of moderation, not more southern strategy."[86]

Not surprisingly, southern Republican congressmen responded angrily to these calls for moderation. In a two-hour meeting with Nixon in August 1970, with Agnew in attendance, they aired their grievances. They were quick to hold Nixon's feet to the fire on any perceived backpedaling on issues important to them. Early in the meeting, according to Dent's notes, Nixon pointed out that "the Ripon Society does not represent the President" and "that what is needed in the South is a good strong base for the future. He emphasized his interest in the South and his strong feeling for the Southern people whom he said have been saving the nation, particularly in the area of national security."[87] Florida senator Edward Gurney spoke for the room when he shared their frustration over the school situation. In particular they were angry about "the recent news story about U.S. Attorneys and Marshals going South to assist with desegregation, [the] IRS tax-exempt status decision on private schools [the IRS would no longer grant tax-exempt status to newly forming private schools with racist admission policies], and the current law suits being instituted by the Justice Department in a number of Southern states [over the failure to desegregate]."[88]

Others warned that they were not sure Nixon could still carry the South if his administration continued to push for more school integration. North Carolina congressman Jim Holshouser "indicated that as of today he did not think the President could carry" his state because of the desegregation efforts, Dent noted. Holshouser added that "within the last thirty days the Administration was giving the appearance of being anti-South for the first time." The president, he noted implausibly, was "now being described as 'Mister Integrator.'" Dent wrote that at this point it "was difficult to understand what exactly Holshouser was saying here." However, Holshouser got very specific about the political danger that loomed. A Nixon administration that backed aggressive desegregation efforts "is hurting with the middle class vote which he says is the basis of the GOP vote in North Carolina. He says that this reaction is not just confined to the Wallace voter."[89]

As the discussion moved on to focus on economic policy, Fletcher Thompson, a Georgia congressman, pulled the curtain back by reminding the president that "the economy question is second only to the race question in the South." Thompson, without any recorded objection from the others at the meeting, "described himself as being biased, but also put everyone else in this category." As Dent recorded: "He said, 'we in the South are motivated by race.' He pointed to the 43 percent vote that Wallace got in 1968 in a three-way race."[90]

Nixon responded to this litany of complaints by saying that whether the congressmen liked it or not, "he must carry out court orders." But he reassured them that he would "like to get rid of any image that would classify this Administration as being militarily integrationist." In his defense, Nixon noted Agnew's popularity in the southern states and "emphasized that the Vice President and the Attorney General were very much on the side of the South." Agnew, as the meeting wound down, returned the favor, assuring Nixon that "these are his good friends" but reminding those gathered that "the President has tremendous sectional pressures on him and other such pressures which were sometimes in conflict with their own desires. He pointed out that the President has to represent the entire country."[91]

The GOP held its own in the midterm elections that year, at least in the South. The Nixon political team began to focus more intently on reelection. Agnew meanwhile was dogged by persistent stories that he would be bumped from the ticket and that his speeches were injecting a new mean-spiritedness into American politics. As the "dump Agnew" whispers continued, his office received letters from southerners who assured the embattled vice president that he had their fulsome support. Indeed, some cited Agnew's place on the ticket as the key to their vote for Richard Nixon.

For example, in July 1971 Ira Day of Raleigh sent one of Jesse Helms's TV commentaries from his *Viewpoint* program to Frank Dale of Nixon's Committee To Reelect the President. In it, Helms complained that Nixon was not paying enough attention to southern conservatives' concerns. "Mr. Nixon could not have won election in 1968 had it not been for the support given by voters with conservative inclinations. He cannot retain this support on the assumption that such voters have no other place to go. They can always stay at home on election day." Of the speculation that Agnew would be dropped from the ticket, Helms was frustrated that "Mr. Nixon has scarcely come to the defense of Mr. Agnew, let alone made clear that he wants Mr. Agnew for his running mate again." But, Helms warned, "if the President is persuaded to replace Mr. Agnew, then he will lose a vast amount of the vital conservative support he enjoyed in 1968." Helms did not expect Nixon to transform himself into "a rock-ribbed conservative—which he is not and could not honestly portray himself as being." However, the president needed to "demonstrate a sense of loyalty to a courageous man who has been a faithful and hardworking member of the Nixon Administration."[92]

Day's letter accompanying the Helms script took a harsher tone regarding Nixon's perceived dithering. Day explained that he had sent money and had worked for the Nixon campaign in the past. He was, however, pausing his efforts and his contributions for now: "I want to see if he is going to dump Spiro Agnew in 1972 and how much more liberal he is going to get." Specifically, Day wanted to see if Nixon would "continue to play up to the union and minority vote, which are the niggers, and when he is going to fulfill his promise when he came to North Carolina about school busing. . . . He has not done one thing to make this promise good to the citizens of North Carolina." Day was not about to shift his vote to the Democrats, after fifty years of voting Republican, but come election time, "I could go fishing that day."[93]

Agnew received support from southern congressmen as well. In July 1972 LaMar Baker of Tennessee read into the *Congressional Record* a strong editorial from the *Nashville Banner:* "Mr. Agnew is a man of notable political stature in his own right; a man who brought to the 1968 campaign the considerable executive prestige he had acquired as Governor of Maryland, admired and respected by fellow executives irrespective of party labels. Staunchly conservative, the designation is more than a tag of convenient classification. His rugged individualism and complete frankness in speaking his mind embrace more than the unswerving Constitutional concept in matters of governmental operation. They relate to the conscientious treatment of citizen responsibility." Nixon had chosen "the man who symbolizes so strongly the working conservatism bespeaking a major strength in support of national policies, both domestic and foreign, upon which the upcoming contest will be predicated. . . . It does not surprise that he is the President's choice. Millions concur."[94]

Agnew also heard from Corbett Thigpen, famous as one of the psychiatrists who wrote the 1957 best seller *The Three Faces of Eve*, about a woman with multiple personalities. In August 1971 Thigpen, a Georgian, wrote to encourage Agnew to keep up the fight, noting "your popularity in the south is as high as it has ever been." What concerned Thigpen was that Nixon still seemed too willing to concede to moderates in the party. He hoped that Agnew could rescue the administration for conservatives. "The Liberals despise you and will put you down at every opportunity," Thigpen observed. "They show no hesitancy in making known in all their media that you have fallen in the eyes of the American public. This is wishful thinking." Thigpen urged Agnew to use his popularity as leverage with Nixon: "Should you consent to be his Vice President again, I would hope that you would make it clear to him that you intend to be more than just a decoration to re-elect him, and that your philosophy will either play a part in the government or no dice."[95]

Jesse Helms himself, on the brink of launching his long senatorial career as one of the South's leading conservatives, wrote in 1972 to thank Agnew for his support. Helms wrote chummily that Agnew had been "'my man' since the day you came to our television station during the early days of the 1968 campaign. I have been very proud of you." The letter also gives more evidence of Agnew's contributions to the switchover campaign aimed at white southern Democrats. "We are very pleased with the progress thus far," Helms wrote. "We have the public support of more than a thousand Democrats who have been active in their party from precinct level to the state level. Two former state chairmen of that party have endorsed us, plus others such as a former state attorney general, supreme court justices, legislators, state treasurer, etc. Needless to say, this has been very comforting to us."[96] Even though Helms trailed Democrat Nick Galifianakis for much of the race, he prevailed in the end in part because of Democratic voters who had indeed switched over.[97]

Agnew campaigned successfully for Louisiana Republican David Treen in 1972. As Ari Berman noted, Treen voted against "nearly every piece of civil rights legislation, including the V[oting] R[ights] A[ct] extension in 1975."[98] Agnew was encouraged to stump for Treen in person because

Fig. 2. Richard Nixon and Spiro Agnew at the 1972 Republican National Convention. Behind the smiles, the two never had a warm relationship. It would sour even more as both became entangled in illegalities during their second term. (National Archives, White House Photo Collection [Nixon Administration], 1/20/1969–8/9/74 [National Archives Identifier, 194277])

Louisiana seemed prime for a Republican gain in the House of Representatives. Gerald Mack, state chair of the Young Republicans, assessed the situation in a letter to Agnew: "Because of the intense unpopularity of George McGovern in Louisiana, this race is our golden opportunity to establish the Republican Party as a viable factor in Louisiana politics." Mack proved prescient when he added, "I sincerely believe that the future of the Republican Party lies here in the South."[99]

The landslide reelection win in 1972 indeed seemed to bode well for continued GOP gains in the South and for Agnew's career. Thoughts inevitably began to turn toward 1976. A Harris poll published after the election named the vice president the leading GOP candidate for 1976. In a projected matchup against Ted Kennedy, Agnew lost nationally, but he led comfortably in the South 53 percent to 43 percent (and by a whopping 59 percent to 39 percent in the Deep South).[100] Frank Montgomery, a GOP county chair from Durham County in North Carolina, relished this look ahead. Montgomery assured Agnew that "a new wind is blowing in the Political Life of the South. . . . If you decide to go for the #1 spot we are for you. I am of the opinion this applies to the Solid South."[101] One cannot help but notice that Montgomery used "Solid South" to mean a solid Republican South.

6

NO CONTEST

Spiro Agnew celebrated his fifty-fourth birthday on November 9, 1972, in grand style. Two days after being reelected vice president, surrounded by three hundred guests in the Cotillion Room of Washington's Sheraton Park Hotel, he basked in the moment. Top-shelf celebrities including Frank Sinatra and Australian tennis star Rod Laver, and minor luminaries such as Marie Lombardi (the widow of Green Bay Packers coaching legend Vince Lombardi) and Barbara Marx (the wife of Zeppo Marx and later the fourth and final wife of Sinatra), raised their glasses to the vice president. The theme of the birthday bash was "The Spiro of '76," playing off the upcoming Bicentennial and Agnew's newly minted status as a front-runner in the next presidential election, still four years away.[1] Little did Agnew know that the occasion would mark the zenith of his political career, capping a rapid ascent for a man only a decade removed from chairing Kiwanis Club luncheons in Maryland.

The vice president's political future looked bright indeed in late 1972. He had a national following across silent majority country with a network of loyal supporters that spread out across the electoral map. He had the strong backing of key Republican Party leaders such as Senators Barry Goldwater and Strom Thurmond. And he had the experience of a full four-year term in the White House under his belt. While Agnew had been a loyal soldier for Richard Nixon's administration and the Republican Party, he could also offer himself as something of an outsider in 1976, if so desired. He had staked out positions in foreign and domestic policy distinct from Nixon's. He was more strident on the leading cultural issues of the day and more hawkish on the Vietnam War. The vice president had been suspicious of the opening to China and was already making the case against affirmative action and the snobbery of the intellectual and coastal elites on the home front. If conventional wisdom held, he would be a leading contender to become the party's standard-bearer in 1976.

Just as Agnew's political fortunes looked optimistic, so too did the prospects for the Republican Party. Only eight years after the devastating national loss to Lyndon Johnson and the sweeping Great Society Congress of 1964, the GOP had retained the White House and picked up twelve congressional seats. Old party affiliations were giving way to a new political order. And while Republicans were still in the minority in both chambers of Congress, there was no question that the once solidly Democratic South and the manufacturing Rust Belt states were continuing a slow but steady generational shift to the right. The fast-growing sections of the country in the Southwest and the exurban edge cities were leaning Republican too. And Agnew—a border state suburbanite who had publicly taken on the media, the universities, and the hoi polloi of Washington and New York—could legitimately lay claim to those emerging demographics.

Agnew had another advantage that became crystal clear to political observers in the first few months of 1973. He had been so far out of Nixon's inner circle of advisors and operatives during the first term that he had absolutely nothing to do with the developing Watergate scandal. In the dark about the break-in and the cover-up, Agnew could plausibly put distance between himself and Nixon chief of staff H. R. Haldeman, presidential assistant John Ehrlichman, former attorney general and 1972 campaign manager John Mitchell, and White House counsel John Dean—all of whom soon would be out of government and on their way to jail in the fallout. As the investigations led by Congress and the special prosecutor ramped up during the first part of the year, there was even the real possibility that Nixon might not be able to finish his term in office. Spiro Agnew was, at least for a moment, a loudly thumping heartbeat away from the presidency.[2]

And then it all fell apart. Agnew's career crashed because of his own past mistakes and sloppiness. Bribes, tax evasion, and other calumny led to his sudden resignation and a pathetic plea of nolo contendere in a Baltimore courtroom in October 1973. The Republican Party's destiny was more complicated. Suffering setbacks in the 1974 and 1976 elections, due at least in part to the implosion of the Nixon-Agnew team and internal party struggles, generational success would eventually follow with national victories in 1980, 1984, 1988, 2000, 2004, and 2016. Control of the Senate (1981) and eventually the House (1995), which had eluded the Republicans for a generation, finally broke the Democratic Party's decades-long stranglehold on Congress. And although Agnew was long gone from Republican power circles by the time those victories came about, his legacy lurked below the surface.

Within a week of his reelection Nixon was already trying to figure out a way to engineer his successor. One thing was clear: he did not want Agnew to be given any kind of inside track for the GOP nomination in 1976. The president told his chief of staff, who was then in his final weeks on the job, "We do not further [Agnew's] interest politically for '76. We don't want him to have the appearance of being the heir apparent, we also don't want to appear to push him down."[3] Nixon and Haldeman settled on a strategy of benign neglect. While they wanted to maintain some leverage over the vice president, they ultimately wanted to keep his political ambitions in check. They viewed Agnew as lacking the personal drive to attain the presidency, more interested in playing golf than in expending the time and energy needed to mount a national campaign.[4] Nixon wanted to find a way to position John Connally as his successor.[5]

Nixon and Haldeman decided that they should offer Agnew a lead role working on the Bicentennial celebration for 1976. Agnew found the proposal offensive and demeaning. In his memoirs he described his expectation of getting a "very big, important assignment" as a reward for working hard as vice president and being a team player during the 1972 campaign. The Bicentennial assignment "made me shudder."[6] Agnew told the president that the Bicentennial was "a loser, because everybody has his own ideas about it and nobody can be the head of it without making a million enemies."[7] He mentioned his interest in positioning himself for 1976, the absolute wrong thing for him to say to Nixon.[8] With conventional wisdom and polling showing that Agnew was indeed the front-runner in the next election, the vice president sought out other ways to raise his stature.

Politically, Agnew still needed to earn gravitas to enhance the perception that he was a legitimate presidential candidate in 1976, and he asked Nixon for the chance to do "Kissinger-type missions in the foreign area." At least to his face, the president agreed that Agnew should "not just do goodwill trips and funerals." Haldeman recorded in his diary that Nixon told him, "We'll handle it, setting him up for some single-shot negotiations, and foreign economic things."[9] Once again Nixon was trying to figure out ways to assuage Agnew while keeping him substantively out of the way. The vice president, however, kept pushing. Just prior to the inauguration in January 1973, and with tensions mounting between the Israelis and the Egyptians, Agnew pitched the idea that he ought to take a trip to the region to visit Anwar Sadat and serve as a shuttle diplomacy–style envoy for Middle East peace. Haldeman described Nixon as "so astonished he didn't know quite how to answer the thing at first, but [he] then made the point that the likelihood of anything good coming out of such a trip was almost zero, and that it would be very unwise for the Vice President to take the risk of being rebuffed at that high level." Nixon seemed to realize that Agnew's appeal was a move of desperation because "he had nothing really of importance to do."[10] Nixon would send him to Southeast Asia instead.

Without much of an understanding of what his role was to be in the second term, Agnew received the oath of office from Chief Justice Warren Burger on January 20, 1973.[11] He now had a second term and a pathway to his party's nomination. And while he didn't have a policy portfolio in the White House that might befit a potential president, journalist Elizabeth Drew believed that his style might be just presidential enough. Already well known for his blunt, red-meat rhetoric, Agnew still carried himself with "a certain dignity" and "a peculiar sort of elegance," Drew observed. He clearly liked the trappings and the attention of office, "his own plane [and] the Palm Springs spa of his new friend Frank Sinatra."[12] Perhaps the lifestyle would be enough to sustain him for the next couple of years if he was willing to do some of the hard work of moving around the country making allies, raising money, and pressing the flesh in anticipation of his next political move. Distance from Nixon and his White House aides would have immediate and unexpected benefits. He was untouched by Watergate, for a moment at least, and it appeared as if Nixon's second term might be overtaken by events that would catapult him into the presidency before the 1976 election.

The Watergate scandal began to unfold within weeks of the inauguration. Not only had Agnew not been a part of discussions about the break-in or the cover-up, he also tactfully steered clear of the topic when it came up in casual discussion. Playing tennis with White House aide and reelection campaign official Jeb Magruder, Agnew asked, "Jeb, what the hell is going on?" Magruder recounted: "My instinct was to be candid. 'It was our operation,' I said. 'It got screwed up. We're trying to take care of it.' Agnew frowned and looked away. 'I don't think we ought to discuss it again, in that case.'"[13] The administration's inner circle began to implode by the spring of 1973 as the Senate Watergate Committee hearings began and Archibald Cox was appointed as an independent special prosecutor. Leaks from the White House undermined key aides, but there was no mention that Agnew was involved. Quite the opposite, he was perceived as in the clear. As Nixon became enmeshed in the scandal, Agnew was viewed by some "as the possible savior of the GOP, the one man untarnished by the spreading stain of Watergate."[14]

Nixon was wise to this growing perception of Agnew's distance from Watergate and asked him to advocate more forcefully on his behalf, shouting on the White House tapes in April 1973, "What the hell is Agnew doing? He's never spoken up once on this goddamn thing."[15] At a crucial juncture late that month Agnew did offer some carefully measured words that might allow him room to maneuver later: "We are inundated with rumor, hearsay, grand jury leaks, speculation and statements from undisclosed sources. It is entirely possible that some of this may be proven later to be accurate. And, if it is, it must be confronted forthrightly at that time."[16] The *New York Times* opined that "some Congressional Republicans are beginning to consider the political benefits that might flow from a Nixon resignation and the resultant accession of Spiro T. Agnew."[17]

The possibility of an Agnew presidency raised hackles within the White House with establishment Republicans who thought him unqualified for office. Henry Kissinger told Nixon that under no circumstances should he resign with Agnew waiting in the wings, citing the vice president's "personality, what it would do to the presidency, and the historical injustice of it."[18] Nixon told his speechwriter Ray Price in the spring of 1973 that he was contemplating resigning over Watergate, but "the only problem [is] you get Agnew. You want Agnew?"[19] On the White House tapes there are multiple instances of Nixon facetiously asking aides about the possibility of Agnew becoming president.[20] But Agnew kept his distance from Watergate and had some straightforward private advice for his boss. Visiting the president at the Bethesda Naval Hospital in July 1973, where Nixon was being kept for several days after being diagnosed with viral pneumonia, Agnew told him to burn the White House tapes.[21] But Agnew's suggestion to suppress evidence was given in the vacuum of his own unfolding legal and ethical problems. U.S. attorneys in Baltimore were already far along in gathering information about kickbacks that the vice president had received, going back to his early political days as Baltimore county executive and continuing through his time in Washington. And while the extent of the investigation was tightly held within the Department of Justice until the late summer of 1973, reporters began to catch wind that the president and the vice president could be removed from office more or less concurrently for their crimes.

The investigation into Agnew's misdeeds is well documented. The exhaustive work of the U.S. attorneys in Baltimore in their forty-page *Exposition of the Evidence Against Spiro T. Agnew* spelled out his offenses chapter and verse. The public statement of Attorney General Elliot Richardson on October 10, 1973, outlined the government's strategy in stark terms. Journalists from the *Wall Street Journal*, the *Washington Post*, and the *Baltimore Sun* painted Agnew as a corrupt politician. His private defense during the summer and fall of 1973—which boiled down to "everyone else in Maryland politics did it, so why shouldn't I?"—may have had some truth in it, but the case against him is difficult to explain away.[22] Agnew's own memoir, *Go Quietly . . . or Else*, released in 1980, seven years after his resignation, defensively justified his actions and placed the blame with Nixon and the White House staff for not stepping up to defend him. More unexplored, however, are two facets of the investigation that tied Agnew's downfall into a larger narrative about his place in American politics and the fissures that were beginning to be exposed within the Republican Party.

As an emerging spokesman for the silent majority, the vice president had carved out a political persona that centered on his relatability. He spoke to an imagined suburbia where a new breed of politicians could present themselves as genuine examples of the voters that they represented. Most national Republican and Democratic leaders in the recent past had been larger-than-life figures: military heroes (Dwight Eisenhower), career politicians (Richard Nixon), Wall Street lawyers (Thomas Dewey), blue bloods (John F. Kennedy, Robert Taft, Franklin Roosevelt, Henry Cabot Lodge), internationalists (Herbert Hoover), and intellectuals (Adlai Stevenson). Agnew created his public persona more in the model of 1964 Republican presidential candidate Barry Goldwater. The vice president fashioned himself as the good neighbor manning the grill at the backyard barbeque, an everyday guy who loved his family and pro football. In politics he was considered tough and candid, but fair and honest. If, however, he was going to be publicly exposed as a bribe taker, a tax evader, and, as was later reported, an adulterer, the image of a just-like-the-voters leader who could speak truth to power would be smashed to smithereens. These kinds of revelations would weaken his ability to call out the media, intellectuals, and anti–Vietnam War protesters at supper clubs, churches, and Lincoln Day dinners across the nation. A public indictment of Agnew's character would separate the message from the messenger. And while the message might continue to resonate with some of the silent majority, the messenger, at least at this point in American political history, still had to have character and honesty as the cornerstones of his image. In the end, when fully uncovered, Agnew's story would reveal him as just like so many other run-of-the-mill politicians; he was willing to lie, cheat, and adulterate for the benefit of his own wealth, power, and gratification. Although Agnew's political persona as the decent man from suburbia fell apart, future Republican politicians took their cue from his earlier success. If you wanted to speak for Middle America, you had to have an honest public persona that matched the wholesome narrative.

A second illuminating element of Agnew's downfall was that the major players in the drama were something of a microcosm of the growing debate within the Republican Party about its direction. The interaction between the key political and judicial actors in the months leading up to the vice president's resignation highlighted a system that honorably chose evenhandedness over party loyalty. Collectively, the GOP leadership pushed Agnew to resign despite divergent political opinions about the party's future.

The U.S. Attorney's Office in Baltimore was on the front line of the investigation into Agnew's misdeeds. By 1973 the office had been trying to clean up state politics for more than a decade. Power in Maryland had traditionally been controlled by the Democrats and allocated between Baltimore and the more rural parts of the state. A border state during the Civil War with the nickname "America in Miniature," Maryland had big cities, suburbs, coastal areas, farms, and mountains, and politically it combined "the worst of the northern big-city machine with the worst of the southern courthouse tradition."[23] But by the late 1960s political, demographic, and economic power had begun to shift away from the city of Baltimore and toward the surrounding counties and the metropolitan Washington, D.C., suburbs. Future Maryland governor Harry Hughes, who was a member of the House of Delegates from the Eastern Shore during the 1960s, described how Baltimore was "in full-scale post-war retreat, with thousands of its inhabitants, most of them white, pulling up roots and moving to the fast-expanding suburbs. They left behind abandoned row houses, empty factories, increasingly failing schools and rising crime."[24]

Stephen Sachs, who was an assistant U.S. attorney in Baltimore in the early 1960s and later became the U.S. attorney (1967–70) and attorney general of Maryland (1978–86), explained that Maryland unfairly got the reputation of being a free and easy state for politicians. "Were our politicians more corrupt or were our prosecutors more adept? I prefer to think the latter."[25] A series of aggressive and ambitious U.S. attorneys took on the state's entrenched political system. Their work led to high-profile convictions of, among others, a U.S. senator, a congressman, the county executives of Anne Arundel and Baltimore Counties, the Baltimore County state's attorney, a state senator from Baltimore, the speaker of the Maryland House of Delegates, and another state delegate who was arrested by U.S. marshals after being physically flushed out at the State House in Annapolis.

George Beall, the U.S. attorney in Baltimore in 1973, was a lifelong Republican whose brother, J. Glenn Beall Jr., had defeated Democrat Joe Tydings for a U.S. Senate seat in the 1970 midterm elections. Agnew had campaigned for Senator Beall.[26] But by early 1973 it was well known among Maryland pols that George Beall's office was investigating kickbacks in Baltimore County with the goal of indicting Dale Anderson, a Democrat and Agnew's successor as county executive in Towson.[27] Richard Cohen, who covered Annapolis for the *Washington Post*, recalled: "It was clear to some people that if they were squeezing Anderson then they were going to get Agnew. In retrospect now you wonder how anybody got away with it because thousands of people knew what was going on. You can't have gotten all these bribes and shaken everyone down for all these years . . . but everybody had a vested interest in keeping it quiet or limited.[28]

Agnew first heard about the possibility that he was under federal investigation in February 1973 from his personal lawyer George White, who telephoned him as he was returning from a diplomatic trip to Southeast Asia.[29] Nixon, for his part, maintained that he was at least peripherally aware of Agnew's legal troubles by April 1973. By the end of July, however, Richardson had informed the president's chief of staff, Alexander Haig, that "he had never seen such a cut and dried case. Agnew was potentially indictable on more than 40 counts."[30] The U.S. Attorney's Office in Baltimore had gathered the sworn testimony of multiple people close to Agnew's extracurricular activities who attested to his crimes. Together they painted a clear picture that as county executive, as governor, and even as vice president Agnew had received "substantial cash payments in return for engineering contracts with the State of Maryland."[31]

The government's case, which would become public at Agnew's court hearing as part of the vice president's plea bargain, outlined the details of the kickbacks. Payments had started in the mid-1960s when Agnew was still county executive and continued until after the 1972 election, with cash drops occurring even in Agnew's office in the Old Executive Office Building near the White House. Lester Matz, an executive in a large engineering firm, initially paid 5 percent of his fees from his Baltimore County contracts in cash to go-betweens who would ferry the money to Agnew.

Matz sometimes paid him directly while Agnew was governor. He testified that he gave Agnew more cash while he was vice president, sliding
the bills across a table in an envelope for work that included contracts
from Maryland and also for possible work with the federal government.
The state's case also benefited from two other trusted Agnew supporters who flipped for the feds. Jerome Wolff and I. H. "Bud" Hammerman
had served as Agnew's bagmen, often splitting the bribes (50 percent for
Agnew and 25 percent each for Wolff and Hammerman) collected from
multiple engineering firms looking to work on state roads or, in at least
one example, a financial institution seeking to fund a state bond. Hammerman was one of Agnew's primary donors, and Wolff became Agnew's
director of the state roads commission. Both outlined the scheme at least
in part to save their own necks. Wolff also turned over "detailed con-
temporaneous documents on which he recorded the dates, amounts, and
engineering firm sources of the monies . . . as his share of the proceeds of
the scheme."[32] The plan was unsophisticated and included code words to
let Agnew know when the bribes were ready to be delivered.[33] State firms
that complained about the kickbacks had their share of work reduced
but not entirely cut off "for fear of further exacerbating the situation."[34]
The cash payments continued to Agnew through December 1972 and
ranged between two thousand and twenty thousand dollars. According
to the testimony of Allen Green, another official at a large engineering
firm who turned state's evidence, payments were made at his vice presidential office and at his residence at the Sheraton Park Hotel in Washington, D.C., for possible federal contracts as well.[35] This led one prosecuting
U.S. attorney to exclaim, "Agnew wasn't greedy; he was quite cheap."[36]

Agnew's need for walking-around money was a personal concern that
he made plain to Matz and the others. He viewed the vice presidency as
a "continuing financial burden" and said that "although his salary as Vice
President would be higher than his salary as Governor, he expected that
the social and other demands of the office would substantially increase
his personal expenses."[37] As a politician who had risen through the ranks
at an incredible speed and without family money or significant outside
investments, he was in fact a pauper by comparison to many of his colleagues and actually lived off his government paycheck. But that didn't

justify the bribes or make them legal. Richardson told Nixon in August that the witnesses were believable and in some cases had irrefutable documents showing that the payments had continued through the vice presidential years.[38]

Elliot Richardson's professional background and standing were sources of high agitation for both Agnew and Nixon. He was everything they were not: wealthy, highly educated, and well connected. Richardson's family had been in New England for generations. After prep school at Milton he had gone on to Harvard. He won a Purple Heart for heroism on the beaches at Normandy, then returned from Europe and tore through his resume, graduating from Harvard Law School, clerking for Supreme Court justice Felix Frankfurter, and serving with distinction as a U.S. attorney, attorney general, and lieutenant governor of Massachusetts. He had publicly opposed Agnew's nomination at the 1968 Republican National Convention and spoke up against him on domestic issues in cabinet meetings. Richardson was well regarded by the press and the Washington establishment and may have had his own presidential aspirations.[39] Agnew recalled Nixon slamming him as "that little Ivy League pipsqueak s.o.b."[40] David Keene, one of Agnew's top political aides, believed that Richardson disdained Agnew from the start: "The fact of the matter was that if you put yourself in the position of a Brahmin from Massachusetts, as he was and is, and think about his political career and then you have him look at Spiro Agnew, he would be disgusted by Agnew—before he knew what Agnew did or didn't do. This is a group of people who wouldn't hire the Irish, let alone a bunch of Greeks."[41]

Richardson served a critical purpose in the Nixon administration, however. During Nixon's second term, and under almost constant fire over Watergate and its aftermath, the Bostonian had emerged as a solid and honest jack-of-all-trades. In the first Nixon administration he had been undersecretary of state and later headed the Department of Health, Education, and Welfare. Nixon then appointed him secretary of defense at the start of his second term, needing a respected voice on his troubled Vietnam policy, but Richardson would serve only four months. As it turned out Nixon needed him even more as a quickly confirmable and consensus choice for attorney general to replace Richard Kleindienst, who resigned in April 1973. Much like George H. W. Bush, who would also serve Nixon in multiple high-profile roles, Richardson fit the part. He staked out his judicial independence even before he was confirmed as the new attorney general in May. While awaiting U.S. Senate approval, Richardson willingly tied the appointment of Archibald Cox as the Watergate special prosecutor to his own nomination as the nation's top lawyer. Richardson gave Cox a broad mandate to follow the evidence wherever it might lead and pointedly invited him to his Senate Judiciary Committee confirmation hearings.[42]

Richardson had much in common with George Beall, Maryland's U.S. attorney. Both came from Revolutionary War–era families that had strong political connections to their home states. Beall's father had been a U.S. senator, and his brother, J. Glenn Beall Jr., was serving as a senator from Maryland during the Agnew investigation.[43] Beall had a pedigree as well. Educated at Princeton and the University of Virginia Law School, he had clerked for the chief judge of the U.S. Court of Appeals for the Fourth Circuit. While a staunch member of Maryland's minority Republican Party, Beall was a different kind of Republican than Agnew. Moderate and carefully spoken, he had the loyalty of his staff, many of who were Democrats.[44] One of the assistant U.S. attorneys, Barnett Skolnik, recalled: "The bottom line is, we took [the Agnew case] to George [Beall] and he said: 'Fellas, do what you have to do. Keep me posted on a more or less daily basis. But you've got a green light. Take it wherever the evidence takes you.' He said what he should have said. We didn't care that Agnew was a Republican, but we were concerned it could be shut down for political reasons."[45]

Agnew worked hard to find bias or partisan political reasons for his prosecution during the late summer and early fall of 1973 as word began to leak out of the Department of Justice that the vice president was in legal trouble. On August 7 the story broke with banner headlines in major newspapers.[46] Republican leaders were speechless. Bush, then the National Committee chair, refused to comment, as did Rogers Morton, Agnew's Maryland political ally who was serving as secretary of the interior.[47] Newspaper articles followed, extolling Beall and his assistant U.S. attorneys for upholding a bold tradition of aggressive prosecution of corruption.[48] Other press reports focused on Maryland as rife with political sleaziness.[49] By the end of August the leaks had become more specific to the investigation, and the FBI, at Agnew's request, undertook an internal investigation to find the source(s).[50] In a rare late-summer sit-down with Nixon, Agnew tried to explain his side of the story. Hoping to appeal to the president's own ordeal in the 1952 election that culminated in the famous Checkers speech, Agnew told Nixon that the case against him involved campaign contributions that had been used to help meet "expenses legitimately incurred by him and his family in their public roles." He argued that the contractors were all well qualified and that there had been no quid pro quo involved. He heatedly denied having received money while he was vice president. Agnew complained about the methods of the Baltimore prosecutors and said that they were trying to "track down everything he had ever bought, and every detail of his personal life."[51] At one point he told the president that he supposed the IRS would be harassing him the rest of his life, saying, "You know, they were even charting up how much I paid for my neckties."[52] A letter from Beall to Agnew's lawyer in August 1973 asked for "all bank statements, cancelled checks, check vouchers, check stubs, check books, deposit books . . . for any and all checking and savings accounts in the United States and elsewhere . . . for the period of January 1, 1967 to the present."[53] The prosecutors were indeed scouring Agnew's professional and personal expenses.

In some of the secondary literature about the investigation there are shaded paragraphs about Agnew's gifts to at least one paramour that were uncovered by the federal investigators and that would have been potentially devastating to his public and private lives.[54] The early 1970s were still on the other side of a fault line when it came to how the press and the political world dealt with marital infidelity by public figures, although the rules were starting to change. Presidents Lyndon Johnson and John F. Kennedy had only recently been given a relatively free pass on the issue. The exposure of Watergate, the Pentagon Papers, and the outing of more private issues of elected leaders had broken new ground in media-political relations during the 1972 campaign, including the disclosure of Tom Eagleton's use of shock therapy, which cost him a place on the ticket. But airing the infidelity of a politician who had publicly preached family values at the expense of a jilted spouse was still a decade and a half away.[55] Investigators, however, had the goods on Agnew's purchases of gifts, including jewelry and a foreign sports car, for a mistress with whom "he had been carrying on for some time" and who was a "regular member of his traveling party."[56] In his book about the Secret Service Ronald Kessler recounted the embarrassment of agents who "felt like pimps" for the vice president.[57]

Agnew had cultivated a public image of rectitude that would have been shattered by credible reports that he had taken kickbacks and used them to buy gifts for a woman who was not his wife. As Garry Wills pointed out in *Nixon Agonistes*, when Nixon laid out his reasons for choosing Agnew to run with him in 1968, the third item on the list was that he was a family man.[58] Agnew never made any mention of extramarital affairs in his memoirs and the prosecutors ruled the topic "out of bounds," but journalists and historians who have studied the investigation believe that it likely played a role in his abrupt decision to resign from office.[59]

By late summer 1973 Agnew and his lawyers recognized that he was in deep legal trouble. Agnew wrote of the investigation: "From the very outset, Richardson treated me, not as the Vice President of the United States, but as a criminal."[60] He quickly realized that the White House was not going to bail him out of his predicament. Nixon decided to let his attorney general continue to pursue the case against Agnew, explaining in his memoirs that he faced the dilemma of eroding his already crumbling credibility by defending his wounded vice president or risking the alienation of Agnew's staunch supporters by staying neutral. He chose the latter.[61]

Nixon answered questions about Agnew's viability as vice president in a press conference in early October. With body language that did not connote confidence, he said that whether Agnew resigned or not, "this was a matter for [Agnew] to decide" and that he ought to be given at least the presumption of innocence.[62] But inside the Department of Justice the case against the vice president continued to strengthen. William Ruckelshaus, the deputy attorney general, recalled: "The case was overwhelming, and got worse and worse for [Agnew] the longer it went on. We took the point of view of devil's advocate in the Justice Department; we tried to make sure that the witnesses were absolutely impenetrable—that their stories held up. We used lie detector tests and all kinds of ways of trying to break them down, just to be sure that we weren't unjustly accusing the vice-president, and their stories just continued to strengthen."[63]

Agnew privately vacillated between resigning, fighting the charges, or asking Congress to try to impeach him in what would likely be a protracted battle. Arizona senator Barry Goldwater was one of the last Republicans who might have been able to save Agnew's political career. Goldwater instinctively mistrusted Nixon's politics and secret dealings, and he saw the vice president as his closest ally and most important ideological fellow traveler in the White House. He instinctively took Agnew's side of the kickback story seriously, again illuminating the vice president's importance to the right wing of the Republican Party, which saw him as their possible standard-bearer in 1976. Visiting Agnew at his home in Chevy Chase, Maryland, on September 9, Goldwater found the vice president "puzzled and angry." He counseled Agnew not to tell the White House about his idea to approach Speaker of the House Carl Albert for congressional hearings on the allegations against him. He also questioned why Nixon allowed his own attorney general to go after his vice president without hearing Agnew's version of things.[64] Goldwater empathized with Agnew's explanation and later wrote, "Every politician must accept campaign contributions. The giver usually wants to hand the donation to the candidate in person. Before the passage of the [post-Watergate] campaign regulations most of these donations were made in cash. No reports were required, and no records were kept."[65] When the two men met again in the middle of September, Agnew told Goldwater that Nixon (via Alexander Haig) had asked him to resign and had also quashed his gambit to go to the House of Representatives and ask for an impeachment trial.[66] Nixon, fearing that Goldwater might publicly support Agnew's cause and thus muck up the impending deal to remove the vice president from office, sent two top aides to Phoenix to brief him in greater detail about the charges against Agnew.[67] After hearing the government's case Goldwater backed off.

The vice president fulminated publicly against the U.S. attorneys, the press, and the leaks about his case until the bitter end. Only days before his plea bargain he rallied the faithful at a speech in Los Angeles where two thousand Republican women interrupted him with applause thirty-two times. Agnew defiantly announced: "I want to say at this point—clearly and unequivocally—I am innocent of the charges against me. . . . I have not used my office, nor abused my public trust as County Executive, as Governor, or as Vice President to enrich myself at the expense of my fellow Americans. . . . I will not resign if indicted."[68] But he also knew that any hope of running for president in 1976 was out.[69] In a last-ditch effort he went to individual members of the House of Representatives who supported the idea of congressional hearings into the charges against him. Led by two Republicans from silent majority territory, Sam Devine of Ohio and Bill Dickinson of Alabama, they got responses from about a hundred members about a breakfast meeting to come to the vice president's defense.[70] But the writing was already on the wall. The meeting was abruptly cancelled, and Spiro Agnew became the first vice president to resign from office since John Calhoun in 1832. All that was left were the formalities and the final acts.

The last meeting between Nixon and Agnew on October 9, 1973, was by all accounts a sad, forced, and bitter encounter that highlighted what little rapport the running mates had with each other even after two national campaigns and almost five years together. Nixon described the meeting with faux sympathy in 1978, saying, "I knew his decision had been very difficult for him."[71]

Agnew's account of the final meeting, written seven years after the fact, was equally strained. He made himself out to be a naïve and loyal soldier taking one for the team and duped by a two-faced Nixon: "I looked at the President, his face gaunt and sorrowful. It was hard to believe he was not genuinely sorry about the course of events. Within two days, this consummate actor would be celebrating his appointment of a new Vice President with never a thought of me. . . . My eyes filled at his solicitous words. . . . I felt no rancor toward Mr. Nixon, only a heavy, burdening sadness. I was about to let a lot of people down."[72] According to Nixon, Agnew asked him for some kind of foreign assignment to soften the blow of his resignation. Assessing the gravity of the charges against him and his limited ability to make a living as a disgraced former vice president who was likely to be disbarred, Agnew gloomily asked Nixon if he could help him "get some corporation to put him on a retainer as a consultant."[73] The two men would never speak again, although Agnew grudgingly attended Nixon's funeral in 1994.

As part of a carefully choreographed script between Agnew's lawyers and the Department of Justice, the vice president submitted a tersely written resignation on October 10, 1973, at 2:05 p.m. to Secretary of State Henry Kissinger. At precisely the same time Agnew arrived at the federal courthouse in Baltimore, where he "strode briskly into the courtroom. He was dressed impeccably, as always, in a perfectly pressed blue suit and blue and tan striped tie, his graying hair slicked neatly back off his tanned but now thin and tight lipped face. There were murmurs as he made his unannounced entrance."[74] Agnew's resignation was relayed directly to U.S. District Court judge Walter Hoffman, who was presiding over a hearing that spectators and observing press thought was going to address the question of newspaper leaks. Hoffman told the stunned audience to refrain from disturbances, forbade anyone from leaving the courtroom during the proceeding, and had the U.S. marshals lock the doors.[75] As Cohen and Witcover wrote, "Each time the judge addressed him in the next few minutes, Agnew would stand, reply, and sit down again. It was a humiliation, a visible ebbing of power."[76]

In exchange for the government agreeing not to pursue jail time, Agnew had to resign from office and accept a judgment of conviction of a felony. He pled no contest to tax evasion. Hoffman admonished the newly private citizen that "a plea of *nolo contendere* is, insofar as this criminal proceeding is concerned today, the full equivalent to a plea of guilty." He asked Agnew if he understood the consequences of the plea agreement, and he responded positively.[77] Attorney General Richardson then addressed the court to spell out the plea agreement, which he argued must be perceived as "just and honorable, not simply to the parties but above all to the American people." Richardson pulled no punches about what the evidence had established: "a pattern of substantial cash payments to the defendant" in exchange for engineering contracts throughout Agnew's political career. He noted that the government could have pressed forward with an indictment on bribery and extortion charges, but that it would have "likely inflict[ed] upon the Nation serious and permanent scars . . . with potentially disastrous consequences to vital interests of the United States. Confidence in the adequacy of our fundamental institutions would have been put to severe trial."[78]

Agnew spoke next. He echoed Richardson's assessment that "intense media interest in the case would distract public attention from national problems—to the country's detriment." He then admitted that he had received payments in 1967 that were taxable and that he did not declare them on his federal or state returns. He denied other "assertions of illegal acts on my part made by government witnesses." He said that he knew state contracts had been given to those who made payments to him, but that "no contracts were awarded to contractors who were not competent to perform the work and in most instances state contracts were awarded without any arrangement for the payment of money by the contractor." He again denied that the payments influenced his decision-making and said that "at no time have I enriched myself at the expense of the public trust."[79]

It then was Hoffman's turn. He noted that in prior sentencing cases for tax evasion when the defendant was a lawyer, he had fined and imprisoned the offender for up to five months "as a deterrent to others who are required to file their returns." But given the attorney general's recommendation, Hoffman handed down a three-year suspended sentence and a ten thousand dollar fine.[80] Agnew left the courthouse, pushing his way through reporters and cameras. He drove directly to Randallstown, Maryland, where he met the rest of his family and attended the burial of his half brother, who had died a few days before. At the wake, Agnew confessed later, he wanted to say to those in attendance, "Stop staring at me. I'm not a freak on display. I'm a human being, just as you are, and I don't want my hurt to be examined so clinically."[81] He ate dinner later that night at Sabatino's, a favorite Italian restaurant in Baltimore, where he ordered linguini with clam sauce, garlic bread, salad, and a sirloin strip steak, along with red wine.[82]

Agnew's friends and colleagues were stunned by the sudden turn of events. Pat Buchanan, his wordsmith and muse, was caught completely unaware and called Haig, who told him, "We've got [Agnew] taking envelopes in the basement."[83] Ronald Reagan, then governor of California, said, "Ted Agnew was and is a friend of mine" and that he was "shocked and saddened as I am sure all Americans are." Democrat Daniel Inouye of Hawaii, who was also a member of the Senate Watergate Committee, said, "Everything is so unreal. I've got to go and straighten myself out."[84] Staffers were equally dumbfounded. The vice president's secretary Lisa Brown told the *Washington Post*, "People were calling over the phone and crying and saying it can't be true."[85] Even in Agnew's father's birthplace in Greece, where the vice president had made a triumphant visit two years before, Agnew's cousin Andreas Anagnostopoulos acknowledged, "It is a sad blow for us, for the family and for the village."[86]

The silent majority Americans who assumed Agnew would fight until the end wrote letters to his office. Leonard Job of Lakeland, Florida, penned a note in mid-October: "I have unbounded faith in you, and I still do regardless of the fact that you are no longer Vice President." Carolyn O'Brien of Hayesville, North Carolina, wrote: "We conservatives were not voting for Nixon, so much as for Agnew. . . . [H]ad you stayed and this mess not come up, you'd have been our next President." Etta Paxton from Wenatchee, Washington, stated: "This is just a note to say I am still backing you. . . . You have more backing out here in the hinterland than you may think." George Gillespie, president of Indiana Christian University in Indianapolis, dejectedly wrote: "We shall always remember you, Mr. Vice President, as our loyal, fearless and beloved leader."[87] But events quickly overtook Agnew's resignation, and he was soon yesterday's news. After briefly exploring the idea of naming John Connally to replace Agnew, Nixon appointed House Minority Leader Gerald Ford. The Yom Kippur War between Israel and a coalition of Arab states, which had started only a few days before Agnew's plea bargain, took over the headlines. And just ten days after Richardson stood in Hoffman's courtroom and made his case against Agnew, the attorney general also resigned his position, but on principle, for defying Nixon's order that he fire Watergate special prosecutor Archibald Cox.

The system functioned appropriately in the legal case of Spiro Agnew. Richardson, Hoffmann, and Maryland's U.S. attorney, George Beall, deserve special commendation for their courage and conviction in following the evidence to its logical conclusion. All three were loyal Republicans. And while certainly some thought that justice had not been appropriately served because Agnew skipped jail time and copped a plea, the majority of the public seemed to perceive the former vice president as a chastened and guilty man. His political career and his legacy had been shredded, and his resignation also may have opened the door for a speedier resolution to the scandal that ultimately truncated Nixon's second term.

Nixon originally thought that pushing Agnew out might satisfy some of his critics by removing the Watergate spotlight from the White House. Goldwater certainly believed that making Agnew a sacrificial lamb was Nixon's major motivation in letting the attorney general take him down. But green-lighting Agnew's resignation without a fight may have undermined Nixon's own position. In his memoirs Nixon drew the lesson that "all [Agnew's resignation] did was to open the way to put pressure on the President to resign as well. This is something we have to realize: that any accommodation with opponents in this kind of fight does not satisfy—it only brings demands for more."[88] Democratic congressional leaders agreed. Massachusetts congressman Tip O'Neill told his colleague Peter Rodino, chair of the House committee that oversaw Nixon's impeachment hearings: "By copping a plea and resigning, Spiro has done the country a great service. He has cleared the deck for the impeachment of Richard Nixon."[89] Agnew had been an unbeknownst insurance policy for the White House because some of Nixon's enemies viewed his possible elevation as an even worse outcome than an outright presidential impeachment. With Agnew gone the path was now clear for Nixon's ouster ten months later.

The week after he resigned Agnew appeared on national television and radio to read a rambling description of the "matters related to my resignation that are misunderstood." In tortured reasoning he explained that absent impeachment or forcing the court to try to indict a sitting vice president, resigning and pleading no contest was his only option. He argued that his resignation preempted any chance of a fair legal fight against the charges levied against him. His logic was that because he left office voluntarily, he carried a presumption of guilt sufficient to prevent his own defense on the merits of the case. The media bore the brunt of his criticism. In his opinion he was driven from office by attacks that were "increased by daily publication of the wildest rumor and speculation, much of it bearing no resemblance to the information being given the prosecutors." Maybe more to the point of the journalists and historians who thought Agnew accepted the plea deal to save his marriage, he noted: "By taking the course of the *nolo* plea I've spared my family great anguish."[90]

Only weeks short of being eligible for his federal pension, Agnew continued to commute from his suburban Maryland home to an office across the street from the White House for the next couple of months. He answered letters and lunched at local haunts with his staff.[91] His pal Frank Sinatra, whom he would later describe as a special friend in "a bracket of one," loaned him money to pay off his court fees and to use for living expenses.[92] In his responses to citizens from around the country who wrote to him, he played the victim and proclaimed, "I can only reaffirm my innocence to you and hope, in this complex and confusing situation, that you will try to understand that I believe the actions I have taken are in the best interest of the Nation."[93]

Before Thanksgiving 1973 the former vice president hosted a thank-you party for his staff at his home, where he and Judy greeted guests at the door and amiably served food and drink. Agnew even played the piano at the end of the evening.[94] For the first few months after his resignation he continued to live a pretend life as a powerful politician. Nixon had ordered six months of Secret Service protection as Agnew figured out his next career move and how he would provide for his family.[95] Making a living was going to take some creativity; Agnew was soon disbarred in a unanimous decision of Maryland's highest court, which found that "it is difficult to feel compassion for an attorney who is so morally obtuse that he consciously cheats for his own pecuniary gain that government he has sworn to serve."[96] Politically dead, Agnew began to reinvent himself as an international lobbyist, a connector for American businesses in the global world of petroleum and political strongmen, and as an author and a bon vivant with famous friends and residences in California and Maryland.

With his Rolodex and name recognition Agnew began to jet around the world trying to open doors for business clients looking for access to the Middle East and Asia. In the first years after his resignation he was spotted at dinner with legendary baseball manager Leo Durocher at Tiberio in Washington and in a prime seat at a Sinatra concert at Merriweather Post Pavilion in suburban Maryland. Occasionally he dashed off letters to the editors of the *Washington Post* and the *Baltimore Sun* when he felt personally maligned, but Agnew initially stayed away from reporters and interviews. Unlike Nixon's post-Watergate life, his occasional visits to Washington were usually below the media's radar. His small company, Pathlite, was based in a Baltimore suburb and funded with seed money from a squirrely businessman with whom he soon had an acrimonious falling-out. Life moved on. The Agnews sold their house in Maryland's suburbs and started splitting their time between Southern California and a more modest dwelling near Annapolis.[97]

Agnew's career took an odd turn not long after he left Washington as he improbably tried his hand at writing fiction. Composing dialogue while on the planes that took him around the world on business, he penned a novel titled *The Canfield Decision*, dedicated to Judy and published in 1976 by Playboy Press. The public relations sheet for "The Story Behind the Book" quoted the new author:

> It was a rude shock. One minute I was a secure Vice President with a clear field for the presidential nomination and then suddenly I was out. Details of the very unusual circumstances will have to wait until I write the whole story. But anyhow, there I was—returned to civilian life without any pension, without any means of livelihood, even unable to practice law . . . trials were still going on, so publication of the memoir would have to wait. The idea of writing a novel occurred to me. I realized that I had an unusual qualification, one possessed by only a few living people—an intimate knowledge of the Vice President of the United States.[98]

The novel focused on a fictional vice president named Porter Canfield who was cheating on his wife and later charged with conspiracy and murder. Written with an eye toward a Hollywood movie option, some of the prose departed from Agnew's political reputation as a wholesome voice of the silent majority: "In the rhythmic twisting and pulsing of the next fifteen minutes, he was conscious only of disjointed impressions: the little animal cries from Meredith; the carefully folded brocade bedspread on the side; the slight creaking of the bed as he reached a crescendo. Then his own flurry of endearments and groan of release during the rocketing to a delicious peak before plunging ecstatically into awareness of every vibrating curve."[99] At another point Agnew discussed the merits of French red wines: "As the dinner entered the salad course, Canfield sipped his third glass of Chateau Margaux appreciatively. One good thing about a President's second term, he reflected, was that California wines were not served all the time."[100] It was a long way from communing with Middle America.

The Canfield Decision sold reasonably well and even got some decent reviews. Economist John Kenneth Galbraith implausibly assessed it in the *New York Times* and complimented the new novelist by saying that while it was not great literature, "I can say that his book has one hell of a plot."[101] The *Harvard Crimson* was less charitable, snorting that the novel "leads one to believe that Agnew's career as a writer will be about as successful as his career as a politician. There is no question that the book would have remained unpublished if anyone else had written it."[102] Agnew sent *The Canfield Decision* to many of his would-be business opportunities, trying to ingratiate himself as a person of importance.[103] He also made a run at Hollywood, using Frank Sinatra's lawyer in Beverly Hills, Mickey Rudin, as a go-between with producers. A return letter from Carl Foreman, who had written the initial script for *The Bridge on the River Kwai* and was then at Warner Brothers, gave the studio's response to *The Canfield Decision:* "I doubt that it is picture material, for many reasons, but especially at this time. While this will no doubt be a disappointment to Mr. Agnew, I am sure the book is selling well and I hope that its reception has been a source of pleasure to him."[104]

On his book tour in the spring and summer of 1976 Agnew received broad national exposure for the first time since his resignation almost three years earlier. And he soon found himself in hot water with the media and political leaders over passages in the book that bordered on conspiratorial anti-Semitism. Israel and the Jewish lobby figured prominently in the novel, and there were several eyebrow-raising sections. Describing the audience at a speech given by his protagonist, for example, he wrote: "The applause was courteous, but hardly thunderous. After all, less than 15 percent of the crowd was Jewish. Down at the press table, where less than 15 percent was not Jewish, the reaction was ecstatic."[105]

In an interview with Barbara Walters on *Today*, Agnew was asked to discuss a section of his book where the characters talk about a Jewish cabal and Zionist influence on American life. He responded bluntly: "I do feel that the Zionist influences in the United States are dragging the US into a rather disorganized approach to the Middle East problem . . . and I feel that because of the Zionist influences in the United States [Israel's] aggression is routinely considered to be permissible." When pushed by Walters, Agnew concluded, "I think the media are sympathetic to the Zionist cause, put it that way."[106]

A week later on *Panorama*, a local Washington news program hosted by Maury Povich, Agnew went even further:

> I don't think there's any question that population-wise, the ratio of American Jews to the US population is infinitesimal compared to the representation of the American Jewish community in the news media. And all you have to do is look at the big organs. You look at *The New York Times*, owned by the Sulzbergers, *The Washington Post*, owned by Mrs. Graham—and you go straight through the networks to see who's in control in many cases—Mr. Goodman, NBC. And I could name literally hundreds of American Jews who are in high positions of policy making in the media.[107]

Gerald Ford, now president, and the leading Democratic candidates in the upcoming 1976 election immediately called Agnew out. Former press secretary Vic Gold and former speechwriter William Safire also took him to task. Safire said: "He has confessed he cheated on his taxes. It wasn't the national-impact media or any Zionist conspiracy that brought him down: it was only the law. Frustrated and vengeful, he has become what we all once took some joy in deriding, a nattering nabob of negativism." Editorial pages around the country chimed in, even from deep within the parts of the country where Agnew was once perceived as a hero. The *Lincoln (Nebraska) Star* opined: "Agnew either is suffering the same strain of paranoia that led to the Holocaust or he is speaking in behalf of his Arab business clients."[108]

Looking for a lifeline, Agnew reached out to former Jewish colleagues and friends for public support. Stanley Fine, who worked as Agnew's volunteer driver during the 1966 gubernatorial campaign and went on to become director of the Maryland State Lottery, received a letter from his former boss that appealed to his "sense of fair play. . . . I believe that you are aware that I am no more anti-semitic than hundreds of American Jews who oppose the Zionist idea."[109] Fine said the letter "totally infuriated me."[110] Agnew did find support from former speechwriter Pat Buchanan, who opined in his syndicated column that the American Jewish community had badly over-reached and was using McCarthyite tactics to intimidate the former vice president. Buchanan, who would later lay claim to Agnew's political heritage in his own three runs for president, justified his support by stating that "to be anti-Israeli on these issues is no more to be anti-Semitic than to oppose forced busing, quotas and scatter-site housing is to be anti-black."[111]

Agnew stayed away from Republican Party politics and the 1976 campaign, and the feeling was mutual. After Nixon appointed him vice president, Ford had quickly cleaned out Agnew's staff. As president he had made a special effort to reach out to Republican liberals, like Charles Goodell of New York, that Agnew had helped defeat in 1970, and he also picked Nelson Rockefeller to serve as his vice president.[112]

After Agnew's book tour ended in the summer of 1976, he went back to work developing his modest international lobbying work and started writing his memoirs. *Go Quietly . . . or Else* was published in 1980 by William Morrow and dedicated to Frank Sinatra. The book focused on Agnew's waning days as vice president and heaped scorn on the press, Elliot Richardson, the U.S. attorneys in Baltimore, and the White House staff. Alexander Haig, Nixon's chief of staff, drew particular contempt for his perceived threats of what the government would do to Agnew if he chose not to resign. Haig told him that Nixon would publicly turn against him if he chose to fight the bribery charges, Agnew claimed. Haig also supposedly said the White House would not help in Agnew's defense or in any post-political career if he chose to go against the attorney general. Even more ominous, according to Agnew, was that Haig had dangled the possibility that Judy Agnew might be prosecuted as well because their tax returns were filed jointly. Haig had warned him that "anything may be in the offing," Agnew wrote, and that "the President has a lot of power—don't forget that," implying that the Nixon White House might have done him bodily harm if he hadn't acquiesced to the Department of Justice.[113] *Go Quietly* was met with a collective yawn. The *Christian Science Monitor* said it was "a book for anyone who wants to reopen the pages of the Agnew affair of seven years ago. But few probably will. . . . Altogether, it's a little too hard to believe."[114]

Ironically, *Go Quietly* took Agnew down an unexpected avenue that would eventually support a $250,000 civil judgment against him. The suit was filed by three Maryland taxpayers who requested that the state be restituted for the $147,500 (plus interest) in bribes that Agnew took while governor. In his memoirs Agnew recounted a conversation with his lawyer George White where he denied taking kickbacks. "The money didn't go to me personally," he wrote.[115] White, now legally freed from attorney-client privilege because Agnew had disclosed the conversation in the book, testified that Agnew had in fact admitted the bribery and also had told him that it had been going on "for a thousand years." Agnew invoked his Fifth Amendment rights against self-incrimination and went down without much of a fight. The *New York Times* editorialized that the civil suit "should put an end to Mr. Agnew's nattering negations of guilt. . . . The country has stronger proof than ever that it was right to get Spiro Agnew out of Washington."[116] The Maryland Court of Appeals upheld the lower court's decision, and Agnew made restitution with interest to the taxpayers. David Scull, a public interest lawyer and one of those who filed the suit, and who also served in the House of Delegates, pointed out that the case coincided with the state's progress in returning ethics to government in Annapolis.[117]

Even in the Reagan White House of the 1980s, Agnew was persona non grata. The two men had developed a warm relationship during the time Agnew was in national politics. At the 1968 Republican National Convention, when Nixon surprised the party faithful by naming the improbable Agnew to be his running mate, Reagan had praised his fellow governor.[118] Ronald and Nancy Reagan welcomed the Agnews to the governor's mansion in Sacramento the following year.[119] But Reagan, who would elevate Agnew's speechwriter Pat Buchanan to communications director in his White House in the mid-1980s, had no use for Agnew during his two terms as president. Nor is there any indication that Agnew sought rehabilitation from Reagan.

Agnew assiduously avoided Nixon during the 1980s, despite living half the year in Rancho Mirage, California, only a couple of hours from San Clemente, where Nixon wrote his memoirs and lived until late in life. Agnew purposely skipped a Palm Springs golf event with Bob Hope, Frank Sinatra, and Ronald Reagan in order to avoid having to talk to Nixon.[120] He refused to take the former president's calls, despite several attempts at communication, because he "felt totally abandoned [by Nixon]."[121] The Agnews also lived just minutes away from Gerald and Betty Ford in California during the 1980s and '90s. But in a series of interviews published after his death in 2006, Ford recalled: "In the fourteen years we've been here in Palm Springs or the desert, I've run into [Agnew] three times—twice at a party at Barbara and Frank Sinatra's. . . . I ran into him once in a golf locker room [and] we exchanged cordial chitchat. Betty has run into Judy [Agnew] several times at the shopping center. We just have nothing in common."[122]

Public sightings of the former vice president were few and far between. In 1987 Agnew appeared as a plaintiff in Federal District Court in Brooklyn, New York, filing suit against an Argentine entity and its American offshoot. Agnew claimed the American company owed him two million dollars for services rendered. The defendants dared Agnew to sue them, arguing that "nobody would believe" the former vice president because of his previous record of corruption. The case offered a glimpse into Agnew's line of work. As the plaintiff in the case Agnew contended that his contacts with the Argentine military junta had produced a large telecom contract with the Argentine Air Force for an American corporation and its subsidiary in Argentina.[123] In court documents Agnew stated that his first visit to Argentina had been in 1980, when he discussed setting up a concert by his friend Frank Sinatra. Agnew described his job as "working for corporations who do business in other countries, to assist them in obtaining contracts." He added, "I have one utility and that's the ability to penetrate to the top people." Under questioning by lawyers for the defense, Agnew offered up the off-topic opinion that Marxists controlled the Nobel Peace Prize committee and dusted off the old complaint of "a left-wing dominance in the United States media and the liberal establishment."[124] Agnew's other clients throughout the 1980s included a German aircraft manufacturer, a South Korean multinational, a French manufacturer of military uniforms, and a Greek dredging company. He also steered American telecom companies to contracts in Taiwan and Saudi Arabia. Agnew's work with the Argentine military was not his only foray into the world of unsavory dictators. He served as a middleman between Iraq's Saddam Hussein and Nicolae Ceausescu of Romania in an arrangement to provide uniforms for the Iraqi military.[125]

Agnew made news again in 1989 when he claimed that he was entitled to a tax deduction from the state of California for the penalty he paid to the state of Maryland in 1982 as part of the restitution for bribes he collected as governor. Although Agnew lost the case he was clearly living well, reporting more than six hundred thousand dollars in wages, incomes, and dividends on his tax returns.[126]

Before he died at the age of seventy-seven in 1996, Agnew made two more public appearances that caught national attention. When Richard Nixon passed away in 1994 he was torn about whether or not to attend the funeral. He eventually accepted the invitation of Nixon's daughters to the service, where many of his old colleagues were present.[127] In CNN's three-and-a-half-hour coverage of the funeral, Nixon's running mate appeared on camera several times but never in the company of the other political luminaries in the audience. CNN anchor Judy Woodruff commented over one shot of the former vice president, "He looks pretty much the same." Correspondent Bruce Morton added, "It's almost the first time anyone has seen him. He really disappeared."[128]

Before Agnew actually disappeared, a white marble bust of him was unveiled in the U.S. Capitol in 1995, thus maintaining the tradition of honoring the vice president, who concurrently serves as president of the

Senate. More than three hundred people, including family, friends, and former staffers, attended the unveiling ceremony, as well as about a dozen U.S. senators. Pat Buchanan and Tricia Nixon Cox, one of the former president's daughters, also attended. The half-hour ceremony, presided over by Republican senator Ted Stevens of Alaska, was awkward. Republican Bob Dole of Kansas, the Senate majority leader who was getting ready to run for president, gave short and carefully worded remarks. Senator Daniel Patrick Moynihan, who had served in the Nixon administration and was now representing New York as a Democrat, cited Agnew's Greek heritage and war service. Moynihan aptly noted his "impassioned beliefs. . . . In a tempestuous time, he was a strong partisan voice, but we would do well to remember that his was not the only [one]." Agnew admitted he was nervous and acknowledged the tension by "remind[ing] those people that, regardless of their personal view of me, this ceremony has less to do with Spiro Agnew than with the office I held, an honor conferred on me by the American people two decades ago."[129] In Maryland, Governor Parris Glendening found Agnew's gubernatorial portrait in storage and returned it to a place of honor in the State House next to his successor in Annapolis, Marvin Mandel.[130] Agnew did not return for that ceremony, but Glendening called him in California and reported that the former vice president "had wondered if he would be restored to his place in history in his lifetime."[131]

Agnew died a little more than a year later. He had been in seemingly good health, according to family members, as he finished out the summer with Judy in their modest eleventh-floor unit at the English Towers condominium complex in Ocean City, Maryland.[132] The official cause of death was acute leukemia, likely a slow-growing form of the cancer that does not always exhibit life-threatening symptoms and can be misdiagnosed as the flu.[133] His hometown paper, the *Baltimore Sun*, poetically noted that he was buried "beneath an oak tree in the gentle hills of suburbia." There were no world leaders or movie stars in attendance, but former Baltimore mayor Thomas J. D'Alesandro III, the brother of Democratic congressional leader Nancy Pelosi of California, attended the service. D'Alesandro told the *Sun* that he had planned to play golf with Agnew the day before.[134] Patrick Buchanan, Agnew's old speechwriter, then in the middle of his second insurgent presidential campaign, paid his last respects to his former boss at the gravesite. Buchanan reflected in his own memoirs: "He is a forgotten man today, but there has never been a Vice President like him, who came to national politics an unknown, ascended to the heights in the esteem and affection of half his countrymen, then fell so low and hard. . . . Had he left the practices of Annapolis back in Annapolis, Spiro Agnew would have been President."[135]

Agnew's political career went too far and too fast for his own good. Within a decade he rose from a local zoning board official to the vice presidency and the world stage. He came out of nowhere, and after resigning in scandal in 1973, he returned to nowhere. But as biographer Justin Coffey pointed out, Agnew is not a tragic figure.[136] Personally, he could not live up to the emerging ethos of what it meant to be a representative of the silent majority. He was not particularly pious, thrifty, or committed to family values. He took kickbacks, cheated on his taxes and his wife, and seemed to enjoy the attention brought by his own celebrity. And yet he played a significant, though largely forgotten, role in defining twenty-first-century conservative populism. Agnew grasped the coming tension that successful national Republican leaders would harness in future elections. He connected the dots between the traditional conservative values of prudence, small government, and patriotism and the populist appeal of the culture wars, anti-intellectualism, and the politics of racial and class resentment. Launched from his white middle-class base, he emerged as a hero to ordinary citizens scattered across the rural South and Midwest and among the soon-to-be-named Reagan Democrats who worked in manufacturing jobs in the Rust Belt. He was their voice.

As we will explore in the final chapter, Agnew was a harbinger of Donald Trump and the modern Republican Party. As much as any other political leader in the early 1970s, Agnew found a way to channel the rage and discontent that many white Americans felt about where the nation was heading in the aftermath of the tumultuous 1960s. His politics were a mirror of the silent majority, unnerved by the anti-Vietnam movement, the progressive march for civil rights and women's equality, and the widening socioeconomic split between city, suburbs, and rural America.

Agnew took on the media, Ivy Leaguers, intellectuals, and politicians who seemed to have forgotten the common folks back home. And while his themes were not necessarily new, he helped reimagine American politics at a critical juncture in the country's history. The clarity of his voice was a signal of what was to come.

7

FROM AGNEW TO TRUMP

Five prominent Washington-based journalists met at the Sheraton Park Hotel in the nation's capital in the summer of 1970 to discuss Spiro Agnew's impact on American society. That a vice president less than two years into his term could inspire such a gathering speaks volumes about how much Agnew differed from most of his predecessors and successors in the No. 2 job. He clearly did not fit John Nance Garner's view that the vice presidency wasn't worth a warm bucket of spit.[1] With an audience looking on, the panel spent an hour focused on how Agnew was redefining political rhetoric, the future of the Republican Party, and societal norms.

Leading off the discussion, syndicated columnist Jack Anderson called Agnew out for misunderstanding the role of the free press. "If we let [Agnew] make the decisions as to what was to be said and what was to be read . . . there would never be one critical word about the Nixon Administration. I don't believe this is the democratic way." Nancy Dickerson of NBC News added, "I think Mr. Agnew's rhetoric has been a very dangerous thing because it has turned off so many young people and so many black people." Warren Rogers from Hearst considered the vice president to be "the single most divisive figure in public life today" because the ideas he constantly attacked "are those things in our society to which we look for improvement and betterment on all fronts." Agnew, he said, was reshaping the GOP by "out-Wallacing George Wallace." Richard Wilson of the Cowles media chain thought Agnew was the most important vice president in a generation because he managed to "coalesce the support of the average voter" behind the Nixon administration.[2]

Agnew's scandal-shortened political career, his reclusiveness following his resignation, and the lack of interest by historians and journalists in exploring his legacy have limited his imprint on American history. As Frank Mankiewicz, an aide to Robert Kennedy and George McGovern, accurately predicted at the same 1970 panel discussion, "I think history will make of [Agnew] a rather minor figure."[3] But the symbolism and tenor of Agnew's vice presidency, what he stood for (and more important, what he stood against), have taken on much greater weight since Donald Trump's rise to political power. As MSNBC's Lawrence O'Donnell noted, Nixon's choice "wasn't just about Spiro Agnew. This was about the future of the party, specifically the future of liberalism within the party. The liberals knew what was happening. The South now felt itself in control of both nominees on the Republican ticket."[4] Agnew's selection was consequential then and remains so a half century later.

Donald Trump has been over-compared to a variety of polarizing political figures of the twentieth century. Is he the second coming of Benito Mussolini, Richard Nixon, Huey Long, or George Wallace, or some combination thereof?[5] While time will tell what the lasting impact of the Trump presidency will be, it is clear that his ascendency and indeed his utter dominance of the Republican Party signals a dramatic moment in the nation's political history. A number of people contributed to the rise of the anti-elite, populist wing of the GOP since the 1960s: Barry Goldwater, Phyllis Schlafly, Ronald Reagan, Jesse Helms, Strom Thurmond, and John Tower, among others. Spiro Agnew's name has to be on that list as well. The modern Republican Party owes part of its soul to Agnew, with a generational assist from Patrick Buchanan, his erstwhile speechwriter and later a presidential candidate in his own right. Buchanan's presidential runs (and his body of work in media and print) bridge Agnew and the Republican Party under Donald Trump.

Trump and Agnew both entered politics and public life from the wrong side of the tracks, so to speak. They share a personal and political history that helps explain their similarities, but there are also notable departures. Both descended, at least in part, from recently immigrated families that strived for a better life in East Coast cities. Both were mediocre students.[6] Agnew served honorably during World War II, while Trump avoided the Vietnam War with draft deferments. Trump came

from new money—his father was a successful real estate developer—
while Agnew's father ran a diner. Trump grew up in a middle-class neighborhood in Queens, and his early career in real estate was spent trying
to gain a foothold in the Manhattan market. Many writers saw the 2016
presidential election as "a different clash of world views: a battle between
Manhattan, the world's capital and the rich, powerful, white-hot center
of everything, and Queens, the most Outer Borro-y of the Outer Bor-
ros."[7] At the Alfred E. Smith Memorial Foundation Dinner in October
2016, a long-standing charitable roast where both presidential candidates appear and make fun of themselves and each other, Trump's performance was widely panned. The usually passive philanthropic crowd of
New Yorkers booed him as he made his way through a series of off-color
jokes that tagged him as both tacky and nouveau riche. *Washington Post*
columnist Jennifer Rubin opined that Trump has an inferiority complex
because he "has gone through his adult life with a chip on his shoulder,"[8]
like the fictional Archie Bunker of *All in the Family*, who also hailed from
Queens. Trump's political views, like Agnew's, are starker because of what
he stands against rather than what he stands for.[9]

Both Trump and Agnew started as Democrats, and Trump's political
career, also like Agnew's, has been consistently marked by opportunism
over ideology. It has been reported that Trump first registered as a Republican in 1987 and then switched his party affiliation multiple times
before finally settling as a member of the GOP just a few years before his
run for president.[10] Agnew became a Republican when he moved to the
suburbs. Because there were so few Republicans in Baltimore County in
the 1950s, he thought it would be easier for him to succeed as a big fish in
a small pond. Agnew's rise to political fortune in Maryland came in large
part because of a fractured Democratic Party, riven by segregation and
unable to coalesce around a single strong candidate for county executive
or governor. The dysfunction of the dominant party helped Agnew to improbable election wins on his first tries in 1962 and 1966. His selection as
Nixon's running mate came about because of a confluence of events that
included Nelson Rockefeller's strategic missteps, his own over-the-top
response to the rioting in Baltimore following the assassination of Martin

Luther King Jr., and the presence of an insecure nominee at the top of the ticket who didn't want a running mate who might outshine him.

Trump similarly picked his political moment with great timing and good fortune. Despite talking about running for president for years, he seemed a long shot to win the Republican nomination in 2016, let alone the general election.[11] The crowded field, the numerous televised debates, and Trump's ability to shake up traditional politics with sound bites and speeches made his outsider status more attractive in the primaries to the types of audiences who decades ago supported Agnew. His rallies featured signs reading "The Silent Majority Stands With Trump." In the general election he had the good luck to run against Hillary Clinton, who had already been well defined on the national stage and rated negatively with many voters for a variety of reasons.[12] Race and gender played a role in Trump's victory as well.[13] A perfect storm of political circumstances allowed Agnew and Trump to ascend to major elective office on their first attempts.

As unlikely national political leaders, both Trump and Agnew savaged the political norms of the day with their open hostility toward the media and their use of rhetoric, high and low, to brand their opponents. Agnew used alliterative tricks and lashed out against the TV networks, New York and Washington newspapers, intellectuals, and anti-war protesters. He also denigrated Democrats and fellow Republicans who were insufficiently loyal to Nixon. Trump has similarly gone after "fake news" and used pejorative terms for his opponents.

Both men's diatribes against the media will likely be remembered for years to come. On a trip to Denmark in the early 1990s, not long before Agnew's death, a bearded latter-day hippie reportedly walked up to the former vice president and declared, "Lay some rhetoric on me, man!"[14] And while Trump's after-presidency career will likely be shorter than Agnew's because of his more advanced age, one can imagine a similar encounter with the forty-fifth president occurring someday.

Agnew used the classic behind-the-podium speech as a critical communication tool, a way to relate directly to his constituents without media filters. Trump does the same, although Agnew stuck to his script far more than Trump does. For Agnew—barnstorming in the pre-Twitter age across silent majority country during and between campaigns in 1968, 1970, and 1972—speechmaking meant raising money, votes, and support for the policies of the Nixon administration. And while he also took time to make major addresses on culturally important topics, his headlines and "good press" were often made in regional newspapers. In the smaller cities and towns Agnew racked up goodwill with his messages of law and order, states' rights, the permissive state of higher education, and getting tough on draft dodgers. He usually spoke to crowds of the faithful, those residing in the broad, white middle class who may have sent a son or a father to fight in Vietnam.

Trump operated much the same way during his first two years in office, using campaign-style speeches at rallies of supporters where he was sure to make news by calling out an opponent or belittling a foreign leader. He too targeted off-the-beaten-path venues; in 2018 alone, Trump spoke in Elkhart, Indiana; Duluth, Minnesota; Wilkes-Barre, Pennsylvania; Charleston, West Virginia; and Great Falls, Montana, to name a few. A distant second to his ever-active Twitter account, Trump's speeches have been his most important in-person method of reaching people. Although he conducts on-the-record interviews with journalists, like Agnew he doesn't trust that the fourth estate can deliver his message as effectively as he can.

That Agnew's relationship with the media would eventually come to define him is odd, given that his initial interactions with the press during his first years as a public official in Maryland were generally positive. But starting with his selection as Nixon's running mate, and soon followed by reports of various gaffes on the campaign trail, Agnew's relationship with journalists soured quickly. He was regularly lampooned as a fool, a bigot, and over his head. The *Washington Post* even compared him to Caligula's horse, which according to legend was made a consul by the Roman emperor. It can be argued that Agnew didn't have the kind of calloused skin required for national political life. He came to the vice presidency with the reputation of already being a prickly sort, so it seems highly likely that he thought he would never get a fair hearing from those who criticized him so savagely during his early years in Washington.[15] But in his most famous speech on the role of television news—the one delivered in Des Moines, Iowa, in November 1969 and described in chapter four—he took on the issue of bias in the media in a way that spoke to both the silent majority and the voters who quietly resented the Washington–New York–Boston corridor of power and prestige. It was the perfect issue for Agnew, and it helped Nixon knit together a new Republican Party, one identified less with profits on Wall Street and more closely tied to the cultural issues that concerned Main Street Americans. Agnew may have been speaking about his own experience that night in Des Moines, but he was also preaching to his fellow middle- and working-class strivers who were ready to believe that the media was biased against them and their values.[16]

After the Des Moines speech Agnew should have been unencumbered by what the press thought of him. It should no longer have mattered how Walter Cronkite or the *Washington Post* characterized him. But it did. Agnew (and Nixon) continued to obsess over national media coverage throughout their time in office. Perhaps their concerns had merit; both men's political careers ended at least in part because of investigative work by some of the same press outlets they frequently attacked. Both had something to hide, after all. In this regard Agnew may ultimately share something else important with Trump, given the forty-fifth president's obsession with his news coverage and the allegations of wrongdoing that the national press kept in front of the American public throughout the first two years of his presidency and beyond.

For Agnew (and Trump), there was value if the media—or the intelligence community or the Justice Department—was weakened by persistent attacks in the public arena. If these pillars of American society and government, normally in charge of checking the executive branch, were destabilized, it raised the possibility in the minds of some voters that they were biased arbiters. The doubts once raised, it then followed that the press (or the FBI), in these voters' view, would not be able to do its job fairly when Agnew's legal issues or Watergate came to a denouement. As Bob Woodward and Carl Bernstein wrote in their classic retelling of Watergate, *All the President's Men*, one White House official told them: "We believe the public believes that the Eastern press really is what Agnew said it was—elitist, anti-Nixon and ultimately pro-McGovern."[17]

In Trump's case some of the same doubts apply to his own legal tribulations and those of his personal and political aides.

Trump's relationship with the media has also been something of a love-hate affair. The New York press made him into a national figure, a tycoon playboy coming out of disco-debauched 1970s and '80s Manhattan. He owed his initial national prominence to where he lived and worked and how the media covered him in that environment. There is no way Trump would have risen to such political heights if he had made his life in, say, Baltimore, let alone Towson, where Agnew moved in the 1950s.[18] Long before Trump began "firing" people as a TV personality on his reality show, *The Apprentice*, the media helped create his persona, covering his moves and utterances as if he were something of a national political figure already.

Trump's hard pivot on the media came early in his presidential run. With his Twitter missives and his desire to speak with reporters directly, without handlers or cautionary talking points, he may have redefined political/media relations. His tell-it-like-it-is attitude appealed strongly to voters fed up with packaged sound bites and poll-tested policies. Like Agnew's willingness to take on traditional political communication, Trump has memorably labeled reporting that is unfavorable to him as fake news. In his first year as president he tweeted the phrase more than 150 times and told a talk show host, "One of the greatest of all terms I've come up with is 'fake.'"[19] Beyond that are his labeling of the press as "the opposition party" or "the enemy of the people," his threats to rewrite libel laws, his ridicule of news organizations as business failures, and his demands that specific journalists be fired.[20] Trump's attacks on the press are planetary leaps away from Agnew's Des Moines speech, but the underlying motives are similar.

Suspicion of bedrock American institutions, ones that rarely have come in for foundational criticism by politicians, has become part of the appeal to and the core identity of the silent majority constituency. It helped make Agnew and Trump alluring candidates to legions of white, Middle American supporters.[21] One of Agnew's primary institutional targets beyond the press was higher education. Agnew challenged the college and university culture on granular issues like curriculum development and whether the liberal arts were an appropriate path of study for most people. At a speech also given in Des Moines in April 1970, as mentioned, he bemoaned the rapid enrollment growth of colleges and universities and worried that "college, at one time considered a privilege, is considered to be a right today—and is valued less because of that."[22]

The vice president called out university professors and administrators and quoted them by name in his speeches. He singled out institutions and maintained a public back-and-forth with academia that was and still is unparalleled in politics. And while criticizing elite liberal arts colleges and universities as ivory-tower havens for lefties who indoctrinate their students is a core part of the Republican Party's mantra today, Agnew was in the vanguard on the issue. In an open "Letter to Spiro Agnew" in 1970, Robert McAfee Brown, a professor of religion at Stanford University, said that Agnew's rhetoric and ideas created "a divisiveness that may well destroy us as McCarthyism threatened to destroy us in the 1950s." Brown accused the vice president of wanting "to impose a kind of political loyalty oath on everybody in the universities, from the president down through the faculty and students."[23] Agnew did not shy away from debate, and in fact he welcomed it in a way that would be almost unthinkable today.

On September 21, 1970, Agnew appeared on *The David Frost Show* in New York to debate four student body presidents from universities across the country.[24] By most accounts Agnew performed well. He engaged the students respectfully and in his usual unflappable manner. Even better, the show's visuals reinforced Agnew's subtle message to his core constituency. The vice president appeared in his usual conservative, well-groomed style, with a solid-colored tie and slick-backed hair. By contrast, the students were more unkempt, long-haired, and dressed in the scruffy fashion of the times. The young people also had a much harder time keeping their emotions in check. Agnew made statements about law and order on campus that were difficult for the twenty-somethings to refute.[25] Even frequent Agnew critics such as columnist Mary McGrory of the *Washington Star* and Anthony Lewis of the *New York Times* praised the vice president for his "coolness and quick articulation" and his ability to bring the "discussion back to the subject likely to arouse the television viewers' emotions: student violence."[26]

Once again the modern-day parallels are striking. Donald Trump and his supporters like to use the catchwords "politically correct" and "snowflake," and they mock the rise of "safe spaces" on college campuses. They charge that liberal professors indoctrinate their students and misshape society. These critiques have a direct line to Agnew's sustained attacks on universities almost fifty years earlier.[27] And today we see that some leading intellectuals, especially conservative foreign policy experts, have been among the most outspoken critics of Trump's rhetoric, just as their predecessors were of Agnew.[28]

Compared to Agnew, however, Trump has leveled more of his animus at other institutions, such as the federal judiciary, the North Atlantic Treaty Organization, the North American Free Trade Association (NAFTA), the FBI, and the intelligence community.[29] And much like Patrick Buchanan's message during his three presidential runs, Trump has consistently harped on the evils of free trade agreements, trade deficits, and traditional foreign policy allies.[30] He has openly criticized the motives of the intelligence community, and he fired FBI director James Comey over his refusal to back away from the investigation into whether Trump's campaign colluded with the Russians during the 2016 elections.[31] While Agnew never went that far, he too took on sacred cows and untouchable political commandments, and his base constituency, like Trump's, rallied around enthusiastically.

Like Trump, Agnew had a penchant for international strongmen and enjoyed friendlier relations with antidemocratic leaders than with traditional allies around the globe. His well-publicized trip to his family's ancestral homeland in 1971 was marked by warm visits with the Greek military junta, which the rest of the world had shunned. His world tours included sit-downs with a who's who of human rights violators, dictators, and repressive regimes. And while some of this can be explained away by the realities of the Cold War, there is little question that Agnew's vice presidential missions and his later career as an international businessman—when he was doing deals with the likes of Saddam Hussein, Nicolae Ceausescu, and the Argentine military—were unencumbered by any kind of democratic moral compass. It has similarly been noted that Trump's closest international relationships have been with repressive leaders.[32] For instance, he raised a howl in the press and on social media over his June 2018 European trip, when he insulted American allies and publicly sided with Vladimir Putin on the question of Russian sabotage of the 2016 election.

Agnew and Trump share a similar tradition-busting pedigree when it comes to taking on members of their own party. Ronald Reagan famously said during his campaign for governor of California in 1966: "Thou shall not speak ill of another Republican." He followed this so-called "11th commandment" throughout his runs for president in 1976, 1980, and 1984.[33] Neither Trump nor Agnew abided by Reagan's directive. Agnew's nomination raised the hackles of the liberal wing of the party, and there was pushback at the 1968 National Convention. The New York Republicans—in particular Nelson Rockefeller, Jacob Javits, John Lindsay, and Charles Goodell—fought openly with Agnew during his years as vice president, and Agnew went so far as to campaign against Goodell in his 1970 election. Liberal Republican governors asked Agnew to tone it down or not campaign in their states.

Inside the White House, to the extent that Agnew had much of a voice, he was perceived as a Vietnam hawk and a lightning rod on emerging cultural issues, earning him the enmity of more-moderate cabinet members. When Agnew ran into his own legal trouble in 1973, his main opponents were Attorney General Elliot Richardson and George Beall, the U.S. attorney for Maryland, who came from the same liberal wing of the Republican Party that he been in conflict with for the previous five years. Agnew did not engender deep support within the establishment wing of the party either. When he looked to Congress for help with his legal predicament in the summer and fall of 1973, his silent majority alliance was not yet wide enough to force the issue out of the courts and into an open impeachment process, where he thought he might have a better chance of publicly pleading his case. He had a marriage of convenience with Republicans like House Minority Leader Gerald Ford of Michigan and Senate Minority Leader Hugh Scott of Pennsylvania, but they were not willing to go to the mat for him when his troubles mounted.[34]

Similarly, Trump has gone out of his way to thumb his nose at the establishment wing of the Republican Party. With claims of his own dubious fealty to the party being hurled at him during the 2016 primaries,

Trump belittled his way to the nomination by flinging public insults at the previous three GOP presidential nominees: Mitt Romney (2012), John McCain (2008), and George W. Bush (2000, 2004).[35] Bush responded, much later, in a speech criticizing Trump's tone, temperament, and judgment with thinly veiled comments such as "We've seen our discourse degraded by casual cruelty" and "Bullying and prejudice in our public life sets a national tone and provides permission for cruelty and bigotry. The only way to pass along civic values is to first live up to them."[36] Trump has also had an on-again, off-again relationship with Speaker of the House Paul Ryan of Wisconsin, now retired, and Senate Majority Leader Mitch McConnell of Kentucky.[37]

The political importance of Pat Buchanan is one of many connections between Donald Trump and Spiro Agnew. As a young policy aide to Richard Nixon starting in 1966, Buchanan had significant impact on issues ranging from abortion to affirmative action to media relations. Buchanan and Agnew took to each other and would remain friends for the rest of their lives.[38] Buchanan believed that Agnew "spoke for the heart of America" and even better, "the Vice President did love to lay the wood on" by speaking without a filter.[39] And fortunately for Agnew, who had been underserved by his parochial Maryland staffers, Buchanan's pen and his worldview were just what he needed to supercharge his message behind the podium and solidify his own shifting bona fides as a real conservative voice.[40] As one of Buchanan's biographers noted, he became "indispensable" to the conservative movement by injecting the polemical, editorial style into Agnew's political speech. Buchanan made Agnew "a conservative for the TV age: watchable and quotable, and a spokesman—it seemed to some—for the ordinary man in the street."[41]

Buchanan stayed with Nixon until the bitter end of the Watergate saga and stuck around for a couple of months to help the new Ford administration get situated. Soon thereafter he returned to his original career of journalism and public affairs. His first book reflected on his time in the White House. *Conservative Votes, Liberal Victories* was one in a series of volumes that Buchanan would author over the next forty-plus years.

Buchanan helps link Agnew to Trump in both politics and policy. After leaving the White House Buchanan set about addressing the question of why "conservatives have failed utterly to translate political support and ballot victories into national policy."[42] There had been good rhetoric but not enough action. All that really had been accomplished by the Nixon-Agnew administration was the reshaping of the Supreme Court by the appointment of four new justices; otherwise, the policies of the New Deal and the Great Society had been left in place. The solution, Buchanan said, was confrontation and open political conflict with the establishment, Democrat or Republican: "The nation is a divided country; but it was not divided by conservatives; and it should not be our business to compromise our principles, to silence our complaints, or to abandon our point of view to 'bring us together.' If the right has a purpose in American politics, it is not to contribute to some false sense of unity, but to articulate the concerns, represent the interests and defend the principles, values and beliefs of our own."[43]

According to Buchanan the media had played a crucial role in keeping the establishment in power and solidifying Great Society policies, despite popular national support for conservative candidates and their philosophy of smaller and less-intrusive government. In his mind only one politician had taken on the issue of press bias head-on: Spiro Agnew.[44] While Buchanan's hope that the right wing of the Republican Party (represented by Reagan) would get "dealt a hand" in 1976 was ultimately dashed, he put his finger on what Republicans had to do in order to return to power. "They needed to convert disillusioned Democrats, including hundreds of thousands [of potential supporters] in Queens and the North Bronx. Not only are the Catholic Democrats of Queens more numerous than the black Democrats of Harlem, they are more disillusioned with their party, and receptive to a political appeal that does not violate Republican principles."[45] One of those disillusioned Democrats living in Queens, while not a Catholic, was Donald Trump.

Buchanan took a break from his revolving TV and newspaper column gigs in the mid-1980s to return to the White House as Reagan's communications director. But Buchanan's real goal was to push the Republican Party toward his more-conservative, populist view of the world. In 1992 he challenged incumbent president George H. W. Bush in the Republican primaries. Chasing the establishment, moderate Bush on the campaign trail, and polling surprisingly well in places like New Hampshire, where he received 37.5 percent of the vote, Buchanan tapped into Agnew's constituency with "pitchfork brigades" of average-Joe supporters backing him. Buchanan's litany of policy prescriptions during his campaigns, now several election cycles old, sounded downright Trumpian: he spoke out against free trade pacts and was violently anti-immigration (calling for a wall on the southern border). He pushed an America-first foreign policy, was strongly anti-establishment, and advocated a return to the values-based nation that liberals had stolen from the people. Given the opportunity to deliver a prime time speech at the opening of the 1992 Republican National Convention, Buchanan stole the show, proclaiming: "My friends, this election is about more than who gets what. It is about who we are. It about what we believe, it is about what we stand for as Americans. There is a religious war going on in our country for the soul of America. It is a cultural war, as critical to the kind of nation we shall one day be as was the Cold War itself."[46]

Several of Buchanan's later books, written as reflections after each of his presidential runs, also sound eerily reminiscent of Trump's message to the same constituency. Much of Buchanan's work centered on how to restore America to what he imagined as pre-1960s Eisenhower-era goodness— or as Trump synthesized it, how to "make America great again." Consider his 1998 book *The Great Betrayal*, which focused on economic policy, trade deficits, and the downsides of NAFTA and immigration. Buchanan sadly saw the old Agnew political coalition slipping into economic obscurity, with America having become "a land of middle-class anxiety, downsized hopes, and vanished dreams, where economic insecurity is a preexisting condition of life, and company towns become ghost towns overnight."[47]

Compare Buchanan's language to Trump's in his 2017 inaugural speech. Trump opened by blaming "the establishment" for protecting itself while shortchanging hard-working citizens. "The forgotten men and women of our country will be forgotten no longer," he promised. The American system had failed too many Americans: "Mothers and children trapped in poverty in our inner cities; rusted-out factories scattered like tombstones across the landscape of our nation; an education system, flush with cash, but which leaves our young and beautiful students deprived of knowledge; and the crime and gangs and drugs that have stolen too many lives and robbed our country of so much unrealized potential. This American carnage stops right here and stops right now."[48]

Doubling down on culture and immigration, both core to Trump's message during his campaign and presidency, Buchanan in *The Death of the West* presaged the national debate about Confederate monuments and white supremacists. He argued, "Millions have begun to feel like strangers in their own land." His coalition of voters, which he had helped Agnew tap into a generation earlier, rallied behind a message that emphasized the changing times and the threat that the country they knew was about to disappear. "In half a lifetime, many Americans have seen their God dethroned, their heroes defiled, their culture polluted, their values assaulted, their country invaded, and themselves demonized as extremists and bigots for holding on to beliefs Americans have held for generations," Buchanan wrote.[49]

Trump picked up the same anthem in an August 2017 press conference where he responded to questions about the rally in Charlottesville, Virginia, where a woman was killed. Trump identified with the white supremacists protesting the removal of Confederate statues, arguing, "You're changing history. You're changing culture."[50]

By the late 1990s Buchanan was no longer welcome in the Republican Party.[51] Trump and Buchanan butted heads electorally in 2000 as Trump considered seeking the nomination of the Reform Party, which Buchanan eventually captured. In the tussle, Trump went so far as to call Buchanan "a Hitler-lover" and an anti-Semite on national television. He added, for good measure, "[Buchanan] doesn't like the blacks, he doesn't like the gays." Watching from home, Buchanan was furious at being belittled by Trump, who had no political experience at all.[52] But he didn't take the bait. Recalling the run-in years later, he said sardonically, "With Trump, you have to realize, these are terms of endearment."[53] Buchanan garnered only 450,000 votes in his run as the Reform Party nominee and finished well behind Green Party candidate Ralph Nader. He retreated to his work, including a fierce critique of the neoconservative foreign policies of the George W. Bush administration that Trump has similarly rejected.[54]

Buchanan's quixotic runs for the presidency galvanized a series of issues for a core constituency who believed in his combative tactics and his out-of-the-box policy prescriptions, just as Agnew's supporters had. Buchanan emerged as a spokesman for conservative white males across party lines, an emerging union of "cultural traditionalists and economic populists, an alliance of nostalgics."[55] He told the *New York Times:* "When the chickens come home to roost, this whole coalition will be there for somebody. . . . There's no doubt these issues can win." By 2016 Trump had changed his tune on Buchanan, and he consulted with him during the primaries, even calling him directly to compliment him on columns. And although they did not speak during the final months of Trump's campaign and the first months of his presidency, Buchanan told *Esquire,* "I was delighted when he got in."[56]

The election of Donald Trump in 2016 did not occur in a vacuum. Trump's strategy and style, the policy issues he emphasized, and his willingness to take down sacrosanct norms in American government and politics had antecedents. Spiro Agnew was central among those who years earlier had begun to lay the foundation for the Trump phenomenon, honing sharp, clever arguments against the media, the elite, and the establishment. They assembled a silent majority ready for a message that would ultimately win the presidency. If this group of voters is "the angriest and most pessimistic people in America, the people we used to call Middle Americans, middle class and middle aged; not rich and not poor . . . who wonder how white male became an accusation rather than a description," then we should remember that it was Agnew who helped get them riled up fifty years ago.[57]

Agnew's vice presidency, and its sudden end in a U.S. district courtroom in Baltimore in October 1973, also paved the way for the emergence of Ronald Reagan as the elected voice of the silent majority. With Agnew out of the picture and no conservative populist with as high a profile on the national stage, Reagan was able to run in 1976 and then win spectacularly in 1980 and 1984. In this regard Agnew served as an important usher for a movement that lacked national visibility between Goldwater's 1964 nomination and Reagan's ascendancy.

It is easy to imagine "what if?" For example, what if the U.S. attorney's office in Baltimore had opted not to go after the former Maryland governor and county executive? Watergate forced Nixon to resign in August 1974, barely ten months after Agnew left office; an Agnew presidency was that close. And a President Agnew might have handled Nixon's pardon differently. He might have handled the end of the Vietnam War differently. The butterfly effect of a hypothetical Agnew presidency could have altered the trajectory of American politics and global affairs.

The early twentieth-century French philosopher Paul Valéry wrote, "Hatred, cruelty, hypocrisy and graft belong to no single party, stupidity to no single regime, error to no single system."[58] And Agnew's errors and mistakes were not unique in this regard. He was a corrupt politician at one level, but he also stood for something powerful. His rags to riches to rags political story; his critiques of the media, higher education, and the establishment; and his rhetoric of resentment helped forge a new national coalition for the Republican Party that for now governs the nation.

Agnew's comet-like political career also played a role in inspiring those institutions that he criticized to work harder and more creatively. Journalism in the post-Agnew era became more inclusive of conservative voices but also dug deeper into government malfeasance, graft, and lies. Higher education became less elite in the 1970s and opened up at both the technical and university levels. The Republican Party reinvented itself and became the dominant national party in the 1980s; it arguably remains so today. That these hugely significant developments can be traced to some degree to Agnew's pugnacity and sense of timing testifies to the fact that, for better or worse, his influence on his country was wider and longer lasting than has been recognized. Indeed, Spiro Agnew continues to be an important figure long after many of his predecessors and successors have receded into the warm bucket of spit of forgotten vice presidents. He is one of the rare public officials, in his or any other American era, who can lay claim to a legacy.

NOTES

Introduction

1. Justin Vaughn, "How to Be a Great Vice President," *New York Times,* June 11, 2016.

2. Devine and Kopko, *The VP Advantage.*

3. Lucas, *Agnew: Profile in Conflict,* 111.

4. One could certainly argue that John McCain's 2008 vice presidential pick, Sarah Palin, rivaled Agnew for lack of significant elected political experience, having served less than a single term as governor of Alaska and two terms as mayor of a small town. Trump, of course, had never held any elective office prior to becoming president, but ran an international business.

5. Evans and Novak, *Nixon in the White House,* 305.

6. Strober and Strober, *Nixon: An Oral History,* 90.

7. Haldeman, *The Haldeman Diaries,* 53.

8. Agnew, *Go Quietly . . . Or Else,* 26.

9. The Nixon team struggled to find policy work for Agnew where he could do no harm. A partial list of his assignments included the National Aeronautics and Space Council, the National Council on Marine Resources and Engineering Development, the President's Council on Youth Opportunity, the Peace Corps National Advisory Council, the President's Council on Physical Fitness and Sports, and the National Council on Indian Opportunity.

10. A panel of 137 communications and rhetoric scholars ranked Agnew's network news speech No. 47 in the top 100 speeches of the twentieth century on the basis of its social and political impact as well as its rhetorical artistry. Lucas and Medhurst, *Words of a Century.*

11. Media Memorandum from Patrick J. Buchanan to the President [Nixon], May 21, 1970. Retrieved from https://www.nixonlibrary.gov/virtuallibrary/releases/jan10/025.pdf. Jim Rutenberg, "In Watergate, One Set of Facts. In Trump Era, Take Your Pick," *New York Times,* June 11, 2017.

12. Perlstein, *Nixonland,* 504.

13. Mieczkowski, *Gerald Ford and the Challenges of the 1970s,* 183.

14. Bradlee, *A Good Life,* 372.

15. Strober and Strober, *Nixon: An Oral History,* 431.

16. Agnew, *Go Quietly . . . Or Else,* 9; Coffey, *Spiro Agnew and the Rise of the Republican Right,* 156.

17. "Spiro Agnew and the Golden Age of Corruption."

18. Agnew, *Go Quietly . . . Or Else,* 222.

19. Thomas Waldron and Susan Baer, "Bittersweet Return for Spiro Agnew," *Baltimore Sun,* May 25, 1995. http://articles.baltimoresun.com/1995-05-25/news/199514 5192_1_spiro-agnew-nixon-administration-bust.

20. The journalist Jules Witcover is probably the most knowledgeable and authoritative scholar on Agnew and has published four books about him. Justin Coffey's *Spiro Agnew and the Rise of the Republican Right* is the first significant look at Agnew's legacy in more than forty years.

21. Lippman, *Spiro Agnew's America,* 134–35.

22. Witcover, *White Knight,* 232.

23. Nixon, *RN: The Memoirs of Richard Nixon,* 313.

24. Scammon and Wattenberg, *The Real Majority,* 209–10.

25. *Life,* May 8, 1970.

26. Scammon and Wattenberg, *The Real Majority,* 21.

27. Michael Barbaro and Alexander Burns, "It's Donald Trump's Convention. But the Inspiration? Nixon." *New York Times,* July 18, 2016.

28. Strober and Strober, *Nixon: An Oral History of His Presidency,* 432.

29. Jeremy Diamond, "Trump: 'I Could Shoot Somebody and I Wouldn't Lose Voters,'" CNN, January 24, 2016, http://www.cnn.com/2016/01/23/politics/donald -trump-shoot-somebody-support/index.html.

30. Michael D'Antonio, "When Donald Trump Hated Ronald Reagan," *Politico,* October 25, 2015, http://www.politico.com/magazine/story/2015/10/donald-trump -ronald-reagan-213288.

31. Michael Barbaro, "Donald Trump Clung to 'Birther' Lie for Years and Still Isn't Apologetic," *New York Times,* September 16, 2016; Michele Gorman, "A Brief History of Donald Trump and Bill Clinton's Friendship," *Newsweek,* May 27, 2016, http:// www.newsweek.com/history-donald-trump-bill-clinton-friendship-464360.

32. Michael D'Antonio, "Is Donald Trump a Racist? Here's What the Record Shows," *Fortune,* June 7, 2016, http://fortune.com/2016/06/07/donald-trump-racism -quotes/.

33. Gallup Daily, "Trump Job Approval." Retrieved from http://www.gallup.com /poll/201617/gallup-daily-trump-job-approval.aspx.

34. Cramer, *The Politics of Resentment.*

35. According to the U.S. Census, Maryland's median household income in 2016

was $73,971, the highest in the country. Maryland also has the second-highest percentage of citizens with a college degree or an advanced degree.

36. Scammon and Wattenberg, *The Real Majority,* 25.

37. Phillips, *The Emerging Republican Majority,* 24.

38. Scammon and Wattenberg, *The Real Majority,* 210.

39. Evans and Novak, *Nixon in the White House,* 305.

40. Ford, *A Time to Heal,* 86.

41. Nixon, *RN: The Memoirs of Richard Nixon,* 365.

1. Refusing to Knuckle Under

1. "Baltimore's New County Executive," *Sun,* December 16, 1962.

2. Albright, *What Makes Spiro Run,* 18–49.

3. Lippman, *Spiro Agnew's America,* 21–22.

4. Albright, *What Makes Spiro Run,* 36.

5. Ibid., 18–49. See also Coffey, *Spiro Agnew and the Rise of the Republican Right,* 7–10.

6. Albright, *What Makes Spiro Run,* 38–41.

7. Cohen and Witcover, *A Heartbeat Away,* 17.

8. Coffey, *Spiro Agnew and the Rise of the Republican Right,* 10.

9. Cohen and Witcover, *A Heartbeat Away,* 18–19.

10. See https://www.census.gov/population/cencounts/md190090.txt.

11. Draft of "Baltimore County's Executive on the Move," Agnew Papers, Series 1: Baltimore County Executive, Box 1, Subseries: Public Statements, 1963–1966, Folder "News Releases—1966."

12. "Dear Fellow Citizen," Agnew Papers, Series 1, Subseries: Correspondence, 1962–1966, Box 1, Folder "Pre-Election Correspondence," n.d.

13. "Baltimore's New County Executive," *Sun,* December 16, 1962.

14. Coffey, *Spiro Agnew and the Rise of the Republican Right,* 7–46.

15. "Baltimore's New County Executive," *Sun,* December 16, 1962.

16. Witcover, *White Knight,* 73.

17. Nelson Rockefeller to Spiro Agnew, November 15, 1963, Agnew Papers, Series 1, Subseries: Correspondence, 1962–1966, Box 1, Folder "Personal Correspondence, 1/63 to 12/63."

18. Spiro Agnew to John Steffy, November 12, 1963, Agnew Papers, Series 1, Subseries: Correspondence, 1962–1966, Box 1, Folder "Personal Correspondence, 1/63 to 12/63." Historians also contend that as Richard Nixon's vice president, Agnew was considered to be a conservative. Biographer Justin Coffey notes: "As Agnew climbed up the political ladder, his views evolved and his political metamorphosis helped earn him a spot on the Republican presidential ticket in 1968" (Coffey, *Spiro Agnew and the Rise of the Republican Right,* 1). Al Haig, Nixon's final chief of staff, remembered

Agnew from his many interactions as a "large, smooth, bullet-headed man" but also as a "bare-fisted conservative" (Haig, *Inner Circles*, 365, 367).

19. Cohen and Witcover, *A Heartbeat Away*, 21.

20. Haig, *Inner Circles*, 365. Many thanks to Stanley Fine for sharing his experiences as a young law student who drove Agnew to campaign stops during the 1966 gubernatorial campaign. Fine also recalled how Agnew was an avid Ping-Pong player who invited him to Annapolis from time to time to play against the governor. Interview with Stanley Fine, audio recording in possession of Charles Holden, January 22, 2017.

21. Mrs. Herman Ahne to Spiro T. Agnew, October 10, 1973, Agnew Papers, Series 3, Subset 3, Box 5, Folder 2.

22. Cohen and Witcover, *A Heartbeat Away*, 32–33.

23. Draft of "Baltimore County's Executive on the Move," Agnew Papers, Series 1: Baltimore County Executive, Box 1, Subseries: Public Statements, 1963–1966, Folder "News Releases—1966."

24. Ibid.

25. Ibid.

26. Thank you to Adeen Postar, library director of the University of Baltimore School of Law, for this information.

27. "Baltimore County's Executive on the Move."

28. Ibid.

29. Ibid.

30. Ibid.

31. Ibid.

32. Whyte, *The Organization Man*, 312.

33. "Members of the Grand Lodge of Ancient Free and Accepted Masons of Maryland," n.d., Agnew Papers, Series 1, Subseries: Public Statements, 1963–1966, Box 1, Folder "Speeches and Addresses 1964–1965."

34. Ibid.

35. Wilson, *The Man in the Gray Flannel Suit*, 5.

36. "The Need for Mental Toughness," June 5, 1963, Agnew Papers, Series 1, Subseries: Public Statements, 1963–1966, Box 1, Folder "Speeches and Addresses 1963."

37. "Candidate's 'Affliction,'" *Sun*, May 15, 1960.

38. Election results in *Sun*, November 9, 1960.

39. "Televised Talks Asked," *Sun*, February 23, 1961.

40. "Agnew Calls Foes Afraid—'They Can't Control Me,'" *Sun*, February 15, 1961.

41. "Steinbock Voted into Agnew Post," *Sun*, February 17, 1961.

42. "Nigerian Furor, Cafe Ban Linked," *Sun*, October 17, 1961.

43. "Coed Prefers Jail: Africa, Yes—American, NO: Finds Robes Make a Difference," *Baltimore Afro American*, September 2, 1961.

44. "50 Years Later, Desegregation of Gwynn Oaks Amusement Park Celebrated," *Sun,* July 7, 2013.

45. "About 100 Arrested at Gwynn Oak," *Sun,* July 8, 1963.

46. "2 Integrate Gwynn Oak While 95 Are Arrested: AFRO Editor Tells of Jailing," *Afro American,* July 9, 1963.

47. "Gwynn Oak Shifts Today," *Sun,* August 28, 1963.

48. "Negro Family Integrates Gwynn Oak in Brief Visit," *Sun,* August 29, 1963.

49. "Statement by Spiro T. Agnew, Baltimore County Executive," July 8, 1963, Agnew Papers, Series 1, Subseries 3, Box 1, Folder "E. O. Statements 1963–1966."

50. "Civil Rights: Leadership—opportunists," December 11, 1963, Agnew Papers, Series 1, Subseries 2, Box 1, Folder "Public Issues."

51. "Civil Rights Statement by County Executive, Spiro T. Agnew Made at Testimonial Dinner, Pikesville Armory, May 4, 1964," Agnew Papers, Series 1, Subseries 2, Box 1, Folder "Public Issues."

52. "Civil Rights, STA statement made at dinner, 5/4/64"; "Civil Rights Statement by County Executive, Spiro T. Agnew Made at Testimonial Dinner, Pikesville Armory, May 4, 1964."

53. "Civil Rights," May 4, 1964, Folder "Public Issues."

54. "Baltimore County's Executive on the Move."

55. "Is the Backlash Here at Last?" *New York Times,* September 7, 1966.

56. "Civil Rights: A Turning Point," *New York Times,* September 19, 1966.

57. "Killer of Hotel Bar Maid Raising Funds for Goldwater," *Afro American,* October 31, 1964. Thank you to Carly Wedding of St. Mary's College of Maryland for finding and sharing this article with the authors.

58. "Brewster Beats Wallace: Alabamian Gets 42% of Vote," *Sun,* May 20, 1964.

59. "President Buoyed by Voter Support of Vietnam Policy," *New York Times,* September 15, 1966.

60. Michael Hatfield, "The 1966 Maryland Gubernatorial Election: The Political Saliency of Open Occupancy," master's thesis, University of Massachusetts, 1975, 51.

61. "1966 County Vote Parallels 1964's," *Sun,* September 18, 1966.

62. "Sickles Gains 7000-Vote Lead over Mahoney in Gubernatorial Race," *Sun,* September 14, 1966.

63. "Agnew Is Pleasant and Direct: Mahoney, Tough-Minded, Dogged," *Sun,* November 5, 1966.

64. "Democrats Fight as Agnew Looks On," *Washington Daily News,* September 6, 1966.

65. Ibid.

66. "Agnew," *Sun,* October 28, 1966; "Agnew Woos Democrats," *Sun,* October 3, 1966.

67. Text of speech, "Civil Rights," July 27, 1966, Agnew Papers, Series 2, Subseries 4, Folder "STA Campaign Speeches: Issues," [n.d., 7/27–11/1/66].

68. "Agnew for Governor," news release, October 15, 1966, Agnew Papers, Series 2, Subseries 4, Folder "Position Paper #4."

69. "Agnew Beats Mahoney for Governor by Over 80,000 as Pressman Trails," *Sun*, November 9, 1966.

70. See https://uselectionatlas.org/RESULTS/datagraph.php?fips=24&year= 1966&off=5&elect=0&f=0.

71. "Agnew Is Amassing Record Rights Gain," September 30, 1967, *Afro American*, 28.

72. "Welfare Cut by Governor Is Denounced," *Sun*, February 18, 1967; "State Police Raise Asked," *Sun*, March 1, 1967.

73. "Agnew Talks with Pickets about Welfare Allocations," *Sun*, March 23, 1967.

74. Coffey, *Spiro Agnew and the Rise of the Republican Right*, 52–53.

75. "Agnew Seeks Racial Peace in Cambridge," *Sun*, July 8, 1967.

76. The text of Brown's speech can be found at http://msa.maryland.gov/mega file/msa/speccol/sc2200/sc2221/000012/000008/html/speech1.html.

77. "Agnew Promises Aid to Cambridge," *Sun*, July 26, 1967.

78. "Agnew Sets Firm Policy on Disorder," *Sun*, July 31, 1967.

79. "Agnew Assails Rap Brown, Analyzes Urban Violence," *Sun*, September 12, 1967.

80. "Bowie Campus Calm Again; Senator Supports Students at College," *Sun*, April 3, 1968.

81. "Transcript of Agnew's Statement Closing Bowie State," *Sun*, April 5, 1968.

82. "10 Years after the Riots: Some Progress Has Been Made," *Sun*, April 5, 1978.

83. "Text of Governor Agnew's Statement to Civil Rights Leaders," *Sun*, April 12, 1968.

84. "Negroes Quit Conference with Agnew," *Sun*, April 12, 1968.

85. Moore was quoted as saying that new rounds of get-tough policing amounted to a "war on the black community" and that "the police are the enemy of the black community. Talk of more policing is not going to ease tension in the black community." See "Anti-Crime Plans Termed 'War on Black Community,'" *Sun*, February 8, 1968.

86. "Text of Governor Agnew's Statement to Civil Rights Leaders." Agnew was here referring to a March meeting of leaders from various civil rights organizations to "reconcile the differences in philosophy within the civil rights movement." The main point of contention at that moment was a rift between state senator Clarence M. Mitchell and Robert B. Moore, head of the Baltimore SNCC. See "Negroes Quit Conference with Agnew."

87. "Text of Governor Agnew's Statement to Civil Rights Leaders."

88. Ibid.

89. Ibid.

90. "Negroes Quit Conference with Agnew."

91. "Agnew's 'Lecture' Triggers Reaction," *Afro American,* April 20, 1968.

92. "Agnew's Riot Stand Praised by Callers, Deplored by Clergy," *Sun,* April 13, 1968.

93. "Negroes Quit Conference with Agnew."

94. Ibid.

95. "Agnew's Riot Stand Praised by Callers, Deplored by Clergy."

2. Role Reversal

1. Rosen, *The Republican Party in the Age of Roosevelt,* 44.

2. Ibid., 41.

3. Quoted in Brinkley, *Voices of Protest,* 51.

4. Quoted in McElvaine, *The Great Depression,* 282.

5. The Liberty League's association with Republicans, which FDR predictably encouraged, persisted despite the fact that John Raskob, one of its leaders, was a Democrat who had managed Al Smith's 1928 presidential campaign. See Farber, *Everybody Ought to Be Rich.*

6. See www.u-s-history.com/pages/h895.html.

7. The most notable of these were the National Industrial Recovery Act and the Agricultural Adjustment Act. See *Schechter Poultry Corp. v. United States,* 295 U.S. 495 (1935); *Butler v. United States,* 297 U.S. 1 (1936).

8. See Brinkley, *The End of Reform.*

9. Weir, *Class in America,* 692.

10. See https://www.pbs.org/newshour/spc/character/links/truman_speech.html.

11. Phillips, *The Emerging Republican Majority,* 65.

12. See www.americanrhetoric.com/speeches/huberthumphrey1948dnc.html.

13. Economic status, however, did not always correlate with Republican allegiance. By the 1950s in the North, a Democratic-leaning and culturally liberal class was forming, composed largely of upwardly mobile businessmen, professionals, and technocrats. See Phillips, *The Emerging Republican Majority,* 33, 44, 63, 67, 69, 74, 76–89, 175, 459, 470.

14. See Shafer and Johnston, *The End of Southern Exceptionalism;* Thurber, *Republicans and Race,* 47.

15. Thurber, *Republicans and Race,* 47.

16. See Nickerson, *Mothers of Conservatism.*

17. Ibid., 20–21; McGirr, *Suburban Warriors,* 155.

18. McGirr, *Suburban Warriors,* 155.

19. Nickerson, *Mothers of Conservatism,* 20–21; see also Phillips-Fein, *Invisible Hands.*

20. See Nickerson, *Mothers of Conservatism;* McGirr, *Suburban Warriors;* Dochuk, *From Bible Belt to Sun Belt.*

21. Phillips, *The Emerging Republican Majority,* 83–86.

22. See https://www.khanacademy.org/humanities/us-history/postwarera/postwar-era/a/the-dark-side-of-suburbia.

23. Phillips, *The Emerging Republican Majority,* 181–82.

24. See www.claremont.org/crb/article/nixons-the-one.

25. Wicker, *One of Us.*

26. Nixon, *Six Crises,* 109.

27. Ibid.

28. Ibid., 122–23.

29. Ibid., 126–27.

30. Quoted in Nelson, *Resilient America,* 32.

31. See historymatters.gmu.edu/d/6456.

32. See www.digitalhistory.uh.edu/disp_textbook.cfm?smtID=3+psid=3633.

33. Viereck, "The Revolt Against the Elites," 136.

34. Lipset, "The Sources of the 'Radical Right,'" 294.

35. Hofstadter, "The Pseudo-Conservative Revolt—1955," 65.

36. See www.imdb.com/title/tt0032551/quotes.

37. See Nash, *The Conservative Intellectual Movement,* 233.

38. Phillips, *The Emerging Republican Majority,* 88.

39. See http://www.people-press.org/interactives/party-id-trend/.

40. Rogin, *The Intellectuals and McCarthy,* 246.

41. Nixon, *Six Crises,* 280.

42. Middendorf, *A Glorious Disaster,* 110.

43. Phillips, *The Emerging Republican Majority,* 224; Gould, *Grand Old Party,* 363.

44. Buchanan, *The Greatest Comeback,* 287.

45. Goldwater, *The Conscience of a Conservative,* 69.

46. A talented team of Goldwater organizers led by conservative activist F. Clifton White blanketed the battleground states with volunteers. Well versed in the arcana of ballot rules and procedures, White's foot soldiers captured control of the delegate selection process. Goldwater attracted some five hundred thousand volunteers, at the time a record for presidential campaigns. His managers also pioneered the technique of direct mail advertising, which soon became a staple of political organizing for both parties. Middendorf, *A Glorious Disaster,* 145.

47. Middendorf, *A Glorious Disaster,* xi, 221–22.

48. Ibid., 123–24; Smith, *On His Own Terms,* xxi–xxxi.

49. See www.washingtonpost.com/wp-srv/politics/daily/may98/goldwater speech.htm.

50. Ibid.

51. In 1966 these ideas would be championed by George Mahoney, Agnew's Democratic opponent in the Maryland governor's race. This election would represent the last opportunity for Maryland voters to express support for Goldwaterite ideology on a statewide Democratic ticket.

52. See www.saturdayeveningpost.com/2012/09/20/archives/reprint/campaign -gaffes.html.

53. Richardson, *To Make Men Free,* 270.

54. See https://archive.org/details/uniformcrimerepo1964unit.

55. Brennan, "Winning the War/Losing the Battle," 71.

56. Middendorf, *A Glorious Disaster,* 246.

57. Buchanan, *The Greatest Comeback,* 290.

3. The Road to 1968

1. Buchanan, *The Greatest Comeback,* 333.

2. McPherson, *A Political Education,* 268.

3. Lemann, *The Promised Land,* 183. See also Lemann, "The Unfinished War."

4. McPherson, *A Political Education,* 268.

5. See Patterson, *The Eve of Destruction.*

6. See Bellah et al., *Habits of the Heart;* Katznelson, "Was the Great Society a Lost Opportunity?" 202.

7. Scammon and Wattenberg, *The Real Majority,* 21, 57.

8. See Dallek, *The Right Moment.*

9. Ibid.; https://en.wikipedia/wiki/california_gubernatorial_election_1966.

10. Buchanan, *The Greatest Comeback,* 99; Nelson, *Resilient America,* 60; Middendorf, *A Glorious Disaster*, xiii.

11. Buchanan, *The Greatest Comeback,* 287.

12. Brooke was the first African American senator and Winthrop Rockefeller the first Republican governor of Arkansas since Reconstruction.

13. See Nelson, *Resilient America,* 60.

14. Flamm, "The Politics of 'Law and Order,'" 95.

15. Scammon and Wattenberg, *The Real Majority,* 37–39.

16. Quoted in Buchanan, *The Greatest Comeback,* 142.

17. Flamm, *Law and Order,* 8.

18. See Flamm, *Law and Order.*

19. Stanley, *The Crusader,* 18–21, 25–26.

20. Buchanan, *The Greatest Comeback,* 51.

21. Ibid., 292–94.

22. Siegel, *The Revolt Against the Masses,* 119; White, *The Making of the President, 1968,* 496.

23. Witcover, *Very Strange Bedfellows,* 9.

24. White, *The Making of the President, 1968,* 160–61.

25. Ibid., 380.

26. Cohen, *American Maelstrom,* 122.

27. Chester et al., *An American Melodrama,* 387–88.

28. Cohen, *American Maelstrom,* 208–9.

29. Ibid., 249–51; Witcover, *White Knight,* 220–21; Gould, *Grand Old Party,* 377–78; Chester et al., *An American Melodrama,* 459–75.

30. Buchanan, *The Greatest Comeback,* 250.

31. Witcover, *White Knight,* 170.

32. Ibid., 26–27.

33. Pinchot, *Where He Stands,* 105.

34. Ibid., 101.

35. Ibid., 64.

36. Ibid., 97, 99.

37. Ibid., 79.

38. Ibid., 95.

39. Buchanan, *The Greatest Comeback,* 14; Witcover, *Very Strange Bedfellows,* 14.

40. Cohen, *American Maelstrom,* 257.

41. Witcover, *White Knight,* 220. See also Chester et al., *An American Melodrama,* 482–96.

42. Witcover, *White Knight,* 226.

43. Ibid., 220–21.

44. White, *The Making of the President, 1968,* 294–95.

45. Witcover, *White Knight,* 227.

46. Ibid., 229–30.

47. Ibid., 230.

48. Ibid., 232.

49. Ibid., 247, 253, 265–66.

50. See https://www.youtube.com/watch?=0zHyH6PHFzc.

51. Buchanan, *The Greatest Comeback,* 315.

52. Wicker is quoted in Klaus Fischer, *America in White, Black, and Gray: A History of the Stormy 1960s* (London: Continuum, 2006), 246.

53. Chester et al., *An American Melodrama,* 609–10.

54. Pinchot, *Where He Stands,* 43.

55. See www.presidency.ucsb.edu/ws/?pid=25968.

56. Spiro T. Agnew, Speech, Grand Rapids, MI, August 24, 1968, Agnew Papers, Series 3.8, Box 8, Folder 28.

57. Spiro T. Agnew, Speech, Casper, WY, September 18, 1968, Agnew Papers, Folder 52.

58. Ibid.

59. Ibid.

60. Spiro T. Agnew, Speech, Milwaukee, WI, September 28, 1968, Agnew Papers, Folder 67.

61. Spiro T. Agnew, Speech, Portland, OR, October 3, 1968, Agnew Papers, Folder 75.

62. Ibid.

63. Ibid.

64. Ibid.; Hubert Humphrey, quoted in Perlstein, *Nixonland,* 109; Buchanan, *The Greatest Comeback*, 354.

65. Chester et al., *An American Melodrama,* 609–10.

66. Spiro T. Agnew, Speech, Midland, TX, October 21, 1968, Agnew Papers, Folder 20.

67. Ibid.

68. Coffey, *Spiro Agnew and the Rise of the Republican Right,* 81.

69. Spiro T. Agnew, Speech, Towson, MD, October 11, 1968, Agnew Papers, Folder 93.

70. Ibid.

71. See www.newyorktimes.com/1996/03/27/us/edmund-s-muskie-81-dies-maine-senator-and-a-power-on-the-national-scene.html.

72. Spiro T. Agnew, Speech, Towson, MD, October 11, 1968, Agnew Papers, Folder 93.

73. Ibid.

74. White, *The Making of the President, 1968,* 425.

75. Chester et al., *An American Melodrama,* 628.

76. Spiro T. Agnew, Speech, Towson, MD, October 11, 1968, Agnew Papers, Folder 93.

77. Ibid.

78. White, *The Making of the President, 1968,* 418.

79. Ibid., 416; Witcover, *White Knight,* 271.

80. White, *The Making of the President, 1968,* 416.

81. Spiro T. Agnew, Speech, Woodbridge, NJ, October 14, 1968, Agnew Papers, Folder 93.

82. Ibid.

83. Ibid.

84. Ibid.

85. Coffey, *Spiro Agnew and the Rise of the Republican Right,* 82–83. Buchanan would become a major influence on Agnew's thought and rhetoric during his vice presidency, as explained in the next chapter.

86. Spiro T. Agnew, Speech, Midland, TX, October 21, 1968, Agnew Papers, Folder 20.

87. Ibid.

88. Spiro T. Agnew, 1968 Vice Presidential Campaign Itinerary, August–November 1968, Agnew Papers, Series 3.8, Box 6, Folder 20.

89. Witcover, *White Knight,* 279.

90. Ibid.; *Washington Daily News,* November 8, 1968.

91. Buchanan, *The Greatest Comeback,* 351. See also Efron, *The News Twisters.*

92. Nixon had even come within twenty thousand votes of carrying Agnew's traditionally Democratic home state of Maryland.

93. See *Washington Daily News,* November 8, 1968.

94. Spiro T. Agnew, 1968 Vice Presidential Campaign Itinerary, August–November 1968, Agnew Papers, Series 3.8, Box 6, Folder 20.

95. *Washington Daily News,* November 8, 1968.

96. *Dallas Morning News,* November 10, 1968.

97. Nixon, *RN: The Memoirs of Richard Nixon,* 365.

4. Becoming the Spokesman for the Silent Majority

1. Agnew, *Go Quietly . . . Or Else,* 35.

2. Nixon, *RN: The Memoirs of Richard Nixon,* 340.

3. Agnew would slowly professionalize his staff. Vic Gold, a veteran political operative who had worked with Barry Goldwater in 1964, later joined Agnew's staff as press secretary. He also would eventually hire special assistants who were up-and-coming young conservatives like David Keene, who would go on to a career in politics and later lead the National Rifle Association, and John Damgard, who would work in government and lobbying for decades. After speechmaking became more important to his own political fortunes, Agnew hired J. C. Helms, who held a doctorate in classics from Harvard, to replace Rosenwald in 1970.

4. Blair returned to Maryland to run unsuccessfully for governor as the Republican nominee, ultimately losing to Democrat Marvin Mandel in 1970. He would go on to serve as a U.S. District Court judge in Maryland.

5. James M. Naughton, "Those Biting Words Are Agnew's Own," *New York Times,* May 30, 1970.

6. Agnew Papers, Subseries 3.7: Public Statements, 1968–1974, Series III, SS 7, Box 1.

7. Agnew Papers, Subseries 3.7: Public Statements, 1968–1974, Series III, SS 7,

Box 1, Memo from Jim Keough to Cynthia Rosenwald, April 3, 1969: "It seems to me there is no reason why the VP cannot, from now on, use whatever humor seems called for in speeches. While a lot of humor would have been out of place this week, I don't think anyone would object from here forward."

8. Agnew Papers, Subseries 3.7: Public Statements, 1968–1974, Series III, SS 7, Box 1, Memo dated March 13, 1969, Subject: suggested jokes from Bob Hope.

9. Magruder, *An American Life,* 59.

10. Haldeman, *The Haldeman Diaries,* 52.

11. Ibid.

12. Agnew, *Go Quietly . . . Or Else,* 36.

13. Strober and Strober, *Nixon: An Oral History,* 91.

14. The two best compilation of Agnew's speeches can be found in *Collected Speeches of Spiro Agnew* and Coyne, *The Impudent Snobs.* The Yale speech, however, was quoted in Curran, *Spiro Agnew: Spokesman for America,* 43.

15. Agnew Papers, Subseries 3.7: Public Statements, 1968–1974, Series III, SS 7, Box 1, Preparation for Ohio State University speech; Memo from Cynnie Rosenwald to Spiro Agnew, May 23, 1969.

16. Agnew Papers, Subseries 3.7: Public Statements, 1968–1974, Series III, SS 7, Box 1, Preparation for Ohio State University speech; Agnew's handwritten notes back to Rosenwald on Office of the Vice President stationery, [n.d.]; Title "Cynnie—some thoughts."

17. John Kroll, "What Vice President Agnew Told Ohio State Graduates in His 1969 Commencement Address," *Cleveland Plain Dealer,* May 3, 2013, http://www.cleveland.com/metro/index.ssf/2013/05/what_vice_president_agnew_told.html.

18. "Bob Gives Agnew a Little Hope," *Columbus Evening Dispatch,* June 8, 1969.

19. Agnew's only son, James Rand "Randy" Agnew, finished a stint in Vietnam in 1969. The vice president's longtime secretary Alice Fringer told one of Agnew's biographers that "Randy is so different from his father that it is hard to believe they are father and son" (Albright, *What Makes Spiro Run,* 280). A Jack Anderson nationally syndicated column on September 5, 1970, detailed Randy's divorce and his new life as a weightlifting instructor in suburban Baltimore, where he was living with a male hairdresser. Jack Anderson, "VP's Son, Wife Separate," September 5, 1970. http://jfk.hood.edu/Collection/Weisberg%20Subject%20Index%20Files/A%20Disk/Agnew%20Spiro%20T/Agnew%20Spiro%20T%20135.pdf. Agnew's son denied what he called "the implications" of Anderson's column. "Son of Agnew Says He Has Left His Wife," *New York Times,* September 6, 1970. Randy remarried in 1973; he has spent most of his life in Florida.

20. Agnew, *Go Quietly . . . Or Else,* 27.

21. Ibid.

22. Reeves, *President Nixon,* 139.

23. Spiro Agnew, Address to the Citizens' Testimonial Dinner, New Orleans, Louisiana, October 19, 1969. In *Collected Speeches of Spiro Agnew.*

24. Lucas, *Agnew: Profile in Conflict,* 114.

25. Letter to David B. Johnson, November 18, 1969, Agnew Papers, Series III, Subseries 3.2, Box 1, Folder—"Chronological Files."

26. Perlstein, *Nixonland,* 431.

27. Lucas, *Agnew: Profile in Conflict,* 114.

28. Ibid., 115.

29. Perlstein, *Nixonland,* 505.

30. Buchanan, *Nixon's White House Wars,* 70.

31. Richard Nixon Presidential Library and Museum, "Silent Majority Speech," https://www.nixonlibrary.gov/forkids/speechesforkids/silentmajority/silent majority_transcript.pdf.

32. For the complete *CBS Evening News* of November 4, 1969: https://tvnews .vanderbilt.edu/programs/201383.

33. Buchanan, *Nixon's White House Wars,* 70.

34. Safire, *Before the Fall,* 352.

35. Buchanan, *Nixon's White House Wars,* 72.

36. Ibid., 70; Safire, *Before the Fall,* 352.

37. Buchanan, *Nixon's White House Wars,* 79.

38. Ibid., 71.

39. Agnew Papers, Subseries 3.7: Public Statements, 1968–1974, Series III, SS 7, Box 2, Des Moines Speech File, "Memorandum for Cynnie Rosenwald from Stanley Blair," November 12, 1969.

40. Agnew, *Go Quietly . . . Or Else,* 28.

41. We wrote about this parallel in December 2016. Charles Holden, Zach Messitte, and Jerald Podair, "Look to Agnew for Insight to Trump," *Sun,* December 18, 2016, http://www.baltimoresun.com/news/opinion/oped/bs-ed-trump-agnew-2016 1218-story.html. Agnew's aide David Keene also opined on this subject in July 2017: Keene, "Removing the Media Manhole Cover," *Washington Times,* July 11, 2017.

42. Lippmann, *Spiro Agnew's America,* 195.

43. Lucas, *Agnew: Profile in Conflict,* 123.

44. Coyne, *The Impudent Snobs,* 7.

45. For Agnew's speech feedback from ABC News, see Agnew Papers, Subseries 3.7: Public Statements, 1968–1974, Series III, SS 7, Box 2, Des Moines Speech File, "ABC News, Memorandum: To: Joe Cook; From: Julie Tarachow Hoover; Subject: Agnew Mail, Inter-department correspondence in response to Agnew's televised speeches," February 27, 1970.

46. Haldeman, *The Haldeman Diaries,* 107–8.

47. Nixon, *RN: The Memoirs of Richard Nixon,* 411–12.

48. Buchanan, *Nixon's White House Wars,* 74.

49. Ford, *A Time to Heal,* 89.

50. Agnew Papers, Subseries 3.7: Public Statements, 1968–1974, Series III, SS 7, Box 2, "Montgomery Chamber of Commerce Speech File," November 20, 1969.

51. Haldeman, *The Haldeman Diaries,* 109.

52. Buchanan, *Nixon's White House Wars,* 75.

53. Haldeman, *The Haldeman Diaries,* 109.

54. Albright, *What Makes Spiro Run,* 242.

55. Ibid., 274, and Agnew Papers, Subseries 3.13: News Summaries, 1969–1974, Series III, SS 13, Box 3, "Digest of News Reports," November 17, 1969.

56. Lucas, *Agnew: Profile in Conflict,* 105.

57. Ibid., 26.

58. Ibid., 107.

59. Evans and Novak, *Nixon in the White House,* 315; Lippman, *Spiro Agnew's America,* 189.

60. Haldeman, *The Haldeman Diaries,* 111.

61. Lippman, *Spiro Agnew's America,* 324.

62. Curran, *Spiro Agnew: Spokesman for America,* 121, 143.

63. Buchanan, *Nixon's White House Wars,* 84.

64. Ibid., 78–79. Both Buchanan and William Safire would have long careers with some of the same media outlets they criticized in Agnew's speeches. Safire was a columnist for the *New York Times* from 1973 until his death in 2009, writing on the opinion page and in the "On Language" column in the *New York Times Magazine.* He won the 1978 Pulitzer Prize and frequently appeared on NBC News's *Meet the Press.* Buchanan, when not running for political office or working in the Reagan White House, had regular shows on CNN, notably *Crossfire* and *The Capital Gang,* and was a panelist on *The McLaughlin Group.*

65. Reeves, President Nixon, 160.

66. Buchanan, *Nixon's White House Wars,* 129.

67. Haldeman, *The Haldeman Diaries,* 128.

68. Isaacson, *Kissinger,* 261.

69. Reeves, *President Nixon,* 197.

70. Buchanan, *Nixon's White House Wars,* 86.

71. The irony of Agnew's words is that he was marginally prepared for his own college experience. He dropped out of Johns Hopkins due to poor grades, lack of interest, and declining resources. He would later go back and get his undergraduate degree at night and a law degree from the University of Baltimore, an institution that slipped in and out of accreditation. As Agnew biographer Theo Lippman wrote: "Many of his [high school] classmates and teachers never knew him, or forgot him soon afterward. His one claim to visibility was his piano playing.... The 1937 class yearbook

lists no achievement or interest under his picture: he is one of only 4 in a class of 163 who were so undistinguished." Lippman, *Spiro Agnew's America,* 25. Agnew said of his undergraduate time at Hopkins: "I was more interested in having a good time than studying" (Albright, *What Makes Spiro Run,* 36).

72. April 10, 1970, memo from Herb Thompson to Babette Ullman on organizing publicity for the Des Moines speech, Agnew Papers, Subseries 3.7: Public Statements, 1968–1974, Series III, SS 7, Box 3, "Des Moines, IA speech file," November 17, 1969.

73. Handwritten note from Lynn Chapman of Platte Valley Bible College in Scottsbluff, NE, Agnew Papers, Subseries 3.7: Public Statements, 1968–1974, "Des Moines, IA speech file."

74. Letter from Orville Johnston to Vice President Agnew, May 19, 1970, Agnew Papers, Series III, Subseries 5, Box 126.

75. Brochure from the Candlelight Club at the University of Wisconsin-Oshkosh, May 26, 1971, Agnew Papers, Subseries 3.7: Public Statements, 1968–1974, "Des Moines, IA speech file."

76. "Agnew Attacks College Policies on Admissions," *Chronicle of Higher Education,* April 20, 1970.

77. Associated Press, April 13, 1970, Untitled, Dateline: Ann Arbor, MI, Agnew Papers, Subseries 3.7: Public Statements, 1968–1974, "Des Moines, IA speech file" in the "Digest of News Reports," November 17, 1969.

78. *Birmingham News,* April 20, 1970 (editorial): "Agnew on Open Admission," Agnew Papers, Subseries 3.7: Public Statements, 1968–1974, "Des Moines, IA speech file," "Digest of News Reports."

79. *Detroit News,* April 15, 1970 (editorial): "Quality vs. Power," Agnew Papers, Subseries 3.7: Public Statements, 1968–1974, . . . "Des Moines, IA speech file," "Digest of News Reports."

80. *Boston Globe,* April 16, 1970 (editorial), Agnew Papers, Subseries 3.7: Public Statements, 1968–1974, . . . "Des Moines, IA speech file," "Digest of News Reports."

81. *New York Post,* April 16, 1970 (editorial): "Agnew Misses the Point," Agnew Papers, Subseries 3.7: Public Statements, 1968–1974, "Des Moines, IA speech file," "Digest of News Reports."

82. Magruder, *An American Life,* 98.

83. Witcover, *White Knight,* 334.

84. The Associated Press reported on April 29, 1970, that a Yale official said Agnew was getting back at Brewster for a speech Brewster made on April 21 in which he said Agnew could be explained "as a pawn in the strategic effort to coopt the right wing to head off a George Wallace candidacy."

85. "Yale Student Petition Supports Brewster's Stand on Panthers," *New York Times,* April 30, 1970, 1.

86. Memo for the Vice President from Pat Buchanan, May 19, 1970, Agnew Papers,

Subseries 3.7: Public Statements, 1968–1974, "Des Moines, IA speech file," "Digest of News Reports."

87. Max Frankel, "Hickel, in Note to Nixon, Charges Administration Is Failing Youth; Protests Close Over 80 Colleges," *New York Times,* May 7, 1970, 1.

88. E. W. Kenworthy, "Educators Say President Didn't Vow to Quiet Agnew," *New York Times,* May 10, 1970, 24.

89. Lippman, *Spiro Agnew's America,* 206.

90. Haldeman, *The Haldeman Diaries,* 161–62.

91. Witcover, *White Knight,* 334.

92. Arthur Schlesinger Jr., "The Amazing Success Story of 'Spiro Who,'" *New York Times Book Review,* July 26, 1970, http://www.nytimes.com/books/00/11/26/specials/schlesinger-spiro.html.

93. Nixon, *RN: The Memoirs of Richard Nixon,* 79.

94. Haldeman, *The Haldeman Diaries,* 175–76.

95. Ibid., 176.

96. Ibid., 179, 183–85.

97. Evans and Novak, *Nixon in the White House,* 329.

98. Buchanan, *Nixon's White House Wars,* 179.

99. Haldeman, *The Haldeman Diaries,* 192.

100. Buchanan, *Nixon's White House Wars,* 183.

101. "Tennessee Political Brief," from Roy Goodearle to Jim Allison, Republican National Committee memo in preparation of the Vice President's visit, September 18, 1970, Agnew Papers, Subseries 3.11: Trips, 1969–1973, Series III, SS 2, Box 1.

102. Maraniss, *Into the Story,* 128.

103. Safire, *Before the Fall,* 323.

104. Ibid., 570.

105. By the end of September the *New York Times* would report that Agnew had raised $700,000 or more at party fund-raising events that added to the $3.7 million he had raised since January 1970, making him "the most gilt-edged GOP asset since Mark Hanna turned his fortune and attention to politics." James M. Naughton, "Traveler Agnew Volubly Verbalizes Viewpoints," *New York Times*, September 20, 1970, E-4.

106. William P. Frank, "GOP Hears Agnew Roast Elite Snobs," *Wilmington (Delaware) Morning News,* October 15, 1970, 1.

107. Coffey, *Spiro Agnew and the Rise of the Republican Right,* 65.

108. Remarks by the Vice President, Flanigan Luncheon, New York, October 5, 1970, Agnew Papers, Subseries 3.11: Trips, 1969–1973, Series III, SS II, Box 4.

109. Evans and Novak, *Nixon in the White House,* 334.

110. Reeves, *President Nixon,* 268.

111. Ibid., 333.

112. Magruder, *An American Life,* 128.

113. The 1970 midterm election results were within the range of the five-election cycle for losses by the incumbent party—not the best result, but certainly not the worst. Only in 1962 with Democrat John Kennedy in the White House did the party in power manage to pick up seats in the Senate (four) while losing four in the House. In 1966 LBJ's Democratic Party lost forty-seven House seats and three in the Senate. In 1974, just three months after Nixon's resignation, the Republicans with Ford in the White House lost forty-nine House seats and four more in the Senate. In 1978 Jimmy Carter lost fifteen House seats and three in the Senate.

114. Buchanan, *Nixon's White House Wars,* 193.

115. Coffey, *Spiro Agnew and the Rise of the Republican Right,* 124.

116. Nixon, *RN: The Memoirs of Richard Nixon,* 495.

117. Haldeman, *The Haldeman Diaries,* 208.

118. Ibid., 233.

119. Ibid., 247.

120. Witcover, *Very Strange Bedfellows,* 175.

121. Robert Semple, "On Tour with Spiro Agnew," *New York Times,* September 19, 1996.

122. During the presidential campaign in 1968 Agnew said that "the Greek military government that took over in 1967 has not proven itself to be as horrendous a specter to contemplate as most people thought it would." Lippman, *Spiro Agnew's America,* 427. See the Associated Press video account of Agnew's visit to Greece at https://www.youtube.com/watch?v=vW5sMxs8u9Q and https://www.youtube.com/watch?v=Rv6HUebqYGA.

123. Oswald Johnston, "Agnew Conduct Upsets Greek Regime's Foes," *Sun,* October 24, 1971.

124. Oswald Johnston, "Cheering Greeks Welcome Agnew," *Sun,* October 17, 1971. Hardliners in the military overthrew Papadopoulos in November 1973. After democracy returned to Greece in 1974, Papadopoulos was tried for treason; he spent the rest of his life in jail.

125. "Richard Nixon, John D. Ehrlichman, and H. R. 'Bob' Haldeman on 20 July 1971," Conversation 263–009 (*PRDE* Excerpt A), *Presidential Recordings Digital Edition* ["Vice President Agnew," ed. Nicole Hemmer] (Charlottesville: University of Virginia Press, 2014–). http://prde.upress.virginia.edu/conversations/4004759.

126. Haldeman, *The Haldeman Diaries,* 332.

127. Ibid., 335.

128. "Richard Nixon, Charles W. 'Chuck' Colson, John D. Ehrlichman, and H. R. 'Bob' Haldeman on 20 February 1971," Conversation 454–009 (*PRDE* Excerpt B), *Presidential Recordings Digital Edition* ["Vice President Agnew," ed. Nicole

Hemmer] (Charlottesville: University of Virginia Press, 2014–). http://prde.upress
.virginia.edu/conversations/4004505.

129. Lippman, *Spiro Agnew's America,* 245.

130. Nixon, *RN: The Memoirs of Richard Nixon,* 674.

131. Agnew, *Go Quietly . . . Or Else,* 38–39.

132. Reston, *The Lone Star,* 444.

133. In June 1972 John Connally would step down as treasury secretary after just
sixteen months in office to head up the "Democrats for Nixon" campaign during the
reelection. He switched parties in 1973 and was again considered to replace Agnew in
October 1973 after the vice president resigned. He ran for president as a Republican
in 1980 but dropped out after faring poorly in the primaries. See also Haldeman, *The
Haldeman Diaries,* 327, 470.

134. Nixon, *RN: The Memoirs of Richard Nixon,* 674.

135. Lippman, *Spiro Agnew's America,* 398.

136. Ibid., 412, 428.

137. Coffey, *Spiro Agnew and the Rise of the Republican Right,* 143.

138. Goldwater, *With No Apologies,* 234.

139. Strober and Strober, *Nixon: An Oral History,* 267.

140. Reeves, *President Nixon,* 219.

141. Lippman, *Spiro Agnew's America,* 244.

142. Agnew, *Go Quietly . . . Or Else,* 39.

143. David Rosenbaum, "George McGovern Dies at 90, a Liberal Trounced but
Never Silenced," *New York Times,* October 21, 2012.

144. George McGovern, "Help Wanted," *New York Times,* August 28, 2008.

145. Memo from Herbert L. Thompson to the Vice President, August 10, 1972,
Agnew Papers, Public Statements, 1968–1974, Series III, SS 7, Box 9.

146. The video of Agnew's 1972 acceptance can be found at https://www.youtube
.com/watch?v=AZ59CBrwSmg.

147. Haldeman, *The Haldeman Diaries,* 495.

148. Ibid., 498.

149. Ibid., 485

150. White, *The Making of the President, 1972,* 300.

151. Ambrose, *Nixon: Volume 2,* 647–48.

152. Crouse, *The Boys on the Bus,* 299, 305.

153. Ronald Reagan would win 525 electoral votes in 1984.

154. The video of Nixon's 1972 victory speech is at https://www.youtube.com
/watch?v=x71wUTELcXY.

155. Suggested Election Night Remarks, November 7, 1972, Agnew Papers, Public
Statements, 1968–1974, Series III, SS 7, Box 10.

5. Dixie's Favorite

1. "Goldwater Sweep in Alabama Carries 5 in House Contests," *New York Times,* November 4, 1964.
2. "Alabamian in House Assails the March," *New York Times,* March 31, 1965.
3. William L. Dickinson to Spiro T. Agnew, April 14, 1972, Agnew Papers, Series 3: Vice President of the United States, 1966–1976, Subseries 4: Correspondence with Congressmen and Senators, 1969–1973, Box 1, Folder—Dickinson.
4. "G.O.P., Aided by Agnew, Surges in South," *New York Times,* December 7, 1969.
5. "If Not Agnew on the Ticket, Then Who?" *Anniston Star,* April 26, 1971.
6. Dent, *The Prodigal South,* 267.
7. Scammon and Wattenberg, *The Real Majority,* 181.
8. "VP Revolt Was Symbol of Protest over South's New Power in GOP," *Washington Post,* August 12, 1968.
9. "Text of Agnew's Speech," *Chicago Tribune,* November 21, 1969.
10. Phillips, *The Emerging Republican Majority,* 253.
11. "Thurmond Break Is Made Official," *New York Times,* September 17, 1964.
12. "Thurmond Joins the G.O.P.," *New York Times,* September 17, 1964.
13. Walter N. Leneau to Strom Thurmond, April 10, 1968, Thurmond Papers, Box 4, Subject Correspondence 1968—Folder Civil Rights 3 (Discrimination, Race Relations), Folder II; April 3–19, 1968.
14. J. A. Arrouet to Strom Thurmond, December 21, 1967, Thurmond Papers, Box 4, Folder I; January 4–March 28, 1968.
15. Colie L. Fox to Ramsey Clark, January 19, 1968, Thurmond Papers, Box 4, Folder I.
16. Peter Stabovitz Jr. to Strom Thurmond, February 22, 1968, Thurmond Papers, Box 4, Folder I.
17. David R. Stack to Strom Thurmond, February 9, 1968, Thurmond Papers, Box 4, Folder I.
18. William P. Jones to Strom Thurmond, March 30, 1968, Thurmond Papers, Box 4, Folder I.
19. Strom Thurmond to William P. Jones, April 3, 1968, Thurmond Papers, Box 4, Folder I.
20. R. B. Ward to Strom Thurmond, April 7, 1968, Thurmond Papers, Box 4, Folder II.
21. C. B. Lashar to Strom Thurmond, April 7, 1968, Thurmond Papers, Box 4, Folder II.
22. Sumter L. Lowry to Strom Thurmond, April 12, 1968, Thurmond Papers, Box 4, Folder II.

23. Margaret H. White to Strom Thurmond, April 9, 1968, Thurmond Papers, Box 4, Folder II.

24. Walter N. Leneau to Strom Thurmond, April 10, 1968, Thurmond Papers, Box 4, Folder II.

25. James W. White Jr. to Strom Thurmond, April 9, 1968, Thurmond Papers, Box 4, Folder II.

26. Mr. and Mrs. Don Harvey to Strom Thurmond, March [misdated] 8, 1968, Thurmond Papers, Box 4, Folder I.

27. Hugh F. Fenzel to Strom Thurmond, April 6, 1968, Thurmond Papers, Box 4, Folder II.

28. Mattie Seegars to Strom Thurmond, May 28, 1968, Thurmond Papers, Box 4, Folder V; May 27–June 7, 1968.

29. Mary Neary to Strom Thurmond, April 20, 1968, Thurmond Papers, Box 4, Folder III; April 20–May 11, 1968.

30. Katharine R. Adams to Strom Thurmond, May 6, 1968, Thurmond Papers, Box 4, Folder III. See also http://exhibits.library.northwestern.edu/archives/exhibits/1968/documents/BlackStudentStatement.pdf.

31. Gladys Walker to Strom Thurmond, May 11, 1968, Thurmond Papers, Box 4, Folder IV; May 13–24, 1968.

32. Annelle Davis to Public Servant & Fellow American, n.d., Thurmond Papers, Box 4, Folder VI; June 13–27, 1968.

33. A. A. Richards to Strom Thurmond, May 27, 1968, Thurmond Papers, Box 4, Folder V.

34. Scammon and Wattenberg, *The Real Majority,* 196.

35. The Very Concerned to Strom Thurmond, April 10, 1968, Thurmond Papers, Box 4, Folder II.

36. John N. Kennemur to Strom Thurmond, April 16 [*sic*], 1968, Thurmond Papers, Box 4, Folder III.

37. "Presidential Quiz No. 13," Thurmond Papers, Box 25—Campaigns—1968 Campaign—Publicity—Oct. 4–31; n.d.

38. Letter from the Solid South Carolina Independent Party, n.d., Thurmond Papers, Box 25—Campaigns—1968 Campaign—Publicity—Oct. 4–31; n.d.

39. See Thurmond Papers, Box 26—Campaigns—1968 Campaign—Presidential Scorecard—Stationary—1972 Campaign—General—Abermathy-Culbertson, Folder I, Oct. 12–Nov. 1, 1968, n.d.; Folder II, n.d.

40. Dent, *The Prodigal South,* 110.

41. Berman, *Give Us the Ballot,* location 1358 of 8563.

42. Dent, *The Prodigal South,* 103.

43. Scammon and Wattenberg, *The Real Majority,* 209.

44. Dent, *The Prodigal South,* 114, 267.

45. "Agnew Makes Bid for 'Protest' Vote," *New York Times,* October 8, 1968.

46. Ibid.

47. "Warning Is Given by G.O.P. Nominee," *New York Times,* October 30, 1968.

48. "Nixon May Win by Landslide," *Florence (South Carolina) Morning News,* October 2, 1968.

49. "Warning Is Given by G.O.P. Nominee," *New York Times,* October 30, 1968. Harry Dent's internal polling, however, showed that by mid-October Nixon had moved slightly ahead of Wallace, 32 percent to 29 percent, with Humphrey at 20 percent. See Dent, *The Prodigal South,* 108–15.

50. "Warning Is Given by G.O.P. Nominee," *New York Times,* October 30, 1968.

51. "Agnew Talks in Charleston," *Florence (South Carolina) Morning News,* October 30, 1968.

52. Phillips, *The Emerging Republican Majority,* 227.

53. Dent, *The Prodigal South,* 135.

54. Berman, *Give Us the Ballot,* location 1400 of 8563.

55. "Memorandum for the President," November 17, 1969, Dent Papers, MS0158, Box 3, Folder 21—Southern GOP; July–December, 1969.

56. "Sen. Fulbright Hits 'Emotionalism' of Agnew's Talks," *Daytona Beach Morning Journal,* November 11, 1969.

57. "A 'Republican' South?" *Florence (South Carolina) Morning News,* December 15, 1969.

58. Harold G. Fyle to Spiro Agnew, December 4, 1969, Agnew Papers, Folder SP 3–75/PRO "Montgomery/Alabama Chamber of Commerce [Executive, 1969–1971] November 20, 1969/PRO.

59. A. L. Pecorado to Spiro Agnew, November 23, 1969, Agnew Papers, Folder "Montgomery."

60. L. Mendel Rivers to Spiro Agnew, November 21, 1969, Agnew Papers, Folder "Montgomery."

61. James M. Collins to Spiro Agnew, December 8, 1968, Agnew Papers, Folder "Montgomery."

62. Jim Allison to Harry Dent, August 29, 1969, Dent Papers, Box 3, Folder 11—Request Engagements—Vice President; April–December, 1969.

63. Phillips, *The Emerging Republican Majority,* 253.

64. Ibid., 326, footnote 28.

65. Ibid., 259.

66. "The White Reaction," n.d., Dent Papers, Box 2, Folder 6—Memos to the President; May–December, 1969.

67. "Memorandum for the President," December 8, 1969, Dent Papers, Box 2, Folder 6—Memos to the President.

68. "Memorandum for Harry Dent," December 11, 1969, Dent Papers, Box 2, Folder 6—Memos to the President.

69. "Agnew Sees Rise in Crime Slowed," *New York Times,* April 25, 1970.

70. "G.O.P., Aided by Agnew, Surges in South," *New York Times,* December 7, 1969.

71. "Memorandum for the President," December 8, 1969, Dent Papers, Box 2, Folder 6—Memos to the President.

72. "G.O.P., Aided by Agnew, Surges in South," *New York Times,* December 7, 1969.

73. See Lassiter, *The Silent Majority;* Kruse, *White Flight.*

74. "2,000 Attend G.O.P. Dinner," *New York Times,* April 25, 1970.

75. Paul McCoy to Spiro T. Agnew, May 17, 1970, Agnew Papers, Series 3: Vice President, Subseries 5, Box 84, Folder—Political Affairs/North Carolina.

76. Herbert E. Myers to "Dear Sir," October 1970, Agnew Papers, Series 3: Vice President, Subseries 5, Box 83, Folder—Political Affairs/Kentucky.

77. "Administration Plans No Forced Busing, Agnew Tells S.C. GOP," *Danville (Virginia) Bee,* April 25, 1970.

78. "2,000 Attend G.O.P. Dinner," *New York Times,* April 25, 1970.

79. "Agnew Sees Protest if Judge Is Rejected," *Morgantown Dominion News,* April 25, 1970.

80. "Mr. Agnew's Blue Plate Special: Grits," *Sun,* April 28, 1970.

81. Haldeman, *The Haldeman Diaries: Inside the Nixon White House,* 194.

82. "Agnew Mellow in Talk Hailing Confederate Heroes," *New York Times,* May 10, 1970.

83. Ibid.

84. Memorandum for the Vice President, October 7, 1970, Dent Papers, Box 6, Folder 1—Politics [1970 Elections], Folder II; September 24–October, 1970.

85. Bernice B. Morten to Spiro T. Agnew, n.d. [return letter is May 26, 1969, from C. Stanley Blair], Agnew Papers, Series 3, Subseries: General Correspondence, Box 26, Folder—Miller, K—Morten, Thurston, 1968–1973.

86. "Editorial," *Ripon Forum,* July–August 1970.

87. Memorandum for the President, August 6, 1970, Dent Papers, Box 7, Folder 1—Southern GOP; January–August, 1970.

88. Ibid.

89. Ibid.

90. Ibid.

91. Ibid.

92. "WRAL-TV Viewpoint," July 15, 1971, Agnew Papers, Series 3, Subseries 5, Box 84, Folder—Political Affairs/North Carolina.

93. Ira W. Day to Frank Dale, July 29, 1971, Agnew Papers, Series 3, Subseries 5, Box 84, Folder—Political Affairs/North Carolina.

94. "Agnew the Logical Choice of Nixon," Congressional Record—Extensions of Remarks (July 27, 1972), E7117.

95. Corbett H. Thigpen to Spiro Agnew, August 18, 1971, Agnew Papers, Series 3, Subseries 5, Box 83, Folder—Political Affairs/Georgia.

96. Jesse Helms to Spiro T. Agnew, August 10, 1972, Agnew Papers, Series 3, Subseries 5, Box 84, Folder—Political Affairs/North Carolina.

97. See also Link, *Righteous Warrior.*

98. Berman, *Give Us the Ballot,* location 3092 of 8563.

99. Gerald Mack to Spiro Agnew, October 9, 1972, Agnew Papers, Series 3, Subseries 5, Box 83, Folder—Political Affairs/Louisiana.

100. "1976: Kennedy to Beat Agnew," *Anniston Star,* November 9, 1972.

101. Frank Montgomery to Spiro T. Agnew, February 1, 1973, Agnew Papers, Series 3, Subseries 5, Box 84, Folder—Political Affairs/North Carolina.

6. No Contest

1. Cohen and Witcover, *A Heartbeat Away,* 147.

2. Just ten days before the U.S. attorney's investigation into Agnew became public, syndicated columnist Stewart Alsop wrote, "It again seems possible that Vice President Spiro Agnew may become President before 1976. It is also entirely possible that he may be elected in his own right in 1976." Alsop, "President Agnew?" *Washington Post,* July 29, 1973, C6.

3. Haldeman, *The Haldeman Diaries,* 534.

4. Ibid.

5. Ibid., 536.

6. Agnew, *Go Quietly . . . Or Else,* 37.

7. Ibid., 38. Nixon would appoint John Warner, secretary of the navy, to be the administrator of the Bicentennial. Far from making "millions of enemies," Warner was later elected to five terms in the U.S. Senate.

8. Cannon, *Time and Chance,* 137.

9. Haldeman, *The Haldeman Diaries,* 535.

10. Ibid., 5

11. See https://www.c-span.org/video/?5799–1/president-nixon-1973-inauguration. Agnew's oath begins at the eight-minute mark.

12. Drew, *Washington Journal,* 34.

13. Magruder, *An American Life,* 226.

14. Cohen and Witcover, *A Heartbeat Away,* 67.

15. Kutler, *Abuse of Power,* 420.

16. A video of Agnew's statement is in the Associated Press archive at https://www.youtube.com/watch?v=wP7eXLccafQ. Also see James T. Wooten, "Agnew Confirms His Faith in Nixon about Watergate," *New York Times,* April 26, 1973.

17. R. W. Apple, "Watergate Fallout," *New York Times,* May 27, 1973.

18. Kutler, *Abuse of Power,* 322.

19. Ibid., 380.

20. Ibid., 460, 557, 559.

21. Agnew, *Go Quietly . . . Or Else,* 87; Nixon, *RN: The Memoirs of Richard Nixon,* 901. Nixon's chief of staff, Alexander Haig, remembered Agnew telling Nixon what to do with the Watergate tapes: "Boss, you've got to have a bonfire." Strober and Strober, *Nixon: An Oral History,* 395.

22. Agnew told Nixon on September 1, 1973, that "state government salaries were meager. [Agnew] was sure that three-quarters of the governors in other states had done the same kind of thing, namely, accepted campaign contributions from contractors doing business with the state. As [Agnew] saw it, the whole trumped up case simply involved campaign contributions that had been used to help meet expenses legitimately incurred by him and his family in their public roles" (Nixon, *RN: The Memoirs of Richard Nixon,* 915).

23. Cohen and Witcover, *A Heartbeat Away,* 49.

24. Hughes, *My Unexpected Journey,* 73.

25. Stephen Sachs interview with Zach Messitte, December 21, 2017.

26. The political/legal circle in Maryland was very tight in the U.S. attorney's office. Tydings had been the U.S. attorney in Baltimore from 1961 to 1963 and prosecuted A. Gordon Boone, speaker of the House of Delegates, in connection with a scandal in the Maryland savings and loan industry. He became a U.S. senator in 1964 but lost to George Beall's brother, J. Glenn Beall Jr., in 1970. Assistant U.S. attorneys under Tydings in 1963 included Stephen Sachs, who later became the U.S. attorney in Baltimore from 1967 to 1970 and prosecuted U.S. senator Daniel Brewster, among others. Sachs would twice be elected Maryland's attorney general, in 1978 and 1982, and would sue Agnew in 1981 to recover the special payments he had received while county executive, governor, and vice president. Another of Tydings's U.S. attorney generals was Benjamin Civiletti, who would go on to be attorney general of the United States under Jimmy Carter.

27. Cohen and Witcover, *A Heartbeat Away,* 3–4. Anderson would be convicted in 1974 of thirty-two counts of tax evasion, extortion, and conspiracy and would serve time in prison.

28. "Spiro Agnew and the Golden Age of Corruption."

29. Agnew, *Go Quietly . . . Or Else,* 41.

30. Nixon, *RN: The Memoirs of Richard Nixon,* 912–13.

31. "Exposition of the Evidence Against Spiro T. Agnew Accumulated by the Investigation in the Office of the United States Attorney for the District of Maryland as of October 10, 1973," 1.

32. Ibid., 12.

33. Ibid. Hammerman testified that it was understood that when Agnew asked how many "papers" he had for him, each "paper" represented a thousand dollars.

34. Ibid., 2.

35. Ibid., 4.

36. Cohen and Witcover, *A Heartbeat Away*, 195.

37. "Exposition of the Evidence," 3, 26.

38. Nixon, *RN: The Memoirs of Richard Nixon*, 913.

39. Ibid., 913.

40. Agnew, *Go Quietly . . . Or Else*, 60.

41. Coffey, *Spiro Agnew and the Rise of the Republican Right*, 177.

42. Zach Messitte, "Where Have You Gone, Elliot Richardson?" *Milwaukee Journal Sentinel*, March 24, 2017, http://www.jsonline.com/story/opinion/contributors /2017/03/24/messitte-gone-elliot-richardson/99576412/.

43. George and J. Glenn Beall Jr.'s father, James Glenn Beall, served as a congressman from the state's Sixth District (western Maryland) from 1943 to 1953. He then served two terms as a U.S. senator from 1953 to 1965.

44. Despite being an overwhelmingly Democratic state, Maryland elected several liberal Republican members to the Senate and House during the 1960s and 1970s, including Charles Mathias to the U.S. Senate and Rogers Morton and Lawrence Hogan to the House of Representatives. Morton would later become chair of the Republican National Committee, and Hogan was the only Republican member of the House to vote for all three articles of impeachment against Richard Nixon in 1974. Hogan's eldest son, Larry, is the governor of Maryland (2014–).

45. Richard Sandomir, "George Beall, Prosecutor Who Brought Down Agnew, Dies at 79," *New York Times*, January 18, 2017.

46. The headline in the *Washington Post* stretched across the page in a large font. Richard Cohen and Carl Bernstein, "Agnew Is Target of Kickback Probe in Baltimore, Proclaims His Innocence," *Washington Post*, August 7, 1973.

47. David Broder, "GOP Left Speechless by Agnew Headlines," *Washington Post*, August 8, 1973.

48. Theodore Kendricks, "The Prosecutor's Staff Upholds Bold Tradition," *Sun*, August 12, 1973.

49. Saul Friedman and Anthony Lame, "In Agnew Land, Corruption Is Rife," *Philadelphia Inquirer*, August 12, 1973.

50. Spiro Agnew, Part 2 of 3, Documents of the Federal Bureau of Investigation, from the BiblioGov Project.

51. Nixon, *RN: The Memoirs of Richard Nixon,* 915.

52. Ibid., 923.

53. Agnew, *Go Quietly . . . Or Else,* 93–94.

54. Multiple authors allude either directly or indirectly to Agnew's indiscretions. See Feldstein, *Poisoning the Press,* 133; Kessler, *In the President's Secret Service,* 35–36; Witcover, *Very Strange Bedfellows,* 351; Cohen and Witcover, *A Heartbeat Away,* 291; and Coffey, *Spiro Agnew and the Rise of the Republican Right,* 198.

55. The outing of the Gary Hart–Donna Rice affair in 1987, which ended Hart's run for the Democratic nomination for president, is traditionally cited as the beginning of a new era in how the press reported on marital infidelity. Ironically, a year after Agnew resigned, Wilbur Mills of Arkansas, the powerful chair of the House Ways and Means Committee, was arrested for intoxication at Washington's Tidal Basin with a stripper, Fanne Foxe, who jumped from his vehicle into the Potomac River. Mills was reelected even after the widely reported incident.

56. Witcover, *Very Strange Bedfellows,* 351.

57. Kessler, *In the President's Secret Service,* 35–36.

58. Wills, *Nixon Agonistes,* 443.

59. Coffey, *Spiro Agnew and the Rise of the Republican Right,* 198; Cohen and Witcover, *A Heartbeat Away,* 291.

60. Agnew, *Go Quietly . . . Or Else,* 98.

61. Nixon, *RN: The Memoirs of Richard Nixon,* 914–15.

62. Nixon's press conference of October 3, 1973, can be viewed at https://www.youtube.com/watch?v=yFbU73y78aM.

63. Strober and Strober, *Nixon: An Oral History,* 431.

64. Goldwater, *With No Apologies,* 256–57.

65. Ibid., 258.

66. With Democrats in charge of the House of Representatives and with Nixon already on the ropes, there was very little reason for the Democratic leadership to help Agnew stave off an indictment and thus interfere with an independent judicial process. Agnew's aide David Keene remembered that Speaker Carl Albert had sought the advice of Congressman Peter Rodino, chair of the House Judiciary Committee, who would have overseen any impeachment hearings against Agnew. According to Keene, Rodino read Agnew's request and said, "Tell him to go fuck himself." Strober and Strober, *Nixon: An Oral History,* 432.

67. Ibid., 258.

68. Lou Cannon, "Agnew Declares He Won't Resign Even If Indicted," *Washington Post,* September 30, 1973.

69. "Agnew Determined to Clear Name, Has No '76 Hope," *Washington Post,* September 29, 1973.

70. Agnew, *Go Quietly . . . Or Else,* 197.

71. Nixon, *RN: The Memoirs of Richard Nixon,* 922–23.

72. Agnew, *Go Quietly . . . Or Else,* 198.

73. Nixon, *RN: The Memoirs of Richard Nixon,* 923.

74. Cohen and Witcover, *A Heartbeat Away,* 341–42.

75. Ibid., 342–43. Hoffman presided in the Agnew case because all nine members of the U.S. District Court in Baltimore recused themselves, citing familiarity with the vice president. The U.S. Court of Appeals for the Fourth Circuit in Richmond, which had jurisdiction over Virginia and Maryland, appointed Hoffman to the case. The judge had been a prominent member of the Virginia Republican Party, running unsuccessfully for attorney general and Congress before serving as party chair. Dwight Eisenhower then appointed him to the federal bench in 1954, and he notably challenged Virginia's attempts to enforce public school segregation. The federal courthouse in Norfolk, Virginia, is named in Hoffman's honor. (See "A Tribute to Walter E. Hoffman," *Washington and Lee Law Review* 54 [1997]; "Walter Hoffman Dies," *Washington Post,* November 23, 1996.)

76. Cohen and Witcover, *A Heartbeat Away,* 343.

77. Ibid., 344.

78. Statement of Attorney General Elliot L. Richardson delivered in United States District Court for the District of Maryland, October 10, 1973.

79. Cohen and Witcover, *A Heartbeat Away,* 348–50.

80. Ibid., 352–53.

81. Agnew, *Go Quietly . . . Or Else,* 19.

82. Cohen and Witcover, *A Heartbeat Away,* 354.

83. Buchanan, *Nixon's White House Wars,* 352.

84. Peter Milius and Mary Russell, "Both Parties Jolted: Nixon Polls Leaders— GOP Saddened," *Washington Post,* October 11, 1973.

85. Lou Cannon, "Stunned Agnew Staff Reacts with Tears and Anger," *Washington Post,* October 11, 1973.

86. "Agnew Relatives in Greece Sad," *Washington Post,* October 11, 1973.

87. Letters of Support, October 16, 1973, Agnew Papers, Series III, Subseries 3, Box 9, Folders 1–2.

88. Nixon, *RN: The Memoirs of Richard Nixon,* 1005.

89. Zeifman, *Without Honor,* 56.

90. Transcript of Former Vice President Agnew's TV and Radio Address to the Nation, *New York Times,* October 16, 1973.

91. Cohen and Witcover, *A Heartbeat Away,* 358.

92. Agnew, *Go Quietly . . . Or Else,* 147, 204.

93. Agnew Response to Letters of Support, "Dear Mr. LeCount," October 16, 1973, Agnew Papers, Series III, Subseries 3, Box 11, Folder 1, October 29, 1973.

94. Cohen and Witcover, *A Heartbeat Away,* 358.

95. Ibid., 362–63.

96. Drew, *Washington Journal,* 261.

97. Nick Thimmesch, "Birth of a Salesman," *New York Times,* October 26, 1975. See also Richard Cohen, "Did Crime Pay? Spiro Agnew, Pay Attention, All You Nattering Nabobs of Negativism," *Rolling Stone*, November 26, 1981.

98. Manuscript with notes of *The Canfield Decision,* Agnew Papers, Series III, Subseries 5, Box 126, Not Yet Classified, [n.d.].

99. Agnew, *The Canfield Decision,* 300.

100. Ibid., 117.

101. John Kenneth Galbraith, "The Canfield Decision," *New York Times,* June 6, 1976.

102. James B. Witkin, "Spiro's Revenge," *Harvard Crimson,* May 13, 1976, http://www.thecrimson.com/article/1976/5/13/spiros-revenge-pbibf-he-had-committed/.

103. Manuscript with notes of *The Canfield Decision,* Agnew Papers, Series III, Subseries 5, Box 126, Not Yet Classified, [n.d.].

104. Manuscript with notes of *The Canfield Decision,* Letter from Carl Foreman to Mickey Rudin, June 25, 1976, Agnew Papers, Series III, Subseries 5, Box 126, Not Yet Classified, [n.d.].

105. Agnew, *The Canfield Decision,* 32.

106. Interview between Barbara Walters and Spiro T. Agnew, transcript, *Today,* May 11, 1976.

107. Interview between Maury Povich and Spiro T. Agnew, transcript, *Panorama*—WTTG-TV, May 19, 1976, 4.

108. Ford: "President Criticizes Agnew for Statements about Jews," *Washington Post,* June 26, 1976; Gold: "Agnew Has Simply Sold Out," *New York Times,* May 28, 1976; Safire: "Spiro Agnew and the Jews," *New York Times,* May 24, 1976; *Lincoln (Nebraska) Star:* May 25, 1976.

109. Letter from Spiro Agnew to Stanley Fine, July 30, 1976, copy in the possession of Charles Holden.

110. Interview with Stanley Fine, January 22, 2017.

111. Patrick J. Buchanan, "Spiro Agnew, Zionism and Anti-Semitism," *New York Sunday News,* July 25, 1976.

112. Mieczkowski, *Gerald Ford and the Challenges of the 1970s,* 58; Hartmann, *Palace Politics*, 35–36.

113. Agnew, *Go Quietly . . . Or Else,* 189. Agnew also did an interview with a local California news program in which he alluded to the possibility that he was a target of assassination, https://www.youtube.com/watch?v=NTCfm3-loeY&t=2s.

114. Robert Hay, "Agnew Case Revisited," *Christian Science Monitor,* August 6, 1980, https://www.csmonitor.com/1980/0806/080603.html.

115. Agnew, *Go Quietly . . . Or Else,* 43.

116. "Go Quietly, Spiro Agnew," *New York Times,* April 26, 1981.

117. David Scull interview with Zach Messite, December 20, 2017.

118. Witcover, *White Knight,* 231.

119. See coverage in the *Sacramento Union* and the *San Jose Mercury*, May 7, 1969.

120. Ambrose, *Nixon, Volume 3,* 477.

121. Bret Barnes, "Nixon Vice President Spiro T. Agnew Dies," *Washington Post,* September 19, 1996.

122. DeFrank, *Write It When I'm Gone,* 102–3.

123. During the time Agnew was working with the Argentine military the country was in the middle of the so-called Dirty War (1974–83). Human rights groups estimated that about thirty thousand people were killed or forcibly "disappeared" during the dictatorship. Many were drugged and pushed from airplanes above the Atlantic Ocean. The Argentine Air Force was among the worst offenders. In 2016 the head of the air force during this period, Omar Graffigna, was sentenced to twenty-five years in prison at age ninety for the kidnapping and torture of two left-wing activists.

124. Frank Lynn, "Agnew Dealings Revealed in Lawsuit," *New York Times,* July 5, 1987.

125. "Spiro T. Agnew, Ex-Vice President, Dies at 77," *New York Times,* September 18, 1996. See also Ambrose, *Nixon, Volume 3,* 541–42.

126. Virginia Ellis, "$24,197 California Refund Sought: Agnew Wants Tax Break on Bribes He Returned," *Los Angeles Times,* April 4, 1989, http://articles.latimes.com /1989-04-04/news/mn-940_1_california-income-tax-return.

127. Coffey, *Spiro Agnew and the Rise of the Republican Right,* 206.

128. CNN video: https://www.youtube.com/watch?v=E8-gVnPEXTM. Agnew's longest cameo comes at the 47:30 mark.

129. The full video of the ceremony can be found in C-SPAN's online archives. Retrieved from https://www.c-span.org/video/?65348-1/spiro-agnew-bust-unveiling.

130. Mandel spent time in prison for fraud and racketeering until Ronald Reagan commuted his sentence in 1981. The U.S. Court of Appeals for the Fourth Circuit overturned Mandel's conviction in 1987.

131. Charles Babington, "Agnew Finds His Niche in State House," *Washington Post,* April 14, 1995.

132. "Spiro T. Agnew, ex-Vice President, Dies in Md. at 77," *Sun,* September 18, 1996, http://www.baltimoresun.com/bal-agnewobit091896-story.html.

133. See the Mayo Clinic's information on acute leukemia: https://www.mayo clinic.org/diseases-conditions/acute-lymphocytic-leukemia/basics/symptoms/con -20042915.

134. Dan Fesperman and Larry Carson, "Agnew Recalled as 'Regular Guy'[:] Simple Burial Service in Timonium Attended by Former Officials," *Sun,* Sep-

tember 21, 1996, http://articles.baltimoresun.com/1996-09-21/news/1996265009_1
_agnew-secret-service-marker.

135. Buchanan, *Nixon's White House Wars,* 354.

136. Coffey, *Spiro Agnew and the Rise of the Republican Right,* 206.

7. From Agnew to Trump

1. John Nance Garner of Texas, Franklin Roosevelt's vice president during his first
two terms (1933–37), equated the vice presidency with a "warm bucket of spit." See
Patrick Cox's paper, "John Nance Garner on the Vice Presidency: In Search of the
Proverbial Bucket," The Center for American History at the University of Texas—
Austin. Retrieved from https://www.cah.utexas.edu/documents/news/garner.pdf.

2. Transcript of the International Platform Committee's Panel Discussion on the
Vice President, Sheraton Park Hotel, Washington, D.C., July 28, 1970. For quotes:
Jack Anderson, 1; Nancy Dickerson, 3; Warren Rogers, 6–7; Richard Wilson, 9.

3. Ibid., 5.

4. O'Donnell, *Playing with Fire,* 308–9.

5. See Ruth Ben-Ghiat, "An American Authoritarian," *Atlantic,* August 10, 2016,
https://www.theatlantic.com/politics/archive/2016/08/american-authoritarianism
-under-donald-trump/495263/; George Will, "How to Cool Down Donald Trump,"
Washington Post, February 26, 2016; Debbie Elliot, "Is Donald Trump a Modern Day
George Wallace?" National Public Radio, *All Things Considered,* April 22, 2016,
https://www.npr.org/2016/04/22/475172438/donald-trump-and-george-wallace
-riding-the-rage.

6. Trump attended the New York Military Academy and Fordham University
before transferring to the University of Pennsylvania, where he received his undergraduate degree in economics. Agnew attended Johns Hopkins but did not graduate and eventually received a law degree from the University of Baltimore. Valerie
Strauss, "Yes, Donald Trump Really Went to an Ivy League School," *Washington Post,*
July 17, 2015.

7. Kevin Baker, "Clinton vs. Trump is Manhattan vs. Queens," *Politico,* September 25, 2016, https://www.politico.com/magazine/story/2016/09/clinton-trump
-2016-debate-nyc-manhattan-queens-214284.

8. Jennifer Rubin, "Trump Reminds Us that He Is a Crude, Mean Boor," *Washington Post,* October 21, 2016.

9. See Archie Bunker on Democrats, https://www.youtube.com/watch?v=7fq
CS7Y_kME. In the 2013 documentary *Our Nixon,* a compilation of home mov-
ies taken by some of the president's closest aides, Nixon laid into *All in the Family*
for its "permissiveness" regarding homosexuality. Meredith Blake, "In CNN's 'Our
Nixon,' President Vents about 'All in the Family,'" *Los Angeles Times,* August 1, 2013,

http://articles.latimes.com/2013/aug/01/entertainment/la-et-st-our-nixon-cnn
-documentary-all-in-the-family-20130801.

10. Hunter Schwartz, "The Many Ways in Which Donald Trump Was Once a Liberal's Liberal," *Washington Post,* July 9, 2015; Jessica Chasmar, "Donald Trump Changed Political Parties at Least Five Times: Report," *Washington Times,* June 16, 2015.

11. Trump had discussed running for president as far back as the 1988 election; he talked about running six times before declaring his candidacy in 2016. See "Before 2016, Donald Trump Had a History of Toying with a Presidential Run," *PBS News Hour,* July 20, 2016, https://www.pbs.org/newshour/show/2016-donald-trump -history-toying-presidential-run.

12. Aaron Blake, "A Record Number of Americans Now Dislike Hillary Clinton," *Washington Post,* August 31, 2016.

13. Ta-Nehisi Coates, "The First White President," *Atlantic,* October 2017, https:// www.theatlantic.com/magazine/archive/2017/10/the-first-white-president-ta -nehisi-coates/537909/.

14. Steven R. Weisman, "The Vice President in Exile," *New York Times,* December 26, 1996.

15. Agnew, *Go Quietly . . . Or Else,* 235.

16. Spiro Agnew, Address to the Midwest Regional Republican Committee Meeting, Des Moines, Iowa, November 13, 1969. In *Collected Speeches of Spiro Agnew,* 87.

17. Woodward and Bernstein, *All the President's Men,* 177.

18. Susan Mulcahy, "Confessions of a Trump Tabloid Scribe," *Politico,* May/ June 2016, https://www.politico.com/magazine/story/2016/04/2016-donald-trump -tabloids-new-york-post-daily-news-media-213842; Emily Nussbaum, "The TV that Created Donald Trump," *New Yorker,* July 31, 2017, https://www.newyorker.com /magazine/2017/07/31/the-tv-that-created-donald-trump.

19. Steve Coll, "Donald Trump's 'Fake News' Tactics," *New Yorker,* December 11, 2017, https://www.newyorker.com/magazine/2017/12/11/donald-trumps-fake-news -tactics.

20. Transcript of Bret Stephens's acceptance speech at the Daniel Pearl Memorial Lecture at the University of California, Los Angeles, February 26, 2017, http://time .com/4675860/donald-trump-fake-news-attacks/.

21. David Frum, "The Great Republican Revolt," *Atlantic,* January–February 2016.

22. Spiro Agnew, Address to the Republican Statewide Fundraising Dinner, Des Moines, Iowa, April 13, 1970. In *Collected Speeches of Spiro Agnew,* 124.

23. Robert McAfee Brown, "An Open Letter to Spiro T. Agnew," *Christian Century Magazine,* October 14, 1970.

24. The participants were Greg Craig of Harvard, Richard Silverman of Washington University in St. Louis, Eva Jefferson of Northwestern University, and Stephen

Bright of the University of Kentucky. Craig went on to a prominent Washington-based political/legal career. He represented Ronald Reagan's would-be assassin, John Hinckley, and later was the director of policy planning in the State Department in the 1990s. He also served as one of Bill Clinton's key defense attorneys during impeachment proceedings against him in 1998 and 1999. He was Barack Obama's first White House counsel from 2009 to 2010. The Justice Department indicted Craig in April 2019 on charges of lying and hiding information related to the Foreign Agents Registration Act and his foreign lobbying work for the government of Ukraine. The indictment stemmed from special counsel Robert Mueller's investigation into Russian meddling in the 2016 presidential election.

25. A clip of the program can be found at https://www.youtube.com/watch?v=eje_lk6tQdg.

26. Anthony Lewis, "Dear Mr. Vice President," *New York Times,* September 26, 1970; Mary McGrory, "Agnew's Agility Routs the Young," *Washington Star,* September 22, 1970.

27. A July 2017 Pew Research Poll found a sharp divide between Democrats and Republicans on the impact of colleges and universities on the United States. A majority of Republicans and Republican-leaning independents (58 percent) believed that colleges and universities have a negative effect on the country. By contrast, most Democrats and Democratic leaners (72 percent) said colleges and universities have a positive effect. See Pew Research Center, "Sharp Partisan Divisions in Views of National Institutions: Republicans increasingly say colleges have negative impact on U.S.," July 10, 2017, http://www.people-press.org/2017/07/10/sharp-partisan-divisions-in-views-of-national-institutions/.

28. See, for example, Max Boot, "Donald Trump Is Proving Too Stupid to Be President," *Foreign Policy,* June 16, 2017, http://foreignpolicy.com/2017/06/16/donald-trump-is-proving-too-stupid-to-be-president/; Elliot Cohen, "A Clarifying Moment in American History," *Atlantic,* January 29, 2017, https://www.theatlantic.com/politics/archive/2017/01/a-clarifying-moment-in-american-history/514868/; John Podhoretz, "The White House Holocaust Horror," *Commentary,* January 28, 2017, https://www.commentarymagazine.com/politics-ideas/the-white-house-holocaust-horror/.

29. David Sanger and Maggie Haberman, "Donald Trump Sets Conditions for Defending NATO Allies against Attack," *New York Times,* July 20, 2016.

30. For Trump on free trade, see "How Donald Trump Thinks about Free Trade," *Economist,* November 9, 2016, https://www.economist.com/news/united-states/21709921-americas-next-president-wants-pull-out-existing-trade-deals-and-put-future-ones. Pat Buchanan has written scores of material on global trade, including *The Great Betrayal.*

31. "Trump v Comey: Who Said What," BBC News, June 22, 2017, http://www.bbc.com/news/world-us-canada-40196105\.

32. Daniel Benaim, "The Problem Isn't Just Who Trump Has Offended—It's Who He Hasn't," *Foreign Policy*, July 11, 2017, http://foreignpolicy.com/2017/07/11/the-problem-isnt-who-trump-has-offended-its-who-he-hasnt/. Trump's relations with strong allies such as Australia, Germany, and England have been particularly troubled.

33. H. W. Brands, "The Real Story of Reagan's 11th Commandment," *Politico*, April 5, 2017, https://www.politico.com/magazine/story/2017/04/11th-commandment-gop-republican-reagan-trump-214982.

34. Agnew's weak standing with Congress by October 1973 is well chronicled. See Perlstein, *Nixonland*, 431; Hartmann, *Palace Politics*, 6; Mieczkowski, *Gerald Ford and the Challenges of the 1970s*, 58; Ford, *A Time to Heal*, 86.

35. Madeline Conway, "Trump and Romney's 10 Harshest Insults," *Politico*, November 25, 2016, https://www.politico.com/story/2016/11/trump-romney-insults-231839\; Dan Nowicki, "Here's a Blow-by-Blow Account of the Donald Trump vs. John McCain Feud," *Arizona Republic*, October 15, 2016, https://www.azcentral.com/story/news/politics/azdc/2016/10/15/donald-trump-vs-john-mccain-feud/91960246/; MJ Lee, "How Donald Trump Blasted George W. Bush in S.C.—and Still Won," CNN, February 21, 2016, http://www.cnn.com/2016/02/20/politics/donald-trump-south-carolina-military/index.html.

36. David Nakamura, "George W. Bush Comes Out of Retirement to Deliver a Veiled Rebuke of Trump," *Washington Post*, October 19, 2017.

37. Philip Rucker and Damian Paletta, "Escalating Feud, Trump Blames McConnell and Ryan for Upcoming 'Mess' on Debt Ceiling," *Washington Post*, August 24, 2017.

38. Buchanan, *The Greatest Comeback*, 353.

39. Buchanan, *Nixon's White House Wars*, 87.

40. Coffey, *Spiro Agnew and the Rise of the Republican Right*, 115.

41. Stanley, *The Crusader*, 54.

42. Buchanan, *Conservative Votes*, 4.

43. Ibid., 8.

44. Ibid., 90.

45. Ibid., 172.

46. Patrick Buchanan's official website: http://buchanan.org/blog/1992-republican-national-convention-speech-148.

47. Buchanan, *The Great Betrayal*, 7.

48. Donald Trump, First Inaugural Address, https://www.whitehouse.gov/briefings-statements/the-inaugural-address/.

49. Buchanan, *The Death of the West*, 5.

50. "Remarks at Trump Tower on Charlottesville," *Los Angeles Times*, August 15,

2017, http://www.latimes.com/politics/la-na-pol-trump-charlottesville-transcript - 20170815-story.html.

51. Stanley, *The Crusader,* 131.

52. Ibid., 332.

53. Sam Tanenhaus, "Charge of the Right Brigade," *Esquire,* May 2017, 82.

54. Buchanan, *Where the Right Went Wrong,* 6.

55. Stanley, *The Crusader,* 186.

56. Tanenhaus, "Charge of the Right Brigade," 83.

57. David Frum, "The Great Republican Revolt," *Atlantic,* January–February 2016.

58. Valéry, *The Collected Works of Paul Valéry,* xviii.

BIBLIOGRAPHY

Newspapers

Anniston Star
Baltimore Afro American
Baltimore Sun
Chicago Tribune
Columbus Evening Dispatch
Dallas Morning News
Danville (Virginia) Bee
Daytona Beach Morning Journal
Florence (South Carolina) Morning News
Harvard Crimson
Morgantown Dominion News
New York Sunday News
New York Times
Philadelphia Inquirer
Ripon Forum
Sacramento Union
San Jose Mercury
Washington Daily News
Washington Star
Wilmington (Delaware) Morning News

Books and Collections

Agnew, Spiro. *The Canfield Decision.* Chicago: Playboy Press, 1976.
———. *Go Quietly . . . Or Else.* New York: William Morrow, 1980.
Albright, Joseph. *What Makes Spiro Run: The Life and Times of Spiro Agnew.* New York: Dodd, Mead, 1972.
Ambrose, Stephen. *Nixon: Volume 2: The Triumph of a Politician, 1962–1972.* New York: Simon and Schuster, 1989.

———. *Nixon: Volume 3: Ruin and Recovery, 1973–1990.* New York: Simon and Schuster, 1991.

Bellah, Robert, Richard Madsen, William Sullivan, Ann Swidler, and Steven Tipton. *Habits of the Heart: Individualism and Commitment in American Life.* Berkeley: University of California Press, 1985.

Berman, Ari. *Give Us the Ballot: The Modern Struggle for Voting Rights in America.* New York: Farrar, Straus, and Giroux, 2015. Kindle version.

Bradlee, Ben. *A Good Life.* New York: Simon and Schuster, 1995.

Brennan, Mary. "Winning the War/Losing the Battle: The Goldwater Presidential Campaign and Its Effects on the Evolution of Modern Conservatism." In *The Conservative Sixties,* ed. David Farber and Jeff Roche. New York: Peter Lang, 2003.

Brinkley, Alan. *The End of Reform: New Deal Liberalism in Recession and War.* New York: Alfred A. Knopf, 1995.

———. *Voices of Protest: Huey Long, Father Coughlin and the Great Depression.* New York: Alfred A. Knopf, 1982.

Buchanan, Patrick. *Conservative Votes, Liberal Victories.* New York: Quadrangle, 1975.

———. *The Death of the West: How Dying Populations and Immigrant Invasions Imperil Our Country and Civilization.* New York: St. Martin's Press, 2002.

———. *The Great Betrayal: How American Sovereignty and Social Justice Are Being Sacrificed to the Gods of the Global Economy.* Boston: Little, Brown, 1998.

———. *The Greatest Comeback: How Richard Nixon Rose from Defeat to Create the New Majority.* New York: Crown Forum, 2014.

———. *Nixon's White House Wars: The Battles That Made and Broke a President and Divided America Forever.* New York: Crown Forum, 2017.

———. *Where the Right Went Wrong: How Neoconservatives Subverted the Reagan Revolution and Hijacked the Bush Presidency.* New York: St. Martin's Press, 2004.

Cannon, James. *Time and Chance: Gerald Ford's Appointment with History.* New York: Harper Collins, 1994.

Chester, Lewis, Godfrey Hodgson, and Bruce Page. *An American Melodrama: The Presidential Campaign of 1968.* New York: Viking Press, 1969.

Coffey, Justin. *Spiro Agnew and the Rise of the Republican Right.* Santa Barbara: Praeger, 2015.

Cohen, Michael. *American Maelstrom: The 1968 Election and the Politics of Division.* New York: Oxford University Press, 2016.

Cohen, Richard, and Jules Witcover. *A Heartbeat Away: The Investigation and Resignation of Vice President Spiro T. Agnew.* New York: Bantam Book, 1974.

Collected Speeches of Spiro Agnew. New York: Audubon Books, 1971.

Coyne, John, ed. *The Impudent Snobs: Agnew vs. the Intellectual Establishment.* New Rochelle: Arlington House, 1972.

Cramer, Katherine. *The Politics of Resentment: Rural Consciousness in Wisconsin and the Rise of Scott Walker.* Chicago: University of Chicago Press, 2016.

Crouse, Timothy. *The Boys on the Bus.* New York: Ballantine Books, 1973.

Curran, Robert. *Spiro Agnew: Spokesman for America.* New York: Lancer Books, 1970.

Dallek, Matthew. *The Right Moment: Ronald Reagan's First Victory and the Decisive Turning Point in American Politics.* New York: Free Press, 2000.

DeFrank, Thomas. *Write It When I'm Gone: Remarkable Off-the-Record Conversations with Gerald R. Ford.* New York: G. P. Putnam's Sons, 2007.

Dent, Harry. *The Prodigal South Returns to Power.* New York: John Wiley and Sons, 1978.

Devine, Christopher, and Kyle Kopko. *The VP Advantage: How Running Mates Influence Home State Voting in Presidential Elections.* Croydon: Manchester University Press, 2016.

Dochuk, Darren. *From Bible Belt to Sun Belt: Plain-Folk Religion, Grassroots Politics, and the Rise of Evangelical Conservatism.* New York: W. W. Norton, 2011.

Drew, Elizabeth. *Washington Journal: Reporting Watergate and Richard Nixon's Downfall.* New York: Overlook Duckworth, 2014.

Efron, Edith. *The News Twisters.* Los Angeles: Nash, 1971.

Evans, Rowland, and Robert Novak. *Nixon in the White House.* New York: Random House, 1971.

Farber, David. *Everybody Ought to Be Rich: The Life and Times of John J. Raskob, Capitalist.* New York: Oxford University Press, 2013.

Feldstein, Mark. *Poisoning the Press: Richard Nixon, Jack Anderson and the Rise of Washington's Scandal Culture.* New York: Farrar, Straus and Giroux, 2010.

Flamm, Michael. *Law and Order: Street Crime, Civil Unrest, and the Crisis of Liberalism in the 1960s.* New York: Columbia University Press.

———. "The Politics of 'Law and Order.'" In *The Conservative Sixties,* ed. David Farber and Jeff Roche. New York: Peter Lang, 2003.

Ford, Gerald. *A Time to Heal.* New York: Harper and Row, 1979.

Goldwater, Barry. *The Conscience of a Conservative.* Shepherdsville, KY: Victor, 1960.

———. *With No Apologies.* New York: William Morrow, 1979.

Gould, Louis. *Grand Old Party: A History of the Republicans.* New York: Random House, 2003.

Haig, Alexander. *Inner Circles: How America Changed the World: A Memoir.* New York: Grand Central, 1992.

Haldeman, H. R. *The Haldeman Diaries: Inside the Nixon White House.* New York: G. P. Putnam's Sons, 1994.

Harry S. Dent Papers. Special Collections, Clemson University Libraries, Clemson, SC.

Hartmann, Robert. *Palace Politics: An Inside Account of the Ford Years.* New York: McGraw-Hill, 1980.

Hofstadter, Richard. "The Pseudo-Conservative Revolt—1955." In *The Radical Right,* ed. Daniel Bell. New York: Doubleday, 1963.

Hughes, Harry, with John Frece. *My Unexpected Journey: The Autobiography of Harry Roe Hughes.* Charleston, SC: History Press, 2006.

Isaacson, Walter. *Kissinger.* New York: Simon and Schuster, 2005.

Katznelson, Ira. "Was the Great Society a Lost Opportunity?" In *The Rise and Fall of the New Deal Order,* ed. Steve Fraser and Gary Gerstle. Princeton: Princeton University Press, 1989.

Kessler, Ronald. *In the President's Secret Service.* New York: Crown, 2009.

Kruse, Kevin. *White Flight: Atlanta and the Making of Modern Conservatism.* Princeton: Princeton University Press, 2005.

Kutler, Stanley. *Abuse of Power.* New York: Simon and Schuster, 1997.

Lassiter, Matthew. *The Silent Majority: Suburban Politics in the Sunbelt South.* Princeton: Princeton University Press, 2006.

Lemann, Nicholas. *The Promised Land: The Great Black Migration and How It Changed America.* New York: Alfred A. Knopf, 1991.

———. "The Unfinished War." *Atlantic* (December 1988).

Link, William. *Righteous Warrior: Jesse Helms and the Rise of Modern Conservatism.* New York: St. Martin's Press, 2008.

Lippman, Theo. *Spiro Agnew's America.* New York: W. W. Norton, 1972.

Lipset, Seymour. "The Sources of the 'Radical Right.'" In *The Radical Right,* ed. Daniel Bell. New York: Doubleday, 1963.

Lucas, Jim. *Agnew: Profile in Conflict.* New York: Charles Scribner and Sons, 1970.

Lucas, Stephen, and Martin Medhurst. *Words of a Century: The Top 100 Speeches, 1900–1999.* Oxford: Oxford University Press, 2008.

Magruder, Jeb. *An American Life: One Man's Road to Watergate.* New York: Atheneum, 1974.

Maraniss, David. *Into the Story.* New York: Simon and Schuster, 2010.

McElvaine, Robert. *The Great Depression: America, 1929–1941.* New York: Three Rivers Press, 1984.

McGirr, Lisa. *Suburban Warriors: The Origins of the New American Right.* Princeton: Princeton University Press, 2001.

McPherson, Harry. *A Political Education: A Washington Memoir.* Boston: Little, Brown, 1972.

Mieczkowski, Yanek. *Gerald Ford and the Challenges of the 1970s.* Lexington: University of Kentucky Press, 2005.

Nash, George. *The Conservative Intellectual Movement in America Since 1945*. New York: Basic Books, 1976.

Nelson, Michael. *Resilient America: Electing Nixon in 1968, Channeling Dissent, and Dividing Government*. Lawrence: University Press of Kansas, 2014.

Nickerson, Michelle. *Mothers of Conservatism: Women and the Postwar Right*. Princeton: Princeton University Press, 2012.

Nixon, Richard. *RN: The Memoirs of Richard Nixon*. New York: Grosset and Dunlap, 1978.

———. *Six Crises*. New York: Doubleday, 1962.

O'Donnell, Lawrence. *Playing with Fire: The 1968 Election and the Transformation of American Politics*. New York: Penguin Press, 2017.

Patterson, James. *The Eve of Destruction: How 1965 Transformed America*. New York: Basic Books, 2012.

Perlstein, Rick. *Nixonland: The Rise of a President and the Fracturing of America*. New York: Scribner, 2008.

Phillips, Kevin. *The Emerging Republican Majority*. Garden City, NJ: Doubleday, 1970.

Phillips-Fein, Kim. *Invisible Hands: The Businessmen's Crusade Against the New Deal*. New York: W. W. Norton, 2009.

Pinchot, Ann, ed. *Where He Stands: The Life and Convictions of Spiro T. Agnew*. New York: Hawthorn Books, 1968.

Reeves, Richard. *President Nixon*. New York: Simon and Schuster, 2001.

Reston, James. *The Lone Star: The Life of John Connally*. New York: Harper and Row, 1989.

Richardson, Heather. *To Make Men Free: A History of the Republican Party*. New York: Basic Books, 2014.

Rogin, Michael. *The Intellectuals and McCarthy: The Radical Specter*. Cambridge: MIT Press, 1967.

Rosen, Elliot. *The Republican Party in the Age of Roosevelt: Sources of Anti-Governmental Conservatism in the United States*. Charlottesville: University of Virginia Press, 2014.

Safire, William. *Before the Fall*. New York: Doubleday, 1975.

Scammon, Richard, and Ben Wattenberg. *The Real Majority*. New York: Coward-McCann, 1970.

Shafer, Bryon, and Richard Johnston. *The End of Southern Exceptionalism: Class, Race, and Partisan Change in the Postwar South*. Cambridge: Harvard University Press, 2006.

Siegel, Fred. *The Revolt Against the Masses: How Liberalism Has Undermined the Middle Class*. New York: Encounter Books, 2013.

Smith, Richard. *On His Own Terms: A Life of Nelson Rockefeller*. New York: Random House, 2014.

"Spiro Agnew and the Golden Age of Corruption in Maryland Politics: An Interview with Ben Bradlee and Richard Cohen of the *Washington Post*." In *The Occasional Papers of the Center for the Study of Democracy* 2, no. 1 (2006), ed. Charles Holden and Zach Messitte.

Spiro T. Agnew Papers. Special Collections, University of Maryland Libraries, Hornbake Library, College Park, MD.

Stanley, Timothy. *The Crusader: The Life and Tumultuous Times of Pat Buchanan.* New York: Thomas Dunne Books, 2012.

Strober, Gerald, and Deborah Hart Strober. *Nixon: An Oral History of His Presidency.* New York: Harper Collins, 1994.

Strom Thurmond Papers. Special Collections, Clemson University Libraries, Clemson, SC.

Thurber, Timothy. *Republicans and Race: The GOP's Frayed Relationship with African Americans, 1945–1974.* Lawrence: University Press of Kansas, 2013.

Valéry, Paul. *The Collected Works of Paul Valéry.* Princeton: Princeton University Press, 1956.

Viereck, Peter. "The Revolt Against the Elites." In *The Radical Right,* ed. Daniel Bell. New York: Doubleday, 1963.

Weir, Robert, ed. *Class in America: An Encyclopedia,* Westport, CT: Greenwood Press, 2007.

White, Theodore. *The Making of the President, 1968.* New York: Atheneum, 1969.

———. *The Making of the President, 1972.* New York: Atheneum, 1973.

Whyte, William. *The Organization Man.* New York: Simon and Schuster, 1956.

Wicker, Tom. *One of Us: Richard Nixon and the American Dream.* New York: Random House, 1991.

Wills, Garry. *Nixon Agonistes.* Boston: Houghton Mifflin, 1970.

Wilson, Sloan. *The Man in the Gray Flannel Suit.* New York: Simon and Schuster, 1955.

Witcover, Jules. *Very Strange Bedfellows: The Short and Unhappy Marriage of Richard Nixon and Spiro Agnew.* New York: Public Affairs, 2007.

———. *White Knight: The Rise of Spiro Agnew.* New York: Random House, 1972.

Woodward, Bob, and Carl Bernstein. *All the President's Men.* New York: Warner, 1974.

Zeifman, Jerry. *Without Honor.* New York: Thunder's Mouth Press, 1995.

INDEX

Page numbers in italics refer to illustrations.

law and order (*continued*)
1968, 91–95; and social change, resentment of, 73–74. *See also* civil rights movement
LeMay, Curtis, 92–93
Leneau, Walter, 140
Lindsay, John, 146
Lipset, Seymour Martin, 56–57
Lodge, Henry Cabot, 3
Long, Huey, 44–45
Lowry, Sumter, 139–40

Mack, Gerald, 159
Magruder, Jeb, 119, 126–27, 165
Mahoney, George, 33, 217n51
Mandel, Marvin, 189
Man in the Gray Flannel Suit, The (Wilson), 24
Mankiewicz, Frank, 111, 193
Marcos, Ferdinand, 114
Maryland: and political corruption, 166, 168–69, 173, 186; and Republican Party, liberal, 234n44. *See also* Baltimore County
Maryland Casualty Insurance, 18
Masons, 23
materialism, 59
Mathias, Charles, 234n44
Matz, Lester, 169–70
McCarthy, Eugene, 137
McCarthy, Joseph, 53, 55–57, 95
McConnell, Mitch, 202
McCoy, Paul, 151–52
McGovern, George, 112, 131, 133, 159
Meany, George, 89
media: on Agnew, 192; as biased, charges of, 5, 110–13, 115, 203; public views on, 197. *See also under* Agnew, Spiro
Middle America, 57; on Agnew's anti-Semitism, 184–85; and middle-class definition, expansion of, 50–51; and politicians' public personas, 167. *See also* silent majority

Middle America Committee, 106
Middle East, 164, 179
Midwestern Regional Republican Conference, 109
Miller, William, 114
Mills, Wilbur, 235n55
Mississippi Freedom Democratic Party (MFDP), 72–73
Mitchell, John, 129–30, 162
Mitchell, Stephen, 54
Montgomery, Frank, 160
Moore, Robert, 39
Morten, Bernice, 154
Morton, Bruce, 188
Morton, Rogers, 8, 86, 126, 172, 234n44
Moynihan, Daniel Patrick, 189
Mueller, Robert, 241n24
Murphy, George, 126
Muskie, Edmund, 88, 93–94, 98, 131
Myers, Herbert, 152

National Commission on Civil Disorders, 83
Neary, Mary, 141–42
Newark race riots, 31–32
Newark, 74
New Deal: electoral legacy of, 75–76; opposition to, 46–47; and southern Democrats, 48. *See also* Democratic Party
New York City riots, 68
Nixon, Richard: cabinet of, 101; Checkers speech, 54; and China opening, 128; and Des Moines speech, 109–10; and election of 1968, 76, 77–81, 89, 95, 97, 98, 137, 143–47; and election of 1970 (midterm), 121–22, 127, 156; and election of 1972, 134, 154, 156–57, 159, *159;* as establishment candidate, 2; as "everyman," 54–55; and Ford, selection for VP, 179; funeral of, 188; and Hiss, relationship with, 53–54; and King arrest, 60–62; and "kitchen debate," 59; and Joseph Kraft influence, 73; and law and order, 73–74; on Montgomery speech, 113; political